Cataloging Government Publications Online

Cataloging Government Publications Online

Carolyn C. Sherayko, MLS, MA
Editor

The Haworth Press, Inc.
New York·London·Norwood (Australia)

Cataloging Government Publications Online has also been published as *Cataloging & Classification Quarterly,* Volume 18, Numbers 3/4 1994.

The development, preparation, and publication of this work has been undertaken with great care. However, the publisher, employees, editors, and agents of The Haworth Press and all imprints of The Haworth Press, Inc., including The Haworth Medical Press and Pharmaceutical Products Press, are not responsible for any errors contained herein or for consequences that may ensue from use of materials or information contained in this work. Opinions expressed by the author(s) are not necessarily those of The Haworth Press, Inc.

The Haworth Press, Inc., 10 Alice Street, Binghamton, NY 13904-1580 USA

Library of Congress Cataloging-in-Publication Data

Cataloging government publications online / Carolyn C. Sherayko, editor.
     p. cm.
     "Also . . . published as Cataloging & classification quarterly, volume 18, numbers 3/4 1994"–T.p. verso.
     Includes bibliographical references (p.) and index.
     ISBN 1-56024-689-8 (acid-free paper)
     1. Cataloging of government publications–United States–Data processing. I. Sherayko, Carolyn C.
Z695.1.G7C28 1994   94-14320
025.3'434'0973–dc20   CIP

INDEXING & ABSTRACTING

Contributions to this publication are selectively indexed or abstracted in print, electronic, online, or CD-ROM version(s) of the reference tools and information services listed below. This list is current as of the copyright date of this publication. See the end of this section for additional notes.

- *Current Awareness Bulletin*, Association for Information Management, Information House, 20-24 Old Street, London EC1V 9AP, England

- *Index to Periodical Articles Related to Law*, University of Texas, 727 East 26th Street, Austin, TX 78705

- *Information Science Abstracts*, Plenum Publishing Company, 233 Spring Street, New York, NY 10013-1578

- *INSPEC Information Services*, Institution of Electrical Engineers, Michael Faraday House, Six Hills Way, Stevenage, Herts SG1 2AY, England

- *Library & Information Science Abstracts (LISA)*, Bowker-Saur Limited, Maypole House, Maypole Road, East Grinstead, West Sussex RH19 1HH, England

- *Library Hi Tech News*, Pierian Press, P. O. Box 1808, Ann Arbor, MI 48106

- *Library Literature*, The H.W. Wilson Company, 950 University Avenue, Bronx, NY 10452

- *Newsletter of Library and Information Services*, China Sci-Tech Book Review, Library of Academia Sinica, 8 Kexueyuan Nanlu, Zhongguancun, Beijing 100080, People's Republic of China

- *Referativnyi Zhurnal (Abstracts Journal of the Institute of Scientific Information of the Republic of Russia)*, The Institute of Scientific Information, Baltijskaja ul., 14, Moscow A-219, Republic of Russia

- *The Informed Librarian*, Infosources Publishing, 140 Norma Road, Teaneck, NJ 07666

(continued)

SPECIAL BIBLIOGRAPHIC NOTES

related to special journal issues (separates)
and indexing/abstracting

☐ indexing/abstracting services in this list will also cover material in the "separate" that is co-published simultaneously with Haworth's special thematic journal issue or DocuSerial. Indexing/abstracting usually covers material at the article/chapter level.

☐ monographic co-editions are intended for either non-subscribers or libraries which intend to purchase a second copy for their circulating collections.

☐ monographic co-editions are reported to all jobbers/wholesalers/approval plans. The source journal is listed as the "series" to assist the prevention of duplicate purchasing in the same manner utilized for books-in-series.

☐ to facilitate user/access services all indexing/abstracting services are encouraged to utilize the co-indexing entry note indicated at the bottom of the first page of each article/chapter/contribution.

☐ this is intended to assist a library user of any reference tool (whether print, electronic, online, or CD-ROM) to locate the monographic version if the library has purchased this version but not a subscription to the source journal.

☐ individual articles/chapters in any Haworth publication are also available through the Haworth Document Delivery Services (HDDS).

Cataloging Government Publications Online

CONTENTS

PLANNING, ORGANIZATION, WORKFLOWS

Planning, Systems Analysis, and Negotiation:
Key Elements for a Successful GPO Tapeload   1

Josephine Crawford

Approaching Automation: A Planning Model for GPO
Tapeloading–One Library's Experience   19

Linda B. Johnson
Sushila Selness

Planning for Tapeloading of United States Documents:
Issues and Concerns   37

Mary Martin

Sharing Expertise to Mainstream Government
Documents Cataloging   57

Beatrice McKay
Norma Carmack

Automation: The Bridge Between Technical Services
and Government Documents   75

Darlene M. Pierce
Eileen Theodore-Shusta

SPECIAL ISSUES IN ONLINE ACCESS

Control of Government Document Serials in Local
Electronic and Organizational Systems   85

Mary C. Bushing
Bonnie Johnson

Cataloging Challenges: Providing Bibliographic Access
   to Florida's Full-Text Electronic State Documents   97

        Mae M. Clark
        Michael D. Esman
        Claudia V. Weston

F.B.I. (Fugitive Bibliographic Information)   121

        Kathleen Keating

Life After the "Earthquake": The Myths and Realities
   of Cataloging U.S. Government Depository CD-ROM
   Documents   131

        Lynne M. Martin
        Catherine M. Dwyer

CASE STUDIES

Processing of Government Publications in the State
   Library of New South Wales   155

        Mark Hildebrand
        Richard Fell-Marston
        Edwina Rudd

The Online Cataloguing of Government Publications
   of Southern Africa at the State Library, Pretoria   167

        Ria Stoker
        Barbara Kellermann

Ball State University Libraries and OCLC
   GOVDOC Service   181

        Diane Calvin

University of California, San Diego's Experience Creating
   and Updating Machine-Readable GPO Records   189

        Joanne Donovan
        Roberta A. Corbin

Online Processing of Government Publications
  at the University Library System, University
  of Pittsburgh   197
          Debora A. Rougeux
          Rebecca L. Mugridge

Index   209

ABOUT THE EDITOR

Carolyn C. Sherayko, MLS, MA, has been Head of the Cataloging Department at Indiana University since September 1989. Prior to that she held the positions of Social Sciences Cataloger/Documents Librarian at The Pennsylvania State University and Documents/Reference Librarian at Appalachian State University. At Penn State, she directed the automation of circulation, processing, and serials control of federal, state, and international documents. She holds the MLS from the University of North Carolina-Chapel Hill and the MA from Appalachian State University. Ms. Sherayko has served on and chaired the ALA/Government Documents Round Table Cataloging Committee and is currently serving on the Subcommittee to revise the GODORT cataloging manual. She has written and spoken on mainstreaming government publications into library processing.

PLANNING, ORGANIZATION, WORKFLOWS

Planning, Systems Analysis, and Negotiation: Key Elements for a Successful GPO Tapeload

Josephine Crawford

SUMMARY. A complex automation project was brought to successful completion when 236,018 Government Printing Office (GPO) cataloging records (purchased from Marcive, Inc.) and 382,792 copy statements were loaded into the library system at the University of Wisconsin, Madison. Since that time, regularly scheduled loads of

Josephine Crawford, Automation Manager, Center for Health Sciences Library, 1305 Linden Drive, University of Wisconsin, Madison, WI 53706.

The author gratefully acknowledges the project contributions of approximately twenty-five librarians on the UW-Madison campus. Without each person's commitment, analytical skills, and creative ideas, the project would never have been completed with the same degree of success. Special mention must be made of the outstanding work done by Susan G. Peters of the Wisconsin State Historical Society Library and Mark Foster of the Division of Information Technology; without their tireless efforts, the project would not have been possible.

[Haworth co-indexing entry note]: "Planning, Systems Analysis, and Negotiation: Key Elements for a Successful GPO Tapeload," Crawford, Josephine. Co-published simultaneously in *Cataloging & Classification Quarterly* (The Haworth Press, Inc.) Vol. 18, No. 3/4, 1994, pp. 1-17; and: *Cataloging Government Publications Online* (ed: Carolyn C. Sherayko) The Haworth Press, Inc., 1994, pp. 1-17. Multiple copies of this article/chapter may be purchased from The Haworth Document Delivery Center [1-800-3-HAWORTH; 9:00 a.m. - 5:00 p.m. (EST)].

current GPO cataloging records have occurred. This article describes the planning process, important decision points, the scope and complexity of the local programming, and efforts taken to maintain and improve database quality.

INTRODUCTION

At the University of Wisconsin-Madison, a committee composed of catalogers, document specialists, one systems librarian, and one programmer planned and executed a project to load retrospective and current cataloging records produced by the U.S. Government Printing Office (GPO) into the campus bibliographic database. The GPO project was successful in shaping a complex load process which pays attention to:

1. differences in cataloging practices between libraries
2. differences in how libraries shelve documents
3. the lack of library staff for major hand-editing projects.

The retrospective load took place on August 4, 1991 and added 236,018 new bibliographic records and 382,792 location/copy statements to the campus database. The same programs, with minor modification and maintenance, are used currently for regularly-scheduled tapeloads of new GPO cataloging.

BACKGROUND

The State Historical Society of Wisconsin, located on the UW-Madison campus, but administratively separate from the University, is a regional depository library which has developed housing agreements with various UW-Madison libraries such as the Center for Health Sciences Library. Approximately half of the depository documents received are retained by the Historical Society Library while the other half are sent to different campus libraries, based upon the item number under which federal documents are distributed by GPO.[1] In addition, two UW-Madison libraries (the Law and Memorial libraries) are selective depositories, with the Memorial

Library distributing some of its documents to other campus libraries. Therefore, there exists the possibility of receiving up to three copies of any federal document, housed in three different libraries and shelved under three different call numbers. Some libraries traditionally catalog all or some documents received with the objective of integrating documents into stack collections; in other cases, libraries shelve uncataloged documents in special areas and provide access by the SuDoc number.[2]

The UW-Madison libraries and the State Historical Society Library share a single bibliographic database mounted on a NOTIS system; an interface between this NOTIS system and a locally-developed online public access catalog exists and functions well.[3] Computer programs written locally are used for loading OCLC records into the database as well as for authority control. The load programs merge separate OCLC tape records created by different cataloging agencies into one shared bibliographic record, whenever the OCLC number is the same. A standing committee of catalogers has developed campus-wide policies and procedures for the shared database for over ten years. AACR2, Library of Congress Rule Interpretations, and MARC standards are followed with one important exception: one bibliographic record is stored in the database to which both paper and microform holdings are attached.

PROGRAMMING OBJECTIVES

As has been documented in the literature, improved bibliographic access via GPO tapeloading is not easy or straightforward given that the tapes are a by-product of the production of the *Monthly Catalog* and that input procedures by GPO catalogers have varied considerably over the years.[4] After much study and discussion of the many issues, the UW-Madison GPO Committee came to the conclusion that more bibliographic access would be gained for serials and that much staff effort would be saved by purchasing the "cleaned-up" GPO records from Marcive, Inc.[5] Supported by library administrators on this important decision, Committee work proceeded on load issues dealing primarily with information about physical access. Eight programming objectives were formulated as follows:

1. Integrate the GPO/Marcive records into the existing database.
2. Reduce the loading of duplicate cataloging records as much as possible.
3. Load accurate location information, including all owning libraries as well as the shelving location within each library.
4. Load the appropriate call number for each copy.
5. Load brief holdings information for serial records.
6. Load public notes to facilitate ease of use.
7. Provide special handling for microforms.
8. For efficiency, make use of the existing load and authority processing routines used for other cataloging records.

These objectives were designed to allow immediate use of the GPO cataloging records in the online catalog, with a minimum of manual clean-up.

ITEM NUMBER MATRIX

Given that the campus distribution of documents is based upon the GPO item number present in the 074 MARC field, a decision table or matrix using the item number was developed to facilitate the computer assignment of location, call number, and other copy information. There are over 11,000 item numbers; each required individual treatment decisions by campus librarians responsible for documents. Some default choices were provided to reduce this workload.

The Historical Society Library assumed the workload of creating an item number matrix in machine-readable form using manual records. An active list (representing item numbers for currently published documents) and an inactive list (representing retired item numbers) were produced for each campus library. Document librarians were then asked to annotate the matrix line-by-line, in order to show the treatment decisions chosen by their respective library. Sometimes decisions were made only after checking the stacks, the online catalog, a documents shelflist, and/or the *Monthly Catalog*.

Figure 1 supplies matrix column definitions and Figure 2 supplies actual examples in order to show the variety of situations encountered and the approach used.

To prepare for the tapeloading of the current GPO/Marcive records, inactive item numbers were removed from the matrix. The Historical Society Library offered new printed lists to campus libraries with suggestions on how to redo "active" lists, encouraging library staff to use more default processing and to rethink matrix decisions in conjunction with revised workflow procedures.[6] Maintained on a monthly basis, the "active" matrix is used for each current load of GPO/Marcive records; editing of the active matrix involves adding new item numbers and making treatment changes on demand.

SYSTEMS ANALYSIS AND COMMUNICATION

Using two test tapes (one purchased from the Government Printing Office and the other from Marcive, Inc.), the GPO Committee examined hundreds of records, identified exceptions and problems, and negotiated programming solutions. During the time that the document librarians were working on their library's treatment decisions, the librarians on the GPO Committee applied their systems analysis skills and wrote load specifications to document ongoing discussions with the programmer. Written and oral reports were given occasionally to interested library staff, with the idea of educating people about the overall computer process, the inherent trade-offs in handling exceptions, and the need to prepare for increased circulation of documents. Questions and concerns from library staff at large inspired new programming ideas which improved the quality and sophistication of the end product.

MATRIX PROCESSING

When the GPO/Marcive tape records are received on campus, they are first prepared by a number of computer processing routines. For instance, the OCLC number is moved from the 001 field to the 035 field and the locally-defined "MGPO" code is added to the end of the 040 field to show that the source of the record is Marcive.[7] The most sophisticated computer routine processes the

FIGURE 1. Matrix Column Definitions.

ITEM NO.
Each item number can have only one line entry per library unless differentiated by use of the SUDOC column or, in rare instances, by use of the START/STOP columns.

SUDOC STEM/NO.
Up to 25 characters of a SuDoc number can be input to control record loading more specifically than possible by item number alone. In most cases, only the SuDoc stem is used, but the load program handles longer numbers equally well. Two special processing symbols can be used:
= Same treatment for all incoming records with the same item number for a given library, irrespective of the SuDoc stem/number on the incoming tape record.
* Default processing for an item number (used when a library prefers to specify different treatment for some SuDoc stems/numbers but does not want to list every possibility).

LOC
A NOTIS location code representing the owning library.

SLOC
A NOTIS sublocation code representing the shelving location or collection within a library.

START
The Start date indicates the year in which a library began to receive documents under a specific item number and possibly a SuDoc stem/number. "N" in this column indicates that the library has received documents for the entire time an item number is/was active. The Start date cannot be used for serials (Holdings column used instead).

STOP
The Stop date indicates the year in which a library stopped receiving documents. "N" indicates the library has received documents for the entire time an item number is/was active. The Stop date cannot be used for serials (Holdings column used instead).

CLASS
A one-letter NOTIS code indicating the classification scheme used to shelve an item.

CALL
Call number assigned to a document before it is shelved. Three possibilities defined:
1) A library can supply a call number which will load into NOTIS with subfielding appropriate to the classification scheme.
2) "YY" in this column indicates that the SuDoc number present in the 086 field should be copied into the call number field, again with appropriate subfielding.
3) "NN" in this column indicates that no call number should load (i.e. for pamphlets).

NOTE
A number from 01 to 99 representing a specific public note stored in a separate program file. Examples: Current issues in Periodical Room; Volumes for 1980- are in microfiche; Latest year only retained; Filed by state and quadrangle number; Retained until cumulation is received.

HOLDINGS
Use to load brief holdings information for a serial or monographic set. Three possibilities:
1) A library can supply holdings data up to twenty characters consisting of numbers, dashes, commas, and optional spaces (e.g. 1976,1980-1986,1988-).
2) "Y" in this column indicates that the loading program should create a holdings string using the Beginning and Ending Dates from the 008 field in the GPO/Marcive record, but only if the incoming record represents a serial title.
3) "N" in this column indicates that no holdings string should load.

MICRO
A microform sublocation takes precedence over the sublocation listed in the SLOC column, if there is an indication that GPO distributed the document in microform and other conditions are met. If a library does not want this to occur, "N" is entered into this column.

FIGURE 2. Examples from the Item Number Matrix.

ITEM	SUDOC STEM/NO.	LOC	SLOC	START	STOP	CLASS	CALL	NOTE	HOLDINGS	MICRO?
2	=	stee	doc	N	N	S	YY	N	N	N
2	A 1.116:	law	doc	N	N	S	YY	N	N	mic
2	A 1.116:R 88/2/	law	doc	N	N	S	YY	48	1980-	N
2	A 1.58/a:	law	doc	N	N	S	YY	N	1977-	mic
2	*	law	doc	N	N	S	YY	N	N	mic

Steenbock Library assigns an equal sign to item number 2 in order to not specify treatment by individual SuDoc stem/no; YY will cause the SuDoc number to load as the call number. The Law Library specifies different treatment for three SuDoc stems and also supplies a default (*) entry for all other SuDoc stems. 48 in the NOTE column indicates that the phrase "Holdings are incomplete" should load as a public note.

ITEM	SUDOC STEM/NO.	LOC	SLOC	START	STOP	CLASS	CALL	NOTE	HOLDINGS	MICRO?
429-N	=	engn	tech	N	N	S	YY	49	N	N
429-N	E 1.19:	phys	stk	N	N	T	LH 7UN299 ER	49	1978-	mic
429-N	*	phys	doc	N	N	X	NN	55	1978-	mic

The Engineering Library assigns the equals sign to item number 429-N. The Physics Library would like a Cutter call number to load for one of its SuDoc stems; hence, the "T" code in the CLASsification column and the LH call number in the CALL column. The Physics default entry specifies loading no call number.

ITEM	SUDOC STEM/NO.	LOC	SLOC	START	STOP	CLASS	CALL	NOTE	HOLDINGS	MICRO?
498-B	EP 6.9	heah	gpor	1978	N	S	YY	N	N	N
498-B-1	=	phys	doc	N	1979	T	LH 7UN3 ST22	N	N	N

The Health Sciences Library supplies a START date of 1978; therefore, no records will load unless the 008 Beginning Date is 1978 or higher. The Physics Library stopped receiving 498-B-1 documents in 1979; none of these records will load for Physics if the 008 Ending Date is 1980 or higher.

ITEM	SUDOC STEM/NO.	LOC	SLOC	START	STOP	CLASS	CALL	NOTE	HOLDINGS	MICRO?
717-C	J 26.1:	law	doc	N	N	S	YY	N	1969-1974, 1976-1979	N
717-C	J 26.1/2:	law	doc	N	N	S	YY	N	1978-1979	N
717-C	J 26.1/3:	law	doc	N	N	S	YY	N	1974-1978	N
717-C	*	law	doc	N	N	S	YY	N	N	mic

The Law Library uses SUDOC stems to specify different holdings data; "mic" in the MICRO column indicates that Law's "mic" sublocation takes precedence over the "doc" sublocation under specific conditions.

ITEM	SUDOC STEM/NO.	LOC	SLOC	START	STOP	CLASS	CALL	NOTE	HOLDINGS	MICRO?
768-B	=	his	gvp	N	N	S	YY	N	N	N
768-B	=	mem	stk	N	N	L	HD5723 A4532	28	Y	N

The Historical Society chooses the same treatment for all documents distributed under 768-B. A "Y" in the HOLDINGS column indicates that the beginning and ending date from serial records should load into the holdings record. If the ending date is 9999, then an open entry will load. The Memorial Library would like the same HD call number and the same, public note to load for all GPO records with this item number.

records against the treatment decisions stored in the item number matrix. Each unique combination of item number, SuDoc number, and library is recognized by the program for matching to a specific line in the matrix. An example is available in Figure 3.

Careful systems analysis was done in order to normalize item numbers and SuDoc numbers to achieve the desired result. Leading zeros in the case of item numbers and all spaces in the case of SuDoc numbers are dropped by the program. However, all punctuation is retained in order to maintain uniqueness.

When comparing a SuDoc number on a tape record against a similar SuDoc stem/number present in the matrix, the program applies implicit truncation at the end of the SuDoc stem/number in the item matrix. An example is available in Figure 4.

The examination of test tapes uncovered many examples of mul-

FIGURE 3. Loading Multiple Locations/Copies.

```
008            ------c19uu9999dcuuuɢɢɢɢrɢɢɢf0--ua0engɢɢ       [ $ subfield
035/1          $a (OCoLC) 01784590                              delimiter ]
040            $a DLC $c GPO $d MvI-ocs $d MvI-ocm $d MGPO
074            $a 763
086/1    0     $a L 16.3:
086/2    0     $a L 35.3:
086/3    0     $a L36.3:177/4
245     00     $a Labor offices in the United States and Canada.
260     00     $a [Washington] : $b Dept. of Labor, Employment Standards
               Administration, Office of Program Development and Accountability.
300            $a v. $c 24 cm.
490/1    1     $a Bulletin - Employment Standards Administration
490/2    1     $a ESA publication
500/1          $a Previously classed: L 16.3:, L 35.3:
550/2    1     $a Vols. prior to 1978 were issued by the Division of State
               Employment Standards.
580/3          $a Continues: Labor offices in the United States and Canada,
               issued by:  United States.  Bureau of Labor Standards.
650/1          $a Labor bureaus $z United States $x Directories.
650/2          $a Labor bureaus $z Canada $x Directories.
710/1    10    $a United States. $b Employment Standards Administration $b Office
               of Program Development and Accountability.
710/2    11    $a United States. $b Employment Standards Administration $b
               Division of State Employment Standards.
760/1    0     $a Bulletin - Employment Standards Administration
760/2    0     $a United States.  Employment Standards Administration.  $t ESA
               publication
780/1    10    $a Labor offices in the United States and Canada
810/1    1     $a United States.  $b Employment Standards Administration. $t
               Bulletin - Employment Standards Administration.
830/2    0     $a ESA publication.
```

Two libraries have matrix entries for the item number 763 which is present in the 074 field; therefore, three call numbers (one for each SuDoc number present in the 086/1, 086/2, and 086/3 fields) load for each library. As time permits, detailed holdings information is added by hand to the database to show what holdings are shelved under each call number.

FIGURE 4. Normalization and Automatic Truncation.

```
SuDoc number present on tape record:    L 38.6:M 56/4
                      Normalized to:    L38.6:M56/4

SuDoc stem present on item no. matrix:  L 38.6:
                      Normalized to:    L38.6:


During the computer processing, SuDoc numbers are normalized and truncated
according to specific rules in order to achieve the desired result.  The
normalization rules are:
    1) Drop all spaces;
    2) Retain all punctuation.

The two normalized data strings match successfully because of automatic
truncation of the SuDoc number present on the tape record -- shown by the
bolding above.
```

tiple item numbers, usually in a single subfield of the 074 field. Given that an unrecognized item number would result in one or more lost copy statements, the programming recognizes multiple item numbers and handles each one separately.[8]

The test tapes also revealed that some GPO cataloging records lack 074 fields. In most cases they represent documents cataloged by GPO yet not distributed on the depository program. In some cases, the missing item number indicates a GPO error. These records load with a special location called "U.S. Non-Depository Record." A line in the matrix labeled MISSING was used to supply this location as well as an internal staff note explaining that the document may not be owned on campus. These records (just over 11,000 in the current database) do not appear in the online public access catalog, but they are available for use by a cataloger if a library acquires one of these documents.

INTEGRATION

Much of the systems analysis involved planning how to integrate the GPO tapeloading into the load and authority processing programs already in use on campus. These load programs have much flexibility built into them in order to save staff time and improve database quality. There are several processing options to account for differences between current cataloging on OCLC, retrospective conversion on OCLC, purchased records of major microform sets, OCLC records for the Center for Research Libraries, and procedural differences between large and small cataloging departments. For example, the program recognizes duplicate bibliographic records by comparing OCLC numbers on tape records to OCLC numbers on database records; depending upon the processing default chosen by a library or an override code added to a particular record, the incoming bibliographic information is either overlaid or dumped (in the latter case, the program may load location or holdings information though).

Integration with existing programs was achieved in two important ways. First, when the GPO/Marcive records are processed against the item number matrix, the output mimics the OCLC/MARC format so that it can be joined up with the OCLC tape also ready for batch loading. Indexing costs are lower by updating the database with both tapes at the same time. Simulating OCLC/MARC requires the matrix processing to clone or copy records whenever multiple locations for a record should load, each clone with a different location and call number. The loader on the same night merges these clones into one database record with multiple locations.

Second, a GPO load option was programmed in order to smoothly integrate GPO/Marcive tape information with manual cataloging information already present in the database. Otherwise, computer processing of OCLC and GPO records remains the same, especially the authority control processing. The GPO load option operates at the bibliographic level *and* copy level, whenever duplicates are detected via OCLC number matching, as follows:

BIBLIOGRAPHIC LEVEL: The GPO load option specifies that the database record takes precedence over the incoming tape record. This was done in order to maintain local cataloging work such as the addition of Medical Subject Headings. However, database records frequently lack item numbers and SuDoc numbers; therefore, the GPO load option copies these numbers from a tape record and adds them to the matching database record when not already present.

COPY LEVEL: A different location/copy match was programmed when there is a database record present already. The other processing options require an exact match at this level on four elements of information: location, sublocation, call number, and copy number.[9] To account for manual cataloging done prior to a tapeload, a relaxed approach was programmed which only requires an exact match on the main location (but not sublocation, call number, or copy number). Two examples are available in Figure 5.

The GPO load option significantly reduced manual clean-up after the retrospective load in 1991. In regards to current tapeloads, it allows library staff to catalog documents using online transfer from OCLC before a tape record arrives; selective cataloging done by hand cannot be "undone" by a tapeload.

MICROFORM HANDLING

Microforms present a real challenge when loading GPO cataloging records. There are issues regarding the bibliographic description as well as how to create accurate location and holdings information. These issues need to be addressed from the perspective of the inherent differences between monographic and serial cataloging records.

Up until 1992, GPO cataloged the paper copy in most cases and added 5xx notes such as "Distributed to depository libraries in microfiche" or "Distributed to some depository libraries in microfiche." Creation of a single bibliographic record dovetailed nicely with UW-Madison cataloging practice.[10] An example from the retrospective load is available in Figure 6.

FIGURE 5. Library/Copy Matching.

	Location	Sublocation
Example 1:		
GPO/Marcive record:	his	gpr
Database record:	law	doc

The Law Library cataloged the document upon receipt and the catalog record is present in the database. The copy owned by the Historical Society was never cataloged. The load program adds a new location to the database representing the copy owned by the Historical Society Library.

Example 2:		
GPO/Marcive record:	**heah**	gpor
Database record:	**heah**	stk

The bolding shows the match on the main location. The Health Sciences Library cataloged the document for the stack collection. A new location/copy is <u>not</u> added to the database by the load program because the library does not own two copies of the same document.

FIGURE 6. Paper/Microform Dual Distribution.

```
008          ------s1984ᵇᵇᵇᵇdcuakᵇᵇᵇᵇbf00010bengᵇd
035/1        $a (OCoLC) 11208525                    [ $ subfield
040          $a GPO $c GPO $d MGPO-R                    delimiter ]
074          $a 1038-A $a 1038-B (microfiche)
086/1   0    $a Y 4.F 49:S.hrg.98-836
110     10   $a United States. $b Congress. $b Senate. $b Committee on
             Finance. $b Subcommittee on Taxation and Debt Management.
245     10   $a 1983-84 miscellaneous tax bills--IX, S. 146, S. 1332, S.
             1768, S. 1809, and S. 2080 : $b hearing before the Subcommittee on
             Taxation and Debt Management of the Committee on Finance, United
             States Senate, Ninety-eighth Congress, second session ... March 16,
             1984.
260     0    $a Washington : $b U.S. G.P.O., $c 1984.
300          $a iv, 218 p. : $b ill., forms ; $c 24 cm.
490/1   1    $a S. hrg. ; $v 98-836
500/1        $a Distributed to some depository libraries in microfiche.
504/2        $a Includes bibliographical references.
650/1        $a Taxation $z United States.
650/2        $a Taxation, Exemption from $z United States
650/3        $a Energy tax credits $z United States
650/4        $a Fishing boats $z United States $x Energy conservation.
650/5        $a Prepaid legal services $z United States
740/1   01   $a 1983-84 miscellaneous tax bills--9, S. 146, S. 1332,
             S.1768, S. 1809, and S. 2080
810/1   1    $a United States $b Congress $n (98th, 2nd session : $d
             1984) $b Senate $t S.hrg ; $v 98-836
```

The tape GPO/Marcive record had two item numbers in a single $a of the 074 field. The load processing placed each item number into its own $a so that both numbers would index online.

Three locations and call numbers loaded into the UW-Madison database for this bibliographic record, based upon the processing combination of two item numbers and one SuDoc number. The first location represents the paper copy received at the Law Library; the second location represents the microform copy received at the Historical Society Library; the third location represents the microform copy received at the Law Library.

The 007 Fixed Field, with the "h" microform code in the first position of the field, loaded into the holdings records attached to the two microform locations.

Some new programming was required when GPO changed its cataloging policy. Beginning in 1992, when distributing a document only in microform, GPO creates a bibliographic record describing the microform edition; if a serial record already exists for the paper format, the two records are linked together using the 776 field. However, when distributing a document in both paper and microform (i.e., dual distribution), GPO continues to create a single record for both versions. Recent programming now indexes OCLC numbers present in the $w of the 776 field in addition to OCLC numbers stored in the 035 and 019 fields. By doing so, the original de-duping and merge process continues to work reasonably well, but not necessarily in every case.[11] There are two underlying problems here: GPO's inconsistent cataloging policy and the delayed implementation of a national solution to the multiple version problem.[12]

A number of techniques were developed to load accurate location and holdings information for microforms, revolving around the treatment decisions in the item number matrix. Document librarians across the Madison campus requested a number of public notes ranging from the general "Some numbers issued on microfiche" to the more specific "Volumes for 1983- are on microfiche." The ability to load a wide variety of notes (using the NOTES column in the matrix) allows for smoother public access immediately after a GPO record is loaded than would otherwise be possible.

The MICRO column sublocation in the matrix takes precedence over the sublocation found in the SLOC column (see Figure 1) under specific conditions. For instance, the program checks to see if the character string "microfiche" follows the item number in the 074 field and if the Bibliographic Level of the GPO record is "m"; if the answer to both questions is yes, the program loads the sublocation from the MICRO column. Other variations on this theme were programmed, with the result that accurate location information loads for monographs in almost all cases.

Even after much brainstorming, a similarly successful technique was not found for serials distributed in microform. Therefore, serial microforms report out after loading so that library staff can change the sublocation and input holdings information directly into the database as necessary. Hand editing may not be needed in cases where an item number has one and only one serial title distributed under it because the correct sublocation is listed already in the SLOC column of the matrix.

TESTING, TRAINING, AND REPORTS

Organized testing and training was essential in a project of this size, as was the ability to print various "condition" reports to check on specific situations. A plan with three phases was developed and followed:

PHASE ONE: Initial testing was done by the programmer and the GPO Committee by reviewing small numbers of test records after processing against the completed item number matrix. Most bugs were caught at this stage, the specifications were updated in minor ways as the programming logic was finetuned, and negotiation and decision-making took place regarding reports.

PHASE TWO: To prepare for the second phase of testing, each documents librarian was asked to contribute a list of item numbers, covering a wide variety of load situations. This testing was expensive but extremely helpful; the entire file of retrospective GPO/ Marcive records was processed against a test matrix of one thousand lines as well as against the production bibliographic and authority files. In this way, the test records looked exactly as they would look when loaded into the production files the following month.

A packet of information on checking the test load was provided to volunteers. GPO Committee members made individual visits to libraries to make sure that document librarians and catalogers understood what was expected of them as testers. Hands-on training was provided in how to search online by item and SuDoc numbers (in order to check specific situations). Only small programming bugs were discovered at this point which raised confidence across campus in the entire project prior to the retrospective load.

By combining testing and training, hands-on familiarity was gained by library staff responsible for documents before the retrospective load. More importantly, the test file enabled document librarians to better understand the result of their matrix decisions. As a result, many changes were requested and the production matrix was heavily edited the week preceding the retrospective load into the production file.

During Phase Two, programming was completed on a dozen condition reports, which printed out just after the retrospective load and continue to print out after each new load. The Microfiche Serials Report has already been mentioned. The Ambiguous Hits Report notifies catalogers about multiple OCLC records in the database with the same OCLC number. Some other reports detect various GPO cataloging errors, such as when the same SuDoc number appears in both the $a and $z subfields of an 086 field. Additional reports print on demand and allow a library to check on the accuracy of location and call number information under specific conditions or for entire sublocations.

PHASE THREE (ongoing): The final testing occurs by checking the production database immediately after each load, normally done by one or two staff members. The most organized effort naturally occurred the morning after the large retrospective load in 1991.

CONCLUSION

The prospect of a GPO tapeload was somewhat controversial due to fears that the records would "dirty" the database and create a database maintenance nightmare. As a result, the "cleaned-up" GPO database was purchased from Marcive, Inc. and every reasonable effort was made to load accurate local information. By designing a flexible and sophisticated decision matrix, each library was provided with the opportunity to control the load of information to best meet its internal cataloging and shelving practices. Reports were provided for small hand-editing projects, but it was not necessary to undertake major projects.

Workloads in several functional areas have grown due to the GPO tapeloads. Reference staff help users to search for documents in the online catalog more than before. Circulation of documents has increased although there has been no organized effort to document the increase statistically. Circulation staff have been plagued by the need to chase down "phantom" documents.[13] The load programs only detect duplicate bibliographic records when OCLC numbers match, with the result that some duplicates do load because of different OCLC numbers; these records are merged by hand as discovered by cataloging staff.

These problems pale in comparison to the enduring benefits of the project. Thousands of cataloging records are loaded into the database yearly at a substantially lower cost than what could be done using traditional methods. Internally, knowledge about documents, systems analysis skills, and project management experience increased among a number of university staff members. Working relationships between involved staff reached new levels of respect and team work, crossing five organizational lines without and within the university to achieve common goals with limited resources. Most importantly, improved bibliographic access on previously hidden documents enables a wealth of information to be more easily available to users. Through public service announcements about the successful project, the image of all involved libraries was enhanced, particularly important during times of shrinking collections and budget retrenchment.

NOTES

1. Each document is assigned to an item number by the Government Printing Office as a way to manage document distribution. Libraries "select" the item numbers for which distribution is desired. An item number may represent a category of publications, a series, or an individual title. For instance, 508-D represents general publications of the National Library of Medicine, whereas 508-H-8 represents the NLM Technical Bulletin, published monthly.

2. A SuDoc number is assigned by the Superintendent of Documents. The SuDoc classification scheme groups together publications by the various departments, bureaus, and agencies of the U.S. Government. The part of the classification number up to and including a colon (e.g., A 1.10:) is called the "stem." Often the stem will contain both the author and a series designation (if a publication is part of a series). The specific book number follows the stem. In some cases, however, the series designation follows the colon.

3. The UW-Madison NOTIS system, operating on a mainframe computer, is used for database maintenance, online transfer of OCLC records, acquisitions, serials control, and circulation. The online catalog developed locally is called the Network Library System (NLS) and operates on an RS6000 UNIX computer.

4. More information is available in the following:

Cornwell, Gary. "GPO Cataloging Records; Background and Issues." *DTTP (Documents To The People)* 17 (June 1989): 83-85.
Jamison, Carolyn C. "Loading the GPO Tapes-What Does It Really Mean?" *Government Publications Review* 13 (1986): 549-559.
Myers, Judy E. "The Government Printing Office Cataloging Records: Opportunities and Problems." *Government Information Quarterly* 2 (1985): 27-56.

5. Working in cooperation with document librarians from three university libraries, Marcive, Inc. provides "cleaned-up" GPO records. Key improvements are: AACR2 serial cataloging records are created in place of GPO's "availability" records; item and SuDoc numbers are moved to their appropriate MARC field; missing OCLC numbers and filing indicators are added to records; map quadrangle records are prepared for easy loading or dumping; and *Monthly Catalog* error corrections are made. Without these improvements, it would not be possible for UW-Madison to load GPO/Marcive cataloging records for immediate public use.

6. The revised workflow is complicated by the fact that normally a document is received before the bibliographic record arrives on tape. Each library reworked

its workflow with some minimal campus guidelines and set in place its own solution to this problem.

7. In addition to online identification of the source of the GPO/Marcive records, the "MGPO" code in the 040 field will also be used by computer programs to prevent redistribution of Marcive's records according to contractual obligations.

8. Prior to December 1991, the MARC formats did not recognize the presence of more than one item number in the same record. Neither the 074 field nor the $a could repeat. Faced with the need to deal with multiple item numbers, the GPO Committee decided to allow the $a to repeat in the 074 field, as a local variation to the MARC format. Therefore, the GPO load program places each item number into its own subfield; the contents of each $a indexes cleanly in the local NOTIS system, helping library staff to retrieve GPO records efficiently. Future programming may move these numbers to separate 074 fields, in order for the campus database to be in complete compliance with the MARC formats.

9. Under the exact match approach, if location, sublocation, call number, and copy number match exactly, then no new location is added to the database record, although some holdings data may load for the matched location/copy. If there is no exact match, then a new location/copy is added.

10. To improve public service, UW-Madison cataloging policy calls for storing a single bibliographic record in the local database, with paper/microform distinctions described in the holdings records subordinate to the bibliographic record. A typical holdings record for microform contains the 007 Physical Format field, an 843 field with the microform publisher, an 853 field with caption information, and an 863 field listing volumes/issues owned in microform.

11. Some cleanup by hand is required in occasional situations. For instance, sometimes there are three or more OCLC records, all describing the same work. These print out for manual review and merging as appropriate. In other cases, formats other than paper/microform might be involved. If the 776 field is present with an OCLC number in the $w, the program may merge in error. Whenever different formats belong on separate bibliographic records according to local cataloging policy, a cataloger may need to intervene manually.

12. For more information, see:

Multiple Versions Forum Report: Report from a meeting held December 6-8, 1989, Airlie, Virginia. Washington, D.C.: Network Development and MARC Standards Office, Library of Congress, 1990.

13. Some records loaded even though a document has been lost, withdrawn, or was never received. To some extent, a library could reduce the number of phantom records when making treatment decisions on the matrix.

Approaching Automation:
A Planning Model for GPO Tapeloading–
One Library's Experience

Linda B. Johnson
Sushila Selness

SUMMARY. Given the availability of machine readable cataloging records for a significant number of United States federal documents, many libraries are either planning to include or have already begun to incorporate such materials in their online catalogs. After reviewing the literature, this article describes a model developed at San Jose State University for planning such automation and the resulting increased access. Model components include a description of the local situation and checklist questions used for a telephone survey. The article also describes the methodology followed in creating the final proposal for bringing federal documents records into the online catalog.

INTRODUCTION

Within the past decade, a number of developments have made the inclusion of United States government document collections in the

Linda B. Johnson is Head of the Government Publications Department at Clark Library, San Jose State University, One Washington Square, San Jose, CA 95192. Sushila Selness is Head of the Government Documents and Microforms Department, Legal Research Center, University of San Diego, 5998 Alcala Park, San Diego, CA 92110.

[Haworth co-indexing entry note]: "Approaching Automation: A Planning Model for GPO Tapeloading–One Library's Experience," Johnson, Linda B., and Sushila Selness. Co-published simultaneously in *Cataloging & Classification Quarterly* (The Haworth Press, Inc.) Vol. 18, No. 3/4, 1994, pp. 19-36; and: *Cataloging Government Publications Online* (ed: Carolyn C. Sherayko) The Haworth Press, Inc., 1994, pp. 19-36. Multiple copies of this article/chapter may be purchased from The Haworth Document Delivery Center [1-800-3-HAWORTH; 9:00 a.m. - 5:00 p.m. (EST)].

library mainstream a real possibility. The circumstances leading to this welcome situation are the availability of machine readable records for post-1976 U.S. government documents, the proliferation of online catalogs in libraries, and the push for greater and easier accessibility to all library collections through those catalogs. Thus librarians continue to search for the best method suited to their particular situations for bringing government document collections into the online environment. Drawn from the experiences at San Jose State University (SJSU), this article briefly describes one practical model for such automation planning and the resulting preliminary and final proposals.

GPO CATALOGING BACKGROUND

Traditionally, due to the high cost of cataloging large government document collections, lack of available machine readable cataloging (MARC) records, the frequently lower use of these collections when compared to the book and journal collections, and a number of unique shelving and classification schemes, government documents in most libraries remained uncataloged and outside the primary access provided by the library's public catalog. Just as traditionally, public service librarians agonized over the lack of easy access to these materials with the resulting underutilization of the collection and less effective service to patrons. (Watson and Heim 1984)

All this abruptly changed with the availability of machine readable tapes for U.S. federal publications–one of the true watershed events in documents librarianship. Almost immediately after the 1976 inception of the Government Printing Office's (GPO) cataloging of U.S. government documents on the OCLC bibliographic utility, documents librarians enthusiastically began envisioning scenarios for the cataloging and automation of their federal materials. At San Jose State these developments were closely followed with a view to their local relevance and application.

LITERATURE REVIEW

A review of the mileposts along this sometimes bumpy but increasingly well-charted road to U.S. document cataloging and automation enabled the SJSU staff to benefit from the trial and error of other librarians. Given such a rich background, they were able to start their planning model with many of the basic questions already answered. Although here discussed as if a linear progression, the events and issues outlined in this literature review more closely represent a fluid chronology with many occurring simultaneously or frequently recurring.

Initially, the articles in the literature were theoretical in nature as they speculated on the opportunities presented by the availability of the GPO MARC records. First came the realization that cataloging of documents in a cost-effective manner was within reach of the majority of libraries rather than the minority. (Myers and Britton 1978; Bower 1984; Foster and Lufburrow 1979; Graham 1983; Walbridge 1982; Powell et al. 1987). These authors uniformly spoke of the not-to-be-missed opportunity of increasing access to government documents. A few felt that cataloged documents appearing in the library online catalog finally put to rest the separate versus integrated government document collection debate by making the actual physical location of the material much less important. (Foster and Lufburrow 1979; Myers and Britton 1978; Graham 1983; Bower 1984).

Then came articles with numerous suggestions as to possible ways to use the GPO MARC records and the associated problems of each method (Walbridge 1982; Bowerman and Cady 1984; Swanbeck 1985; Plaunt 1985). One of the most ambitious suggestions was the proposed pilot study and detailed model for a full-function documents control system developed exclusively for documents' collections (Stephenson and Purcell 1986, 196-197).

At the same time, a growing number of articles described the actual "hands-on" reality of cataloging and automating as consortia such as the Research Libraries Group (RLG) or individual libraries either loaded the GPO tapes (Jamison 1986), cataloged on a bibliographic utility (Higdon 1984; Stanfield 1986; Maclay 1989), or contracted with a vendor for a customized tape or catalog cards (Walbridge 1982; Plaunt 1985). A few of the articles began to note the timeliness of the appearance of the cataloging (Bower 1984; Powell et al. 1987) or the quality of that cataloging (Foster and Lufburrow 1979; Bower 1984; Powell et al. 1987). One discussed the technical characteristics of the tapes themselves (Jamison 1986).

All this discussion of the tapes and the quality of the cataloging was accompanied by a growing realization that there were some rather serious problems with the tapes and cataloging (Higdon 1984; Swanbeck 1985; Stanfield 1986). Such concern culminated in the seminal article and American Library Association summer meeting presentation by Judy Myers. In these she reviewed the history of the GPO cataloging and the particular problems created by the records on tape. She outlined the corrections needed to bring the records to an acceptable national cataloging standard. More importantly, Myers proposed a cooperative cleanup project of the tapes so that libraries could use those records for loading into their online catalogs without each library having to clean up the records independently (Myers 1985 and 1987).

Happily, Myers' suggestions inspired a project begun in 1987 and completed in 1989 (Tull 1989, 4) by librarians at Rice University, Louisiana State University, Texas A&M, and the vendor, Marcive, Inc. with Myers serving as a consultant. The methodology used and the results of this project are excellently documented by two articles (Tull 1989; Bolner and Kile 1991).

In the post-tape clean-up world, the articles focus on the quality and timeliness of the records using the tapes (Mooney 1989), the problems and solutions when profiling with a vendor tape service (Romans 1992), a creative solution to the problems encountered when matching records using a tape loading vendor service (Mooney 1990), authority control issues (Wallace 1992; Meyer 1992), and changes or refinements in the Government Printing Office's cataloging and tape production procedures (Baldwin 1992).

Others touch upon retrospective conversion options and planning (Tull 1989; Rocha 1991) as well as ambitious retrospective conversion projects such as the one which brought documents into the integrated online catalog of three college libraries (Regueiro et al. 1992). As more and more libraries have document records in their online catalogs, the concerns increasingly revolve around on-going maintenance issues and reorganization of documents departments as seen by discussions on the GOVDOC-L computer conference.

Finally, there are explorations of the many implications of having these records more widely available (Kinney and Cornwell 1991).

SAN JOSE STATE MODEL

Keeping in mind all the questions and answers documented in the literature, staff began to approach the cataloging and automation of government documents at San Jose State University. After many years of planning, library staff implemented Innovative Interfaces' INNOPAC, the online public access catalog (OPAC) in the Spring of 1991. Initially the OPAC contained bibliographic records and corresponding holdings for the main collection, but excluded satellite collections such as government documents, media materials, microforms and others. However, there was an immediate movement to address the inclusion of those collections. The Government Publications Department eagerly accepted the invitation to make a proposal to the library administration to provide library patrons with online bibliographic access to currently received U.S. depository documents.

To create that automation proposal, a planning model was used. As background for the model, it was decided that government document records should be accessible via the same online catalog that accesses the rest of the library holdings. In that way patrons would not have to search a separate database to locate government documents. Even though the government documents collection is shelved separately from the main library collection, eventually, access to all library materials would be from the single OPAC source with location information guiding the patron to the appropriate area. One of the purposes and advantages of an integrated online catalog is to treat collections such as documents like any other library resource.

Additionally, the proposal would address the barcoding and security tagging of the collection as well as the creation and maintenance of holdings records. It was decided to take this opportunity to begin circulating documents using the online system and to open the closed stacks to direct patron access. Other subjects to be covered were the overlaying and de-duping of documents records already in the database, the U.S. depository requirement for a shelflist or other inventory mechanism, and staff training issues.

Finally, although not the main thrust of the model, brief statements were to be made about future inclusion of state, regional, and international documents. This was important now that sources of MARC records for some of these collections, such as the availability of California documents records on the Research Libraries Information Network (RLIN), had been identified.

The result of this effort was a preliminary automation proposal followed by a final proposal, all created by using a model designed to select the best method for cataloging, placing in the OPAC, and circulating U.S. federal documents at SJSU. The San Jose State model offers a practical solution to the planning process which can be adapted to most library situations.

DEFINING PARAMETERS: THE LOCAL SITUATION

The first part of the model calls for a description of the particular library situation. For instance, San Jose State has been a selective depository for government publications, both federal and California state, since 1962. Approximately 50 percent of the depository items available from the GPO are selected. Additionally, SJSU very selectively collects regional materials and international documents, primarily United Nations.

The Government Publications Department is administratively part of the User Services and Facilities Planning Division, but is separated both physically and in terms of public and technical service operations from other library departments. Handling both reference and circulation functions, the department's public service desk is staffed 80 hours per week serving the general public as well as the university community. The department staff consists of the department head, a reference librarian, two library assistants, and four student assistants. In addition to technical service responsibilities, the staff, exclusive of the student assistants, share reference desk coverage during all library service hours.

The bulk of the collection is housed in closed stacks on the second floor of the main library along with the department's reference, technical processing, and staff office areas. Less frequently used materials are housed in a closed-access storage deck in the auxiliary library facility. Storage material is made available to patrons within 24 hours from the time of their request. Some high use items such as the *Code of Federal Regulations* and the *United States Code* are in open stacks within the department. The majority of federal documents are shelved by the Superintendent of Documents (SuDoc) call number. However, a few have been classified and cataloged with Library of Congress (LC) call numbers and are housed either in the main stacks or in the department open stack area.

About 220 selected periodical titles are cataloged by the Serials Department and have bibliographic records with corresponding summary holdings and check-in records on the Serials Control module of Innovacq. These periodical titles, both paper and microform will be excluded from the automation proposal because the OPAC records are directly linked to the corresponding holdings and check-in records on Innovacq. OPAC users can view all linked records without additional commands to switch modules. Only U.S. monographs and other non-cataloged continuations including microforms, will be included in the proposal.

DEFINING PARAMETERS: THE GIVENS

Once the local situation has been delineated, the second step in the model is to review the issues already resolved. These will vary from institution to institution.

For instance, at San Jose State, all subsequent decisions are affected by the fact that the library has an INNOPAC online catalog for all materials. The scope of this integrated system is the current base system storage capacity of 900,000 bibliographic and 1,200,000 item records. The tapeload of the main collection was estimated to be 700,000 bibliographic records leaving a 200,000 record capacity for growth before a system upgrade will be needed. It is estimated that approximately 1,000 GPO MARC records will be generated per month for current receipts. Loading these into INNOPAC will have to be carefully coordinated with the tapeloads of other auxiliary collections to insure adequate system capacity and to allow for timely planning of a system upgrade.

The cost of additional storage capacity in the OPAC as well as the staff resources needed to plan and implement a retrospective conversion project are prohibitive at this time. It is estimated that such a retrospective conversion tapeload of post-1976 GPO records for a depository selecting 45-50 percent of the GPO items would involve 250,000 records. Hence, the proposal addresses only the loading of GPO MARC records for current receipts of monographs and continuations not already cataloged by the library.

A benefit of the somewhat limited scope of the project due to the financial restrictions is the "hands-on" experience which will be gained prior to the automation of the entire documents collection. By first planning for and implementing the automation of only current U.S. depository receipts, the segment of the collection which has been packaged by experienced vendors, SJSU benefits from the extensive experience of libraries that have already loaded these records. This project will serve as a precursor to the more complex and individualized task of cataloging and automating retrospective federal, California state, regional, and international material. With these benefits, such a phased plan is an option staff might very well have chosen to follow even in times of lush funding.

Based on these parameters, a review of the literature, conversations with colleagues, and discussions on GOVDOC-L (the government information computer conference) batch tapeloading of records using a vendor service rather than an in-house record by record cataloging project was selected.

CHECKLIST OF UNIVERSAL ISSUES

Once the particular institutional parameters have been laid out, the third part of the planning model calls for identifying and defining the issues which remain to be settled. These then become the basis for the requirements or specifications which any system or vendor must meet for successful automation. The following checklist outlines these universal issues.

1. What type of automated system will be chosen if it has not already been selected?
2. What is the available budget as compared to the necessary costs? Is there adequate funding to convert all documents

such as federal, state, regional, international? If federal only, what portion can be afforded?

3. What group of records will be selected–monographs, serials, continuations, microforms, computer files, CD-ROMs?

4. Is any part of the collection already in machine readable cataloging format? What percentage? Have those records already been loaded into the online catalog if one exists?

5. Will other functions such as circulation, acquisitions, and/or serials control of government documents be automated?

6. What impact will automation of each of the above functions have on departmental workflow related to such tasks as barcoding, creating holdings records, generating spine labels, security tagging, etc.?

7. Based on percentage of depository item number selections, approximately how many GPO MARC records a month will be exported or loaded into the OPAC?

8. Who will be involved in planning and implementation–Cataloging, Serials, Acquisitions department staff members? Who will be involved in writing the specifications? Will formal committees or informal groups be used?

9. What criteria such as cost, customer service, quality of records, etc., will be used to evaluate and choose the vendor?

10. What are the staff training issues arising from the current size, expertise, and personnel classifications of staff? Who will be trained? Where will the work be done? What terminals and other equipment will need to be ordered? Where will the circulation function occur?

11. What is the impact of government document records appearing in the online catalog? These include possibilities such as an increase in government document interlibrary loan transactions, increased circulation due to increased access, and authority control work in an automated and integrated environment which was previously not required.

12. What will be the impact on department procedures and internal operations of such tasks as revision of existing department guides and handouts, documentation of internal policies and procedures to be added to the department manual, and revision of job descriptions to reflect new duties?

METHODOLOGY

The fourth step of the model is to select a method to gather the necessary information to answer the checklist questions. Due to time factors and the availability of resources, SJSU chose to conduct a highly informal survey of selected academic institutions to assist in the evaluation of the two possible vendors which had already been identified. The survey was neither statistically designed, nor were institutions randomly selected. Each institution merely possessed at least one of our two parameters–INNOPAC online catalog and either Marcive or OCLC as a GPO tape service vendor. In order to identify libraries with those characteristics, we used the roster of automation mentors available from the U.S. GPO (U.S. Government Printing Office 1990). Using this list of government information professionals willing to share their expertise with online catalogs, personal contacts, and discussions at local depository meetings, ten institutions were selected (Appendix A).

Survey questions were designed to answer specifically the checklist questions and generally to elicit the information needed for selection of the best alternative for the SJSU situation. Over the course of a month, these libraries were contacted by phone by a single individual and asked the survey questions (Appendix A). Responses varied in length and thoroughness with two of the ten responses being too brief to provide any useful data and another being so unrelated to the San Jose State situation that it was not helpful.

After reviewing the data, the initial impression was that no two situations are the same nor does the staff proceed with cataloging and automation in the same manner. However, using survey results, the final step of the model tried to approximate the local situation and requirements as closely as possible. The planning model gave an evaluation of the two vendors, weighing the advantages and disadvantages of each including cost comparisons.

PRELIMINARY PROPOSAL

A substantial focus of the preliminary proposal presented to library administrators using this model centered on the impact the cataloging and automation will have on the staff work load and department workflow. The implementation of the proposal will bring drastic changes in department operations with the introduction of such tasks as barcoding, security tagging, generation of spine labels, creation of holdings records, and database maintenance functions. Without doubt, there will also be significant increases in public service, both reference and circulation, and interlibrary loan demands.

Although technically outside the scope of the model as defined, the proposal briefly touches upon a method of cataloging regional and international documents which would bring them into the OPAC and the automated circulation system. This will be more fully explored at a later date.

Given the significant body of literature available on U.S. government documents automation and cataloging, and the number of issues already resolved, our model is extensive enough to answer SJSU's planning needs and those of other libraries at the same stage of automation development.

One drawback of the model as currently constructed is that it does not include a specific decision or implementation plan. It simply states that based on a comparison of the evaluation of the two vendors, library staff and administrators will make the final decision taking into account budget and other factors. In times of short staffing, limited resources, and ever-increasing service demands, it is difficult to find the necessary time and resources within the Government Publications Department to implement the proposal. Without definite cooperative arrangements with other library departments which will be involved or impacted and a realistic time frame for the project, such a technically ambitious undertaking will languish.

FOLLOW-UP SURVEY

Building upon the original checklist and survey questions, staff designed a more complete and focused list of questions. These were used in a telephone survey targeted to over twenty institutions using or planning to use either the Marcive or OCLC GPO tape service vendor and ideally having the Innovative Interfaces, Inc. OPAC.

The following questions were designed upon consultation with the Head of the SJSU Cataloging Department who in this stage of the project became a prime resource person.

1. What is the government document unit like? How many GPO items are selected, how many hours a week is the public service desk staffed and what staff serves on the desk?
2. How many staff are in the department and what is their classification level? Who is involved in the automation work, what other responsibilities such as public service desk hours, committee assignments, etc., do those people have?
3. What was the scope of your automation proposal (e.g., current and/or retrospective documents)?
4. Who was involved in planning for the automation and what was the structure (e.g., committee, task force, staff consultants, other)? Do you have any idea how long the planning took?
5. Which vendor was chosen and why? Are you happy with the customer support?
6. Did your proposal include both serials and monographs? Do you have special policies/procedures for serials?
7. From where does the cataloging expertise come? Is cataloging done in the government publications unit and/or technical processing unit? Who is responsible, how many hours a week, what level of staff? When and how are item records added?
8. How is authority control handled and by whom?
9. What are the quality control issues? How do you verify that you have the items included on the tape? What percentage of the records are "good matches"? Do records need further editing, and if so, what level of staff does this? How do you handle records describing a format other than the piece in hand?
10. What is the workflow material follows from the point of receipt to placement on the shelves? Who does what? Have you identified any innovative and/or time-saving technical processing methods? Has the time required for cataloging and technical processing increased or decreased with automation?

11. How much staff training was needed and who did it? What existing expertise was available in the government publications unit?
12. How are documents circulated? Do you have any barcoding procedures?
13. How often do you receive the tapes and what is the average time lag between receipt of the GPO shipment and the appearance of records in your library OPAC? How is patron access to material provided during that time lag period?
14. What has been the impact of automation on your department's public services, interlibrary loan, technical services, and circulation activities?
15. Do you have a written automation proposal you can share with us?
16. Is there anything else we have not covered which you feel we should be aware of or should address?

SITE VISIT AND FINAL PROPOSAL

Drawing upon the pool of surveyed libraries, staff chose to visit the site which was already using a vendor to supply tapes for loading document records into their OPAC, most closely approximated the SJSU situation in other aspects, and was geographically close enough for an affordable trip. During that visit, staff focused primarily on the workflow established for the material, the technical processing procedures, and any first-hand insights overlooked in the telephone interview.

Upon returning home, all the information gathered in both the planning model stage and the final proposal stage was reviewed and weighed. To this was added the information received during countless telephone conversations with the Marcive and OCLC vendors. Such personal contact was necessary as there were many very specific questions arising throughout the entire planning process which were not answered in the vendors' literature.

Staff then selected the vendor best-suited to the particular situation. In order to have reached that decision, the majority of the components of the proposal had been thoroughly discussed, researched, and documented. All that remained was to gather them together in written form, fleshing them out where needed.

The final proposal itself was divided into a summary statement, the scope of the proposal, the vendor recommendation accompanied by a table comparing the two vendors in eleven areas (Appendix B), a workflow chart, staff assignments, an explanation of the role of other library units, an implementation timeline, and a budget. The proposal has been sent to library administration for discussion and a funding decision. A copy is also available at the Government Publications service desk for the review and comments of all library staff.

The cataloging and inclusion of some of the government document collection in the library's OPAC will eventually streamline technical processing and, more importantly, provide a level of patron access on a par with that available for the library's other collections. But as with all such complicated and multi-part projects, deliberate, thoughtful and well-informed planning such as that embodied in the planning model and the preliminary and final proposals is the key to a successful outcome.

REFERENCES

Baldwin, Gil. 1992. History of GPO Cataloging and Tape Production. *DTTP* (Documents to the People) 20 (December): 207-211.

Bolner, Myrtle Smith, and Barbara Kile. 1991. Documents to the People–Access Through the Automated Catalog. *Government Publications Review* 18: 51-64.

Bower, Cynthia. 1984. OCLC Records for Federal Depository Documents: A Preliminary Investigation. *Government Information Quarterly* 1: 379-400.

Bowerman, Roseann, and Susan A. Cady. 1984. Government Publications in an Online Catalog: A Feasibility Study. *Information Technology and Libraries* 3(December): 331-342.

Foster, Selma V., and Nancy C. Lufburrow. 1979. "Documents to the People in One Easy Step," In *New Horizons for Academic Libraries,* ed. Robert D. Stueart and Richard D. Johnson, 453-455. New York: K.G. Saur Publisher.

Graham, Peter S. 1983. Government Documents and Cataloging in Research Libraries. *Government Publications Review* 10: 117-125.

Higdon, Mary Ann. 1984. "Federal Documents Processing with OCLC: The Texas Tech Experience-Planning, Utilization, the Future." In *Government Documents and Microforms: Standards and Management Issues,* ed. Steven D. Zink and Nancy Jean Melin, 89-97. Westport: Meckler.

Jamison, Carolyn C. 1986. Loading the GPO Tapes-What Does It Really Mean? *Government Publications Review* 13: 549-559.

Kinney, Thomas, and Gary Cornwell. 1991 "GPO Cataloging Records in the Online Catalog: Implications for the Reference Librarian," In *Government Documents and Reference Service*, ed. Robin Kinder, 259-275. New York: The Haworth Press, Inc.

Maclay, Veronica. 1989. Automatic Bibliographic Control of Government Documents at Hastings Law Library. *Technical Services Quarterly* 7(1): 53-64.

Meyer, Christina Perkins. 1992. The Dreaded "A" Word: Authority Control and the GPO Records. *DTTP* (Documents to the People) 20 (December): 213-218.

Mooney, Margaret T. 1989. GPO Cataloging: Is It a Viable Current Access Tool for U.S. Documents? *Government Publications Review* 16: 259-270.

_____. 1990. Matching Library Holdings Against GPO Tapes: Issues, Concerns, and Solutions. *Government Publications Review* 17: 421-428.

Myers, Judy E. 1985. The Government Printing Office Cataloging Records: Opportunities and Problems. *Government Information Quarterly* 2: 27-56.

_____. 1987. "Background Materials to Accompany Automated Bibliographic Control of Government Documents: Current Developments, Judy Myers, ALA, June 29, 1987." Photocopy.

Myers, Judy E., and Helen H. Britton. 1978. Government Documents in the Public Card Catalog: The Iceberg Surfaces. *Government Publications Review* 5: 311-314.

Plaunt, James R. 1985. Cataloging Options for U.S. Government Printing Office Documents. *Government Publications Review* 12: 449-456.

Powell, Margaret S., Deborah Smith Johnston, and Ellen P. Conrad. 1987. The Use of OCLC for Cataloging U.S. Government Publications. *Government Publications Review* 40: 61-76.

Regueiro, Judith E., Margaret L. Breen, Kathleen Knox, and Susan Williamson. 1992. Creating a U.S. Government Documents Database for an Online System, The Tri-College Project. *Government Publications Review* 19: 59-73.

Rocha, Sinai P. 1991. Planning for Online Access of Government Documents. *DTTP* (Documents to the People) 19 (June): 113-117.

Romans, Larry. 1992. Profiling the GPO Tapes for Loading Into the Local Library. *DTTP* (Documents to the People) 20 (December): 219-228.

Stanfield, Karen. 1986. Documents Online: Cataloging Federal Depository Materials at the University of Illinois. *Illinois Libraries* 68: 325-329.

Stephenson, Mary, and Gary R. Purcell. 1985. The Automation of Government Publications: Functional Requirements and Selected Software Systems for Serials Controls. *Government Information Quarterly* 2: 57-76.

_____. 1986. Documents Librarianship II, Current and Future Direction of Automation Activities for U.S. Government Depository Collections. *Government Information Quarterly* 3: 191-199.

Swanbeck, Jan. 1985. Documents Librarianship: I, Federal Documents in the Online Catalog: Problems, Options, and the Future. *Government Information Quarterly* 2: 187-192.

Tull, Laura. 1989. Retrospective Conversion of Government Documents: The Marcive GPO Tape Clean-Up Project. *Technicalities* 9(8): 4-7.

U. S. Government Printing Office. Superintendent of Documents. Library Programs Service. 1990. Directory of Libraries with Online Documents Catalogs. *Administrative Notes* 11 (May 30): 3-7.

Walbridge, Sharon. 1982. OCLC and Government Documents Collections. *Government Publications Review* 9: 277-287.

Wallace, Julia F. 1992. Post-Load Cleanup. *DTTP* (Documents to the People) 20 (December): 228-232.

Watson, Paula D., and Kathleen M. Heim. 1984. Patterns of Access and Circulation in a Depository Document Collection Under Full Bibliographic Control. *Government Publications Review* 11: 269-292.

APPENDIX A

MODEL SURVEY

A. Libraries Surveyed

Ball State University	California State Univ. Fullerton
Harding University	Hastings Law School
Occidental College	Southern Illinois, Carbondale
Swarthmore College	Univ. of Calif., San Diego
Univ of Calif., Santa Cruz	Univ. of Illinois, Urbana

B. Survey Questions

Preliminary: Name of Library:
Person contacted:

Introduction: Give name and institution and explain what you are trying to do, for example:

"I am conducting an informal survey of libraries that are planning, or are in the middle of, integrating MARC records for government documents in their local online systems. We, at SJSU hope to learn from your experience and be able to put forward a proposal that is cost effective for us in terms of staff time as well as in the cost of the tapes."

Questions:

1. Can you describe what you are doing in terms of getting bibliographic records for government documents into your OPAC?

2. How did you go about planning for that? Who was involved in planning and implementation (e.g., technical services people, government documents people and administration)? Where did each of these groups come in or what role did each play?

3. Which service are you using?

    OCLC, Marcive, Other?

4. Which documents are you loading?

    Federal, State, Local, International?
    Serials or Monographs in each category?

5. Are records for current receipts being loaded?

6. What about retrospective conversion?

7. How do you handle creating online records for documents for which MARC records are not available through your selected service?

8. Timeliness?

    How often do you receive tapes?
    What is the average time lag between GPO shipment and receipt of records?

9. Quality Control?

    What percent of records are good matches?
    Do records need further editing? If yes, who in terms of what level of staff does this?
    How do you handle records describing a format other than the piece in hand (e.g., microform vs. paper)?

10. What are your other processing experiences/procedures related to barcoding, targeting with Tattle Tape, spine labels, creating holding records for monographs, creating check-in records and holdings statement for serials, and binding serials?

11. What staffing and work flow changes were necessitated because of the automation? Do you anticipate further changes in the future, both short term and long term?

12. How is authority control for access points handled?

13. How is circulation handled?

14. Is a separate interlibrary loan policy needed? If so, what is it? (This is particularly important if OCLC attaches holdings symbols to records in its master database.)

15. What other significant problems have you encountered that we should be aware of?

APPENDIX B

VENDOR COMPARISON CATEGORIES

1. Tape production factors
2. Availability of current records
3. Availability of retrospective records
4. Record overlay issues
5. Vendor customer support
6. Authority control issues
7. Quality control issues
8. Availability of local records in national database for resource sharing/ ILL
9. Timeliness of tape availability
10. Cost
11. Labeling issues

Planning for Tapeloading
of United States Documents:
Issues and Concerns

Mary Martin

SUMMARY. The automation of cataloging for U.S. government documents, once thought impractical, has created new opportunities for libraries because of the availability of MARC records for tapeloading. Faced with a difficult task of retrospective conversion of records for huge documents collections as well as receiving up to 35,000 individual pieces annually, the concept of loading MARC tapes presents a new method of including these records into local online catalogs. One new approach is to create or load "brief" or "temporary" cataloging records into the online catalog, which are later "overlaid" or "matched" by customized MARC records purchased from a vendor. This article describes one library's experience in planning for and implementing this process of "matching" records, thus enabling government documents to be available for use through the online catalog within days of receipt, with full bibliographic access to follow.

The automation of government documents records has evolved into a process that links the issues involved. Honnold Library at The

Mary Martin is Head, Government Publications and Microforms Department, Honnold Library, Claremont Colleges, Claremont, CA.

The author would like to express thanks to Candace Czerwinski, the Library Assistant who supervises the U.S. documents section and Bill Spivey, the Libraries' Systems Programmer as well as many others who are responsible for the success of the tapeloading project at the Libraries of The Claremont Colleges.

[Haworth co-indexing entry note]: "Planning for Tapeloading of United States Documents: Issues and Concerns," Martin, Mary. Co-published simultaneously in *Cataloging & Classification Quarterly* (The Haworth Press, Inc.) Vol. 18, No. 3/4, 1994, pp. 37-55; and: *Cataloging Government Publications Online* (ed: Carolyn C. Sherayko) The Haworth Press, Inc., 1994, pp. 37-55. Multiple copies of this article/chapter may be purchased from The Haworth Document Delivery Center [1-800-3-HAWORTH; 9:00 a.m. - 5:00 p.m. (EST)].

37

Claremont Colleges has had the benefit of not being among the first libraries to do this, and so learned from preceding efforts. Opportunities to learn the "how to's" and "pitfalls" included attending full-day American Library Association/Government Documents Round Table Preconference workshops on various issues involved in the automation of government documents records (Loading . . . 1992), as well as being able to discuss the project at length with many other librarians undertaking similar projects at their own institutions. It soon became apparent that the government publications staff lacked the specific information or experience in writing specifications for "customizing" a database to be loaded into an already existing database. As the project progressed, we determined that we needed to focus on the issues from a variety of perspectives and in a detailed manner.

BACKGROUND

The Government Publications and Microforms Department of Honnold Library has approximately 650,000 documents, including the international, state, and local collections. The U.S. documents collection is the largest with about 450,000 documents, and presents the most formidable record conversion task. The international documents collection is cataloged by the main cataloging department and is in Library of Congress (LC) Classification order. The state documents collection is in California State Documents classification scheme order (Caldocs). The State Library provides cataloging for California state documents on RLIN and also loads these records into Melvyl (the University of California online catalog). The records are then downloaded from Melvyl by Honnold Library's California Documents library assistant into a dBase IV file, in anticipation of loading into the local Innovative Interfaces, Inc. online catalog in the near future. The database program, which converts MARC records into field labelled dBase IV records to which holdings information can then be attached, was developed by Margaret Mooney of the University of California at Riverside, and is called CALDOCS. Eventually, we hope to include records for all government publications in the online catalog.

PLANNING TASK FORCE

One of the first issues that became evident upon launching our "Automation of Government Documents Project" was that it would take the combined efforts of many managers and staff members in the Library. The formation of a broad-based task force, which would consider interdepartmental issues and effects appeared to be an excellent way to communicate and solicit ideas and questions from all concerned. Therefore, an interdepartmental group was formed consisting at various times of the Library Director, the Associate Directors for Technical Services and Collection Development, the Head of Cataloging, the System's Programmer, the Head of Circulation, the Library Assistant in charge of maintenance of the U.S. Collection, the Head of Government Publications and Microforms, and two Campus (branch) Librarians. This group met biweekly, and later on monthly, for about nine months. It disbanded when we began our current tapeload and online check-in of publications.

TAPELOADS
OR TRADITIONAL CATALOGING METHODS?

Any discussion of this subject always takes on larger proportions than just the issues of whether or not to catalog U.S. Government documents in the traditional manner or purchase tapes of MARC records. When considering some of the current trends, such as integrating government documents into a library's main collection as well as combining general and documents reference service, many previously irrelevant factors assume new significance. Mary Alm's article serves as an example of articles that have been written about libraries including documents records in the online catalog (Alm 1989). From a different perspective, Van De Voorde wrote a candid analysis of the approach taken by the Iowa State University Library in merging reference desks, even though this was not undertaken as a result of the automation of documents records (Van de Voorde 1989). Downsizing of staff and collections makes proposals such as these attractive on the surface. Qualitative analyses about the kind of service the library wishes to offer, and how detailed the access to collections needs to be to provide that service should be a part of any decision-making. Ideally, government publications should be given minimal individual cataloging time and maximum qualitative reference service.

Libraries with large cataloging departments have greater flexibility when considering whether or not to catalog all documents individually. The size of the collection, the percentage of depository items selected, retention policies, and future cataloging resources influence these decisions.

Traditional cataloging methods will always have to be used for those documents for which there are no MARC records available for tapeloading. At this time, this includes a major portion of the U.S. documents distributed before mid-1976 as well as state, local, international and nongovernmental publications. The only resource for cataloging for these documents is one of the bibliographic utilities. This could be more work than many cataloging departments would be able to absorb at one time.

Local situations can also influence the decision on the type of cataloging to apply. For example in Honnold Library, the main library periodical stacks are in title order and not cataloged. Notable exceptions to this rule are government and reference publications. This makes the conversion of the government documents serials records extremely time consuming and would be a drain on the resources of the Cataloging Department. In these times of "downsizing," anything that can be automated with the aim of cutting down on staff time needed for processing is welcome in most libraries.

The really difficult task for a project such as this is in setting up a workable interface between the government documents departmental procedures and those of other departments not attuned to government publications' idiosyncrasies, while working within the parameters of the local online system. Cataloging problems characteristic of government publications include: one series title published annually for twenty different countries; monthly statistical publications that cumulate annually but do not supersede (meaning the monthly cannot be discarded); many publications that issue revisions and interfile updates on an irregular basis; monthly publications with individual unique titles; publications that come in mixed format (microfiche, paper, and/or CD-ROM) for the same title; multipart series that supersede gradually throughout the space of a year or more; and many more.

These problems exist regardless of the methods used to catalog government publications, but tapeloading has the advantage of saving time. Honnold Library chose to purchase tapes from a vendor for its U.S. Government publications for a number of reasons including: the size of the retrospective collection, the workload of our Cataloging Department, the abundance of monographs in microfiche format, the need for timeliness in turn around time for availability of documents, and the sheer enormity of sending 20,000 additional documents each year out of the Government Publications and Microforms Department for cataloging and processing.

There are several vendors of MARC records for U.S. Government publications (often referred to as the "GPO tapes"). The tapes in question contain cataloging records produced by the U.S. Government Printing Office, Library Programs Service through OCLC. The tapes are processed differently by different vendors, so tapes purchased from LC are not going to be the same as those purchased from OCLC. Many vendors purchase the tapes and customize the records for libraries by preparing fields for local holdings and location information, as well as other automated processes the library may wish to utilize (e.g., binding). Vendors for this type of service include Marcive Inc., OCLC's GovDoc Service, and Autographics, Inc. Honnold Library worked exclusively with Marcive, Inc. Other libraries have described experiences of working with OCLC and Brodart, Inc. (which no longer offers this service) (Dobbs 1990; Regueiro et al. 1992).

We also never really considered merging Government Publications reference with the main reference desk, or the collections with the library's main collections. We made a decision that our reference service required more intensive training and interaction with patrons, and that to merge with Main Reference would mean a change in the type of service we wished to provide. Therefore, we proceeded with the project all the while thinking of Government Publications and Microforms as a separate department.

CUSTOMIZING RECORDS FOR TAPELOADS

The next important step involves adapting the records for local needs. It is essential to begin to learn about the library's automated system and what it can and cannot do with these particular MARC records. Some questions will arise when working with a vendor to customize MARC records. Local online systems interact differently with particular vendors' products. Do not assume that the vendor knows the local system parameters in detail. Good sources of advice, initially, are other libraries with the same system. As planning progresses, continue drawing upon their expertise to assess the decisions made locally. "It's not who you know, but who you know to ask." No two libraries' experiences are the same, but information can increase the options and broaden perspectives.

The tapeloading project at Honnold Library is being carried out in three phases. Phase 1 encompassed the loading of the Serials Supplement tape, which is a tape of serials currently published three or more times a year and cataloged by the U.S. Government Printing Office. This tape was "profiled" to reflect only serials for which records were needed. The records have been suppressed from public display until check-in and holdings records are created by a cataloger assigned to the Government Publications and Microforms Department for this purpose. Many libraries load the serials records as part of the retrospective tapeload. Since it was decided to profile for that tapeload very carefully, the decision was made to go ahead and load the Serials Supplement tape in January 1993. The serials records will then be deleted or "profiled out" of the general retrospective tapeload.

Phase 2 of the project began in January 1993, when we began loading current monthly tapes. This procedure is a little more complicated, because of the time lag between receipt and cataloging of publications (Mooney 1989). In all fairness, GPO has decreased the time lag in cataloging for monographs, and cataloging copy for some appear in OCLC by the time of receipt. Microfiche titles are still being cataloged from the backlog, and do take considerably longer. This policy applies to titles published only in microfiche. Publications distributed in dual format (paper and/or microfiche) are cataloged upon receipt of the paper copy.

Microfiche Cataloging

The GPO has now changed its policy on this and will be cataloging items in the format distributed to depository libraries. For serial titles, new serial records will be created for the microfiche version of the publication and linked to the paper record. Both records will be distributed on the tapes. A 533 field note in the record will indicate the dates of the issues distributed in microfiche (Baldwin 1992). In addition, GPO places the item numbers for paper and microfiche in separate 074 fields. The ambiguity of format necessitates some procedure which will identify those titles which were actually received by the depository in microfiche. One way is to either have the vendor or your system search for the presence of "MF" as part of the item number in an 074 field or the phrase "distributed to some depository libraries in microfiche" and to adjust the location information accordingly.

In Honnold Library, when shipments of documents are received from GPO, temporary records are entered into the online catalog. These records contain an 086 field since the U.S. collection is shelved in SuDoc (Superintendent of Documents) call number order. When the tape is loaded, it "overlays" any record for which there is a match on the 086 field (SuDoc class number). Since many publications, particularly microfiche, for which cataloging records are being received now, were actually received in late 1992, the items must be pulled from the collection, and item records attached to the bibliographic record loaded by the tape, which is then "unsuppressed" (i.e., made visible in the OPAC). This procedure will be eliminated once all microfiche are cataloged by means of brief records, before filing into the collection.

Retrospective Profiling

The retrospective tapeload is Phase 3 of the project. As a result of tapeloading done by other libraries, we learned that many records are often loaded for documents not actually owned by the library. There are a number of reasons for this as outlined later. The decision was made to profile, or select records for inclusion in the retrospective tape, very carefully, by checking the shelves against a list of available SuDoc stems provided by Marcive. The department shelflist was determined to be very inaccurate because extensive weeding had been done; therefore, the common method of profiling for record selection by selecting "item numbers" from the "List of Item Numbers Available for Selection by Depository Libraries" seemed to be unacceptable. Profiling by SuDoc stem will reflect more accurately what is on the shelf.

Such details are very specific to each depository library and often glossed over when profiling. However, they are often the cause of most inaccuracies in the inclusion of records on the tapes. Libraries that receive all of the records available, usually regional libraries who theoretically receive everything GPO distributes (and more) have less of a problem than selective libraries do. More detail concerning "missing" and inaccurate records is described later, as well as a possible solution.

Holding Locations

Many libraries use the 049 MARC field to designate a "holdings code," which causes a location to appear in a designated place in the record your system generates for the online catalog. Each branch library, campus, or collection designates unique codes for this purpose, which are entered into the selection profile. The location codes show a holdings location in the libraries and are expressed in both the bibliographic record and the item record. In the Innovative Interfaces, Inc. catalog the location coded into the bibliographic record allows the patron to limit their search to a specific location in the libraries; whereas the location coded into the item record supplies the location in the patron display of the record in the online catalog. Holdings notes generally reflect the libraries, holdings for specific serial titles. The Libraries of The Claremont Colleges have our holdings code placed in a field, by Marcive, which our system loader program then takes and displays in our "patron display box" in the OPAC. Claremont uses the 949 field which is highlighted in patron display for viewing holdings notes.

Call Numbers

The record processing profile tailored by the library for Marcive provided for the SuDoc call number (086) to be transferred into a field which the tape loader program written for us by Innovative Interfaces

Inc. transfers to a local call number display field in the online catalog (949). The online catalog has a separate government documents number index, so patrons can search by a Gov Docs call number without it being confused with Library of Congress call numbers. Claremont deletes the LC call number from incoming documents records. If there are records for documents with LC call numbers already in the online catalog, they do not overlay, as described in the next section on duplicate records. The catalog does display these numbers integrated with LC call numbers when the patron uses the "show nearby on shelf" display mode. This is because there are some records with LC call numbers in the index. The first screen one sees after a call number search is a browse screen that shows just the main entry and call number. One hopes that rather than going directly to the collection with a printout of the browse screen, patrons will move to the next screen which shows location and status.

Other libraries such as California State University at Fullerton put a prefix before the call number (e.g., "Gov Docs") in order to make it more clear for patrons. One drawback at Claremont Colleges is that Innovative Interfaces system limits the number of characters that can display in the location area; therefore, since SuDoc numbers can be very long, part of it could be cut off.

If the documents collection is shelved and classified in SuDoc order, then one will wish to use that number as the call number in the online catalog. If the library classes documents in LC order, then the loader profile would have that number placed in the call number field. The beauty of this process is that any classification number from a MARC record (such as SuDoc or CalDoc) can be placed in the call number field. There are questions such as: Is it possible to have two separate call number indexes? Is that preferable? How will they interfile? How will they display? which should be answered before loading tapes.

Duplicate Records

One issue to consider with tapeloaded records is the likelihood of receiving duplicate records for documents already in the main library collection classified with LC numbers. We avoided duplication of records by having the loader program not overlay a record when an OCLC number is present. Since our brief records do not have OCLC numbers, if one is present, then a record has been downloaded from OCLC, and an LC call number assigned. LC call numbers do not appear in the GPO tapes as per Claremont's record processing profile. The library has a number of publications in the online catalog with 086 fields. We can get a printout of records that do not overlay, and may be duplicates, to deal with in whatever way we wish. The sources of these records are probably a mixture of depository publications sent from the Government Publications and Microforms Department to the main stacks or documents firm ordered for the main collection by individual fund managers. Even if one knows the source of these duplicates, it may not be easy to identify them categorically for inclusion or exclusion in the tapeload. Should these records be completely overlaid by the new, incoming cataloging records? Or, should portions of them be overlaid, thus protecting variable fields? Should one load the duplicates and clean up the problem later? System management reports can be run, based on certain parameters which will identify any records which did not overlay based on a particular field. Careful selection of which fields will be protected, allows for some selectivity in this matter.

Availability Records

Many records on the GPO tapes are not true catalog records, but are "availability" records, which were published in the *Monthly Catalog* to advertise their availability for sale. The most common example of an availability record would be a record for a single issue of a serial published three times or less per year. Even though GPO is stopping this practice, the problem still needs to be addressed in a retrospective tapeload (Baldwin 1992).

GPO is also putting CONSER numbers in serial records which have linking records. The creation of "mother-daughter" records for maps now makes it easier for a library to catalog one "mother" record for all the individual quadrangle topographic map sheet and "daughters" for a state, if so desired. These efforts help with the problems presented by availability records.

Missing Records and Cleanup Efforts

Studies have shown that the library may not own a document for every record loaded and vice versa. For example, GPO has been known to include records with the same SuDoc class numbers as non-depository documents, and to catalog some titles which were never distributed to depository libraries (Mooney 1990). Contributing to this are other problems including errors and poor cataloging from 1976-1981, such as mis-tagged fields and non-standard subject headings, as well as missing SuDocs and item numbers. In addition, many corrections made by GPO did not appear on the tapes (Myers 1985).

In 1987, a major project was undertaken in a cooperative venture by Marcive, Inc. and three academic institutions, Texas A&M, Louisiana State, and Rice Universities, with Judy Myers of the University of Houston as consultant, to enhance the GPO tapes by modifying their content and organization. These cleanup procedures included: adding changes made in the *Monthly Catalog* to the tape database, adding missing OCLC, SuDoc, and various other numbers, deleting availability records, deleting duplicate records for multipart monographs, and adding codes to indicate a library's microfiche holdings. Nearly 78,000 records were deleted (Bolner and Kile 1991). Remaining problems with the tapes that cannot be addressed by profiling include: records for missing copies because of claims never filled, lost copies, or withdrawn copies. Actually, an unintentional result of the Marcive cleanup was that item numbers were attached to records which were never distributed by GPO. Marcive is addressing this problem. Some documents have no records, and appear to have eluded cataloging by GPO. Several groups of records (i.e., some NASA (National Aeronautics and Space Administration) and DOE (Department of Energy) records) do not appear on the tapes, and no one, (GPO, Library of Congress or the vendors) seems to know why.

Other problems are a result of GPO cataloging practices such as serials within series, multipart monographs, analyzed sets, dual format items, and serial title changes (Wallace 1992).

ONLINE PROCESSING AND CHECK-IN ISSUES

Time Lag

As briefly described earlier, one of the recurring issues in documents processing is that of how to handle the time gap between when publications are received and the appearance of cataloging records on tape. The GPO Cataloging Section receives publications at almost the same time they are shipped to depository libraries. Shipments are put together in the Library Distribution Branch by the Classification Section (a branch of the acquisitions process), assigned a SuDoc number, and sent to the Cataloging Section as an actual box at that time. On average, the time lag for cataloging of documents can be up to six months.

As of June 1993, GPO admitted to a cataloging backlog of 20,000 titles, but only 500 of those are current year titles. (GPO catalogers handled 36,000 titles in 1992-1993 fiscal year.) Cataloging priorities continue to focus on current year titles, contracting out for some of the backlog, quality-control analysis of all cataloging, and additional training for the GPO catalogers. In the interest of speedy availability, GPO is doing "abridged" cataloging for some publications such as NASA technical reports and ERIC reports. After some problems with missing numbers in the technical report number field, this application appears to be proceeding smoothly.

A common way of handling the time lag is to enter "temporary," "skeletal," or "provisional" records, which are later linked to or overlaid by complete cataloging records. This involves two problems: entering the information into the "item" records, and ensuring that it is indeed "overlaid" with the correct bibliographic record. Depending on the features of the local system, information must be entered into the item record whether one is creating brief records and tapeload overlaying or doing copy cataloging.

The overlay point can be any of several, but Claremont chose the 086 field, which contains the SuDoc number. Brief records are created using Innovative Interfaces's "key new records" function. Within the library this function has been customized to ask for only certain pieces of information crucial to the bibliographic and item records. Only such information as title, author, call number, item number, location, notes, circulation status, barcode number, and a few other preliminaries are keyed in. All keying is done by a full-time Library Assistant III and a graduate student. These unique records are available for patron view and a list containing the SuDoc number, item number, record number, and title is created for the department to use in rectifying these records. Usually overlays do not occur as expected because the brief record had not yet been keyed so there was nothing on which the full record could overlay. Very few of the non-overlays are the result of error when keying in the SuDoc number.

More frequently, GPO catalogers have changed the SuDoc from that provided on the shipping list or made a mistake in the SuDoc field during classification. A typical example occurred when a Commerce Department publication record was loaded from the Marcive tape and the SuDoc number started with the letter "D" instead of "C" as expected. Sometimes simple errors such as misplaced colons or slashes are the only problem (which are real problems when utilizing a computer matching process!). Even with these difficulties, the overlay based on the 086 field works beautifully for the most part,

Several vendors (e.g., Marcive, Bernan, Autographics, Inc.) now offer services that may solve many of these problems associated with the time lag issue. Shipping list services, such as those offered by these vendors, send machine readable versions of the daily depository shipping lists which are created at GPO at the time of classification to library subscribers. These records serve as temporary records until they are overlaid by the full bibliographic record. A unique number is entered into the database which can be used for overlay purposes. Labels, barcodes, and catalog cards are also available, if desired. The tradeoff will hopefully be in staff time, as well as in the timeliness and availability of records for newly received publications. All vendors enter corrections and changes to the bibliographic records issued by GPO into the database. However, this only benefits retrospective tapeloads and changes that cause a new record to be issued with the same OCLC number, as it would "overlay" the old record when loaded.

Classification Changes

GPO issues numerous changes in SuDoc classification numbers each month. Making these changes on local records and the documents themselves is a very labor intensive process. Marcive makes these corrections to its database, if it receives them in time, so that the record distributed may have already been corrected. OCLC's GOVDOC Service also processes changes to GPO records before sending tapes to subscribers. When selecting a vendor, one should clearly understand the corrections made by the vendor and the timing of those corrections.

Authority Control

Marcive and other vendor services can provide authorities processing for the records. As part of Marcives' standard service, it looks at traceable headings in the records and upgrades them to current LC usage. As an optional service, it can supply a file of just the authority records that pertain to your bibliographic file of GPO cataloging. There is also an "Authorities Notification Service" available in tape or paper format, as well as a choice between full and brief authority records. We chose authorities processing for the retrospective database, but decided to forgo it for the current tapes because of the cost. The INNOPAC system identifies new subject headings with each tapeload so that libraries can continue the authority control process.

A very good analysis of authorities processing for GPO tapes was presented by Christine Meyer of the University of Minnesota. Among her recommendations were: do buy matching LC authority records; and do buy complete, and not minimal authorities records; don't get paper lists as one will never find the time to review them; and don't let catalogers talk you into loading the records into a separate file and reviewing them one by one. As Meyer states, "The whole point of loading GPO records is to provide good access to a large body of materials at low cost, not perfect access at high cost." (Meyer 1992, 216-217). Unfortunately, too many libraries, including Claremont, do not have enough staff to do authorities control processing.

Serials Check-in

Many libraries that tapeloaded GPO cataloging records opted not to build serials check-in records before loading the tapes. Claremont chose to have a separate periodicals tape loaded first, and have the check-in records created using those records. Several questions should be considered in regard to automating serials check-in. What are the features of serials check-in, particularly in regard to mono-graphic series? Will the system automatically link monographic series records with a series note? Even the most sophisticated systems require great ingenuity in solving the problem of annual reports or serials within series. When keying a brief record, a series note could be entered thereby allowing the patron to search directly by title for a particular volume in the series or the series itself could be searched. We have chosen not to include series notes. When the overlay takes place, the series note arrives with the fully cataloged bibliographic record and will thereafter be available to patrons in their searching.

Most serials check-in modules are created for the ease of checking-in regularly issued publications, not those of the irregular or occasional variety. Claiming modules must be adjusted to incorporate the special requirements of the depository program. A new claims policy was introduced by GPO in February 1993, which limits claims to a "core list," among other restrictions (New Claims 1993). The claiming module is a system within Innovative Interfaces' online system that alerts the library staff to those issues of a periodical title that have not arrived when expected. It is very helpful for the library to maintain complete holdings but when dealing with a depository title's issues standard methods for finding a replacement can't always be utilized. When an issue cannot be provided by GPO, due to the title's not being on the list of titles eligible for claiming or due to the fact that GPO's claims copies are exhausted, or even due to the agency bypassing the depository program for an issue or two, the specific government agency must then be contacted or an alternate vendor consulted. Bindery modules must also be adjusted to accommodate depository retention policies.

These problems are not insurmountable, but require creative solutions and a thorough understanding of the capabilities of the local system. For a more in-depth view of automated check-in records in an Innovative Interfaces system, there is an interesting article about the online check-in of documents at the University of California-San Francisco (Maclay 1989).

Flexibility

Another major consideration must be that of how the local system handles the idiosyncrasies of government publications. Is it versatile enough to allow for diverse types of publications such as "slip opinions" from the Supreme Court, which arrive individually, and are later received as bound volumes? Is it possible to reflect the availability of Census Bureau publications in both paper and CD-ROM format? Many of these problems are being creatively dealt with by libraries that have forged ahead with automation of holdings.

Quality Control

In spite of the amount of information gathered before loading the tapes, we had problems with what the tape processing vendor and the local system vendor did. Changes had to be made after the first tapeload. The tape vendor forgot to take out the 086 field as requested for the tapeload. There was a problem with the system vendor misunderstanding the original request that the loader profile provide for overlay on 086 and 074. The vendor interpreted this to mean 086 or 074, and records with the same 074 (of which there can be many) incorrectly overlaid each other. The term for this is "cannibalization" of records and it was rectified after the first tapeload. The system vendor has stated that the loader program can not overlay on two fields at once. This is really too bad because that process would make quality control almost foolproof (Mooney 1990).

The tape is loaded into a separate file, which is suppressed from public view and records are made available to the public when ready. Some records need at least brief individual attention. The retrospective tape, however, will most likely go directly into the system. An advantage to keying the brief records in-house is that by directly handling each title, the correct location code and circulation status can be assigned individually and one knows that when the overlay occurs, it has done so because of an exact match by SuDoc between loading of the brief and the full records, thus maintaining database integrity. With a service where a brief record is provided and uniquely numbered for future overlay, the possibility of the SuDoc changing between arrival of the full record, and the possibility of the patron actually looking for the publication under a different number, while the "correct" one would be supplied by the full bibliographic record, we found undesirable. When the specifications for the record processing profile were written, and the system vendor wrote our tape loader program, the shipping list services were not yet available. It was necessary at that time to create a custom system which works well.

Once problems are worked out, however, the rewards are marvelous. Although some may argue, checking-in a document online and putting on a pre-printed label has to be faster than pulling cards out of a catalog and writing or typing labels! Most of the tedious labor intensive tasks can be eliminated. Many of the specialized notes can be handled by placing processing notes in the record ready for the next check-in.

A final quality control check should be performed to assure the integrity of the database by verifying that the library actually owns the document for which a record was loaded. For the retrospective load, Honnold Library chose to produce "smart" barcodes based on the bibliographic records loaded. These barcodes have the SuDoc number and a partial title printed on them in addition to the scannable barcode number. They will only be applied to the documents if the information matches. Non-matches will be "proof" of any records for which we do not have documents. These records will be deleted from the database at some time in the future.

STAFFING CHANGES

One of the most important considerations in automating government publications access is the impact on patrons. Instead of depending upon serendipitous discovery or the hope that a busy librarian will take pity, patrons will have access to the wealth of information through the online catalog. If the experience of most libraries that have done this is any indication, the use of government documents will double or triple. At the University of New Mexico, reference to documents increased at all public service points, and circulation of documents increased 43 percent the first year, and 156 percent from 1988 to 1991 (Keating 1993, 528). The University of Florida Libraries, following a load of the GPO cataloging records, experienced an immediate and potentially overwhelming increase in reference referrals and interlibrary loan (Comwell *Effects,* 1992). This has implications for everything from reference service to shelving.

The commonplace assumption that automation should immediately reduce personnel is proving to be unfounded. A reduction in staff time for technical processing may be offset by the need for more staff because of increased use of the collection. This is something not always anticipated. In terms of reference service, there are those who believe that only the most intelligent and persistent patrons can find their way through government publications without qualitative assistance. Most government information is considered "primary source" material. Patrons are often looking for the actual information, not an analysis.

POTENTIAL FOR FUTURE COOPERATION

One feature of an online catalog is the ease of identifying what an individual library owns, either through on-site or remote access. Such access makes the possibility of regional cooperation in providing service to depository library users an achievable goal. If libraries can collect "cooperatively," then they can share collection responsibilities with other libraries in their area. Recent changes at GPO coupled with budget crunches facing most libraries, make any possible "downsizing" of collections attractive. In addition, the availability of information in electronic formats is changing the nature of government information dissemination. The days of huge paper collections are numbered. This is not to say that certain publications will not remain available in paper format, but because of costs associated with publishing, they will decrease. Hopefully, this will make being a depository library more affordable.

REFERENCES

Alm, Mary L. 1989. Government Publications Cataloging On-Line: A Look at Its Impact at UNC. *Colorado Libraries* 15 (June): 28-30.

Baldwin, Gil. 1992. History of GPO Cataloging and Tape Production. *DTTP* (Documents to the People) 20 (December):207-211.

Bolner, Myrtle Smith and Barbara Kile. 1991. Documents to the People–Access Through the Automated Catalog. *Government Publications Review* 18:51-64.

Cornwell, Gary. 1992. Effects of Online Cataloging on Usage of Documents in Regional Federal Depository Libraries. *Administrative Notes* 13 (June 16):18-20.

Dobbs, Christopher C. 1990. Quality Control in Implementing OCLC GOVDOC Current Cataloging Service. *DTTP* (Documents to the People) 18 (September):166-170.

Keating, Kathleen and Linda St. Clair. 1993. The Perils of Being Ahead of the Curve: The Impact of GPO *Monthly Catalog* Records on a University Library. *Government Publications Review* 20:523-529.

Loading the GPO MARC Tapes, 1992 Preconference of ALA/Government Documents Round Table. 1992. *DTTP* (Documents to the People) 20 (December):207-232.

Maclay, Veronica. 1989. Automatic Bibliographic Control of Government Documents at Hastings Law Library. *Technical Services Quarterly* 7 (1):53-64.

Mooney, Margaret T. 1989. GPO Cataloging: Is It a Viable Current Access Tool for U.S. Government Documents? *Government Publications Review* 16: 259-270.

_____. 1990. Matching Library Holdings Against GPO Tapes: Issues, Concerns, and Solutions. *Government Publications Review* 17:421-428.

Meyer, Christine Perkins. 1992. The Dreaded "A" Word: Authority Control and the GPO Records. *DTTP* (Documents to the People) 20 (December):213-218.

Myers, Judy. 1985. The Government Printing Office Cataloging Records: Opportunities and Problems. *Government Information Quarterly* 2:27-56.

New Claims Policy Announced. 1993. Administrative Notes, 14 (February 28):1-5.

Plaunt James R. 1985. Cataloging Options for U.S. Government Printing Office Documents. *Government Publication Review* 12:449-456.

Regueiro, Judith E., Margaret L. Breen, Kathleen Knox, and Susan Williamson. 1992. Creating a U.S. Government Documents Database for an Online System: The Tri-College Project. *Government Publications Review* 19:59-73.

Romans, Larry. 1992. Profiling the GPO Tapes for Loading into the Local Library. *DTTP* (Documents to the People) 20 (December):219-228.

Tull, Laura. 1989. Retrospective Conversion of Government Documents: The Marcive GPO Tape Clean-Up Project. *Technicalities* 9 (8):4-7.

Van De Voorde, Philip E. 1989. Should Reference for U.S. Government Publications and General Reference Be Merged? *Government Publications Review* 16:247-257.

Wallace, Julia F. 1992. Post-Load Cleanup. *DTTP* (Documents to the People) 20 (December):228-232.

Sharing Expertise
to Mainstream Government
Documents Cataloging

Beatrice McKay
Norma Carmack

SUMMARY. In 1989 Trinity University Library began a project to copy catalog the pre-1976 titles in its U.S. Depository Collection. In light of the fact that the documents unit is too small to carry out this specialized project alone, several librarians and paraprofessionals have shared their time and expertise to ensure the success of this project. Trinity University/Marcive's pioneering role in tapeloading GPO catalog records is briefly discussed. Also discussed are additional ways in which the library is integrating some of the documents cataloging and maintenance responsibilities into the technical services department.

INTRODUCTION

Trinity University's Maddux Library became a selective depository for U.S. government publications in 1964. We select 48 percent of depository items and hold 168,000 volumes and over 300,000 microfiche. The regular collection numbers about 700,000 volumes

Beatrice McKay is Serials Cataloger and Norma Carmack is Documents Librarian at Trinity University's Maddux Library, 715 Stadium Drive, San Antonio, TX 78212.

[Haworth co-indexing entry note]: "Sharing Expertise to Mainstream Government Documents Cataloging," McKay, Beatrice, and Norma Carmack. Co-published simultaneously in *Cataloging & Classification Quarterly* (The Haworth Press, Inc.) Vol. 18, No. 3/4, 1994, pp. 57-74; and: *Cataloging Government Publications Online* (ed: Carolyn C. Sherayko) The Haworth Press, Inc., 1994, pp. 57-74. Multiple copies of this article/chapter may be purchased from The Haworth Document Delivery Center [1-800-3-HAWORTH; 9:00 a.m. - 5:00 p.m. (EST)].

and serves a primarily undergraduate student body of about 2,400. Trinity is an independent university with a focus on the liberal arts and sciences.

The library employs 16 librarians and 43 support staff. The documents staff of two full-time paraprofessionals is supervised by a librarian for whom government documents is one of several responsibilities. The documents unit operated independently of technical services for many years, and with good reason: when documents are uncataloged and housed in a separate collection, the documents processing functions of receiving, shelflisting, labeling, shelving and claiming require no coordination with a cataloging department.

On the other hand, when a library decides to include records for documents in its public catalog, bibliographic control of those records brings a new dimension to the work of the documents unit. No longer are access and control limited to the *Monthly Catalog of United States Publications* and other governmentally and commercially produced printed indexes. Rather, these now become a function of the locally maintained catalog.

In Trinity's case, we began adding documents records to the public catalog in the early 1980s, yet we have only recently begun to understand and respond to the need to exploit the expertise of the cataloging department in order to enhance the quality of the documents records in the public catalog. There are at least two reasons for our delayed response to such a major shift in the treatment of documents. First of all, for nearly twenty years, the documents unit had been a completely separate entity from technical services and cataloging. Because the documents staff had always taken care of documents, it was easy to assume that they would continue to do so.

A second reason is the method by which we acquired documents records for the catalog: tapeloading. Tape- or batch-loading of large numbers of records into an online catalog is indeed a different sort of process than title-by-title cataloging. As Judy Myers expressed so well, "Library staff processing of high-quality computer-selected records can often be reduced to checking the records which the computer identifies as problems, and adding any local data which the computer cannot add, such as the circulation bar code numbers. Computer-selection of records can increase cataloging productivity by another order of magnitude . . ."[1] Because traditional cataloging was not required of documents staff, it was easy to assume that coordination with the cataloging department was unnecessary. When catalogers stumbled over documents records, they tended to ignore them, for the general understanding persisted that documents belonged to another world.

As time passed, however, we gradually began to realize that catalog records for documents needed attention and maintenance not unlike that for other materials. We also recognized that the small documents staff has neither the time nor the knowledge to make and carry out cataloging decisions. If we are to share a catalog, we must also share our expertise. The library user neither knows nor cares to know that records for documents are handled differently from records for other materials. The user is interested only in finding accurate information clearly expressed in the OPAC. Thus, to best serve our users through the provision of a high-quality database, we are gradually learning to lower the traditional walls between the documents unit and the cataloging department. In this article, we intend to describe a project which takes advantage of cataloging staff expertise to add pre-1976 documents to the catalog. To provide a context for our work at Trinity, we begin with a brief history of documents in public catalogs in general and in Trinity's catalog in particular. Following the project description, we will discuss the various ways in which we are moving toward a more integrated, mainstream approach to documents work.

A BRIEF HISTORY OF DOCUMENTS IN PUBLIC CATALOGS

Documents in Public Catalogs Before 1976

Since 1976, when GPO began creating catalog records using OCLC, increasing numbers of libraries have been incorporating U.S. documents into their public catalogs. Prior to that time, however, documents records were rarely included in public catalogs. In a 1975 article discussing the retrieval problems encountered when documents are integrated with the general collection, Sharon Edge noted that at that time, the *Monthly Catalog*, not the public catalog, was the principal means of access to documents.[2] A survey conducted during that same period confirmed the lack of catalog access to these materials: 93 federal depository libraries associated with four-year colleges or universities responded, and only three of them, or 3.2 percent, catalogued all depository documents they received.[3]

The size of its documents collection strongly influenced a library's decision about cataloging the collection. Alice Bahr summarized general practice by saying that, "Typically, numbers dictated organization. Libraries that selected small numbers [of documents] cataloged them . . . ," while those that selected higher percentages of depository items tended to keep a separate, uncataloged documents collection. Still other libraries chose to keep most documents in a separate collection while cataloging and classifying selective titles with the regular collection.[4] There are exceptions to the rule, among them the University of Illinois Library, which has a long-standing policy to fully catalog all depository items with the exception of ephemera.[5]

Why were documents thus excluded from the public catalog? Bernard Fry explained in 1977 that it was because "traditional methods of cataloging are uneconomical to apply to large collections."[6] Not only lack of funds, but also lack of personnel formed an obstacle to cataloging large, previously uncataloged collections: "the combination of traditionally understaffed and low-budget document departments could not afford the enormous cost of cataloging new materials."[7] Cause and effect were thus self-perpetuating. Because documents collections were not cataloged, staffing levels and skills matched the requirements of traditional documents processing: receiving, checking in, labeling, shelving, and claiming. On the other hand, because staffing levels and skills were low, it was not feasible for documents staff to provide cataloging for the collection.

If it was too expensive to catalog documents collections, why was that so? Simply put, "Quality records were sparse, necessitating original cataloging . . ."[8] The primary source of those "quality records" was the Library of Congress (LC), from which libraries were able to buy printed cards for some titles. In the years preceding 1976 (when GPO began contributing records online to OCLC) the

Library of Congress cataloged about 3,000 depository titles per year.[9] In 1973, this amounted to only about 20 percent of the 16,770 entries listed in the *Monthly Catalogs* for January through November of that year.[10]

Categories of materials chosen for cataloging by LC generally included "currently published monographs consisting principally of important factual information concerning the economy, social environment and political life of the United States. . ."[11] By 1975/76, the percentage of *Monthly Catalog* entries bearing a Library of Congress card number had increased to about 36 percent, but not all items with an LC card number actually had cards available.[12] Even if libraries with large collections acquired all available LC printed cards (i.e., for 20-35 percent of each year's depository items), 65-80 percent of the remaining annual receipts would require original cataloging, a considerable undertaking.

In addition to acquiring LC printed cards, a relatively small number of libraries could also obtain documents records from OCLC, at the time still a fledgling utility. Organized in 1967, OCLC included as members 49 academic libraries in Ohio. Shared cataloging began in 1971. By 1975, about 300 libraries (mostly through regional consortia) in 28 states were participating on a permanent basis. As of July, 1974, about 44 percent of the records in OCLC (or 413,000) had been contributed by the Library of Congress and 56 percent (or 520,000) by participating libraries. Thus, documents records which figured in the database were easily accessible by member libraries.[13]

Documents in Public Catalogs from 1976 Forward

A gradual evolution began in 1976, one which is still ongoing and which is resulting in more and more libraries including records for documents in public catalogs. Two crucial factors in this change were (1) GPO's decision in 1976 to adopt standard cataloging practice in order to contribute records to OCLC and (2) the contributions of commercial firms to enhance the usefulness of the GPO tapes.

Since 1895, when publication of the *Monthly Catalog* began, GPO's intent in describing government publications had not been to catalog them, in the sense that librarians use the term. Rather, its purpose was to create a list each month of items published the previous month, along with price and availability. When in 1976 GPO began creating records in MARC format and following Anglo-American cataloging rules, it was still with a view to creating the *Monthly Catalog,* only now making use of the magnetic tapes which resulted from their cataloging on OCLC.

GPO is not primarily a cataloging service; its charge is, among others, to publish the *Monthly Catalog* and to distribute depository items. Nevertheless, as GPO continued to create standard catalog records for documents, the agency inevitably began to play an increasing leadership role in documents cataloging. In 1981, "conformance [to Anglo-American cataloging rules and Library of Congress subject headings] ushered in GPO's new role as cataloging authority for U.S. government materials . . ."[14] GPO has gradually responded to needs expressed by librarians, attempting to balance GPO's primary purpose with the reality of its role as a *de facto* provider of catalog records. As these needs are sometimes in direct conflict, the balance is a difficult one to attain.

Unlike in earlier years, when "quality records" were scarce, they were now available, thanks to GPO's use of OCLC and to OCLC's general accessibility. The increasing availability of this network shared cataloging made it easier for libraries to obtain records for their public catalogs.

However, record-by-record cataloging via OCLC was prohibitively expensive for most large collections. What libraries needed was a means to batch load large numbers of high quality records at a low per-record cost. When GPO began creating tapes of standard MARC records for the purpose of putting out the *Monthly Catalog,* librarians hoped that GPO would distribute the tapes to depositories, ready to load into their local online catalogs.[15] There were, however, two obstacles to batch loading of the GPO monthly tapes. The first was a complete lack of documentation to accompany the tapes, so that loading of the tapes locally was very problematic. The second was the cumulative effect of GPO cataloging practice over the years, which resulted in a problem-filled database. Myers[16] and Swanbeck[17] describe in detail the problems involved.

In addition to GPO's decision to use OCLC for cataloging and for production of tapes, a second important factor in the trend toward including documents in the public catalog was the contribution of commercial firms. First, Marcive's cooperation with depository libraries at LSU, Rice, and Texas A&M University facilitated the cleanup of the database of records created by GPO on its monthly tapes since 1976. (See Bolner and Kile[18] and Tull[19] for a description of this important project.) Secondly, vendors such as Marcive and OCLC's GOVDOC service allow libraries to select records for only those titles they receive as depository items. Third, they manipulate the tapes acquired from GPO/LC to facilitate smooth loading into local systems. Finally, they attempt to compensate for the problems caused by GPO practices. For example, Marcive does not distribute duplicate serial and multi-volume monograph records (called "availability records") which have been a by-product of the production requirements of the *Monthly Catalog*. This helps decrease the number of duplicate records in the library's catalog. (GPO has recently modified its practice in such a way as to omit these records from the *Monthly Catalog* tapes.)

As a result of the two factors discussed above, an increasing number of libraries began to include documents in their catalogs during the 1980s. The evolution has been a slow one, however. "In the decade since the GPO catalog records in MARC format became available, only a handful of libraries were using them to provide full cataloging of the depository collections. The majority of depository libraries still were not providing users with the most effective means of gaining access to government publications–listing them in the public access catalog with all the other library materials."[20] In 1984, only 16 of 391 depository libraries responding to a GPO survey said that they had bought the GPO tapes.[21] A 1988 survey of 93 ARL libraries with online public catalogs revealed that only 11 percent cataloged all of their documents.[22]

It should be noted that both of these surveys were taken before the above-mentioned cleanup project and before other enhancements to the services were provided by commercial vendors. Thanks in part to these advances, today more and more libraries with automated catalogs are beginning to tapeload catalog records for documents. Approximately 130 libraries have loaded the GPO/Marcive database and/or are subscribing to Marcive's monthly tape service. OCLC's GOVDOC service provides approximately 160 libraries with tapes of current GPO cataloging records.[23] New services are helping to fulfill depository requirements (e.g., Marcive's Shipping List Service). GPO is trying to respond to libraries' needs (e.g., elimination of "availability records" from its monthly tapes; providing cataloging for the format which is actually distributed to depositories, rather than the format placed in the archives).

Bernard Fry saw clearly indeed into the future when in 1977 he said, "The advent of network shared cataloging and the availability of GPO-LC produced catalog tapes and cards offer for those libraries able to use them new opportunities for service to their publics . . . In the long term, however, most libraries are likely to adopt shared cataloging successfully for government publications at all levels in order to increase efficiency, reduce waste, and provide faster service."[24] Now, fifteen years later, we can confirm that shared cataloging through the national utilities has been a boon to libraries with small documents collections and for cataloging of pre-1976 titles. At the same time, the value that commercial vendors have added to the GPO tapes has made batch-loading of catalog records a practical and economical undertaking for libraries with larger collections.

A HISTORY OF DOCUMENTS
IN THE TRINITY UNIVERSITY CATALOG

Since 1964, our federal documents have been maintained in a separate collection in a Superintendent of Documents (SuDoc) classification number arrangement. The *Monthly Catalog* and other printed indexes provided access to the collection. This approach was less-than-satisfactory because these indexes were time-consuming to use, and using them at all often depended on staff suggestion. Jane Mackay, former documents librarian at Trinity University, was concerned that this important collection was often neglected and under-utilized. To enhance access to the federal documents, she submitted a grant proposal for LSCA Title II funds to produce a microfiche catalog of documents holdings in the seven depositories in the San Antonio area and in the regional depository collection at the Texas State Library. The grant proposal was approved, and a COM catalog of 65,000 records was produced in 1980.[25] Her methodology made use of item numbers to retrieve data from the GPO Monthly Catalog Computer Tapes for the period July 1976 through December 1980. Trinity's records were then extracted from the "grant database" and incorporated into our COM catalog. An additional 30,000 records were batch loaded into our database by Marcive in 1984, extending the coverage from 1976 through 1984. The following year Trinity librarians worked with Marcive staff to create a system for automatically adding current GPO records to the Library database.

As many other libraries have since discovered, incorporating government documents into the public catalog sharply increases the awareness and use of documents. Our students and faculty were now able to locate documents in the catalog without assistance much of the time, and the reference staff became more effective in responding to documents questions.

RETROSPECTIVE CATALOGING PROJECT

Background

In the spring of 1989, we initiated work on a project to catalog the pre-1976 titles in the federal depository collection. This project became a reality largely as a result of Cat/Ref Committee discussions and planning during 1987 and 1988. A small group of monographs had been successfully searched in OCLC by paraprofessional staff in 1987, and the level of copy cataloging did not appear to be unusually difficult. However, it was generally agreed that the success of the project would depend on the quality of the OCLC searching, since one title would often present many choices of copy. Using trained and experienced OCLC searchers would best ensure high quality copy cataloging. As a final point of consensus, the reference librarians/bibliographers would review each agency's publications and withdraw titles for disposal according to GPO guidelines. What remained would be cataloged.

While the exact number of pre-1976 titles could not be determined, it was estimated to be at least fifty thousand (after weeding). This group included titles received on deposit between 1964, the first year of depository status, and the beginning of GPO tapeloaded coverage in 1976. During these years, the selection rate ranged from 50 percent to 75 percent. The size of this uncataloged collection had also increased as a result of library policy which called for transferring all United States publications from the main collection to the documents unit. In addition, large numbers of documents had been acquired from the disposal lists of other depository libraries.

While the size of this older, uncataloged collection was not large in comparison to those generally found in libraries with a longer history of depository status, it contained numerous sets and series of scientific or historical importance. Among the significant works were complete runs of U.S. Geological Survey *Bulletins* and *Professional Papers,* a complete set of the *War of the Rebellion,* substantial holdings of military history publications covering the First and Second World Wars including reports of the Nuremberg Trials, a complete run of the earlier *Bulletins* issued by the U.S. Department of Labor Women's Bureau between 1919 and 1946, a nearly-complete run of the Smithsonian Institution's Bureau of American Ethnology *Bulletins,* and many others. All librarians at Trinity agreed that access to these older documents could best be achieved by including them in the public catalog.

Missing Records

During the initial planning, very little attention was given to the problem of post-1976 publications which had not been included in the GPO tapeloads. Their number was unknown but thought to be small. Once the project was underway, it soon became apparent that the number of "missed" titles could vary widely from agency to agency, as evidenced by the hundreds of Government Accounting Office (GAO) Reports which had somehow slipped out of sight! This project has given us the perfect opportunity to correct a problem which pervades tapeloaded catalogs.

Workflow

As a first step, the documents librarian coordinated a review of the entire collection of federal documents and compiled a report which spelled out the relative importance of each agency's publications based on curricular needs, general library usage and requirements, and significant holdings within the agency classes. This report, "U.S. Documents: Collection Development and Cataloging Priorities," serves as a framework for the project and includes specific details on retention policies, weeding assignments, and cataloging priorities for each agency.

Our collection of approximately one thousand uncataloged Smithsonian Institution publications was an ideal choice for a "test run," since it was a very "clean" collection which did not require weeding. The hit rate in OCLC was over 90 percent, which surpassed all expectations. Our project to copy catalog the older documents appeared to be a feasible one.

To begin, the documents librarian coordinates the review and weeding activities of the reference librarians/bibliographers and then notifies the senior documents assistant that a specific section of the SuDoc classification is ready to be cataloged. To avoid any misunderstanding, this notification is always a written one. The senior documents assistant performs several of the initial steps in the cataloging process:

1. Searches the NOTIS database by the SuDoc numbers of a selected agency and obtains a printout of all numbers found in the system.
2. At the stacks, checks the titles in the collection against the printout and places those not found in NOTIS on a book truck.
3. Searches this truck of uncataloged titles in OCLC and downloads the appropriate catalog records into NOTIS. Since these titles will appear in the OPAC immediately, signs are placed on the affected shelves directing users to ask in the documents office for missing titles.
4. Sets aside titles which lack OCLC copy in the "copy not found" category.

At this point, the truck of documents is sent to the cataloging department where the copy cataloging supervisor and one copy cataloger share the work. This particular assignment of duties came about because as manager, the copy cataloging supervisor was not under the same pressure to maintain a certain monthly level of production. Furthermore, the copy cataloger chosen for the project was not assigned at the time to any other special project and had a minimal backlog. Both staff members work only on monographic titles; many of the serial titles have already been cataloged, and exact holdings information is being done as a separate project.

When the truck of documents arrives in the copy cataloging unit, the copy catalogers

1. Search the titles in NOTIS.
2. Verify and correct description and subject and name headings.
3. Add location information to the 049 of the bibliographic record, according to the instructions of the senior documents assistant.
4. Create a standard holdings message to display in the OPAC: "Check documents stacks for holdings."
5. Return the truck of documents to the documents unit.

Once the truck is back in the documents unit, the senior documents assistant:

1. Creates a holdings statement for multivolume monographs and periodicals.
2. Records the cataloging statistics.
3. Orders shelflist cards.
4. Retains a record of all titles in the "copy not found" category.

The amount of time required per truck depends on the type of material. For example, "bound withs" take much more time than single item monographs. Under normal circumstances, however, about 300 titles per month can be cataloged. In addition, because this project is lowest priority for the copy cataloging unit, the rate of cataloging may also vary depending upon the status of other concurrent projects. For instance, during 1991 and 1992, NOTIS implementation and barcoding of the collection preempted copy cataloging of documents. To date, approximately 20 percent of the estimated fifty thousand uncataloged pre-1976 documents have been cataloged.

SHARING EXPERTISE

As our retrospective cataloging project demonstrates, Trinity's documents unit is too small to undertake all the functions related to maintaining a cataloged documents collection.[26] In the absence of a full-time documents cataloger, we have found ways to draw upon the skills and knowledge of librarians in other departments.

The first cooperative effort was the one required for the retrospective cataloging project described above, and which has benefitted from the work of two copy catalogers. Following that successful partnership, the maintenance cataloger initiated a maintenance project intended to provide correct locations in the catalog for documents received in microfiche.

In the process of doing routine cleanup on the database, the maintenance librarian had become aware that many records for documents received in microfiche gave no indication in the OPAC of their physical format or of their location in microfiche cabinets. (Laura Tull has noted in her article on the Marcive cleanup project that, because of a policy of not creating original records during the project, participants had not addressed the lack of microform cataloging records on the GPO tapes.)[27] The post-1976 congressional publications constituted a particularly severe problem for users who retrieve documents from open shelves or microfiche cabinets. Over 50 percent of these publications are received in microfiche format, and many committees have had one or more changes in format over the years. Reference staff receive a continuous stream of location questions from confused users. It became apparent to the maintenance librarian that these records could not be reliably corrected without working from the microfiche themselves.

In September 1992, following discussions with the documents librarian, the maintenance librarian loaned one of her student workers to documents for whatever length of time necessary to correct these records. Guidelines and training for searching and for making corrections to fixed fields and locations were carried out by the maintenance librarian, with ongoing supervision being handled by the senior documents assistant. A new location message in the OPAC for document microforms was established to lead patrons to the microfiche cabinets rather than to the shelves. Approximately

1,200 titles a month are being corrected. Projected completion date is the end of 1994. Access to the congressional documents is being greatly enhanced by this maintenance project, initiated by one of Trinity's catalog librarians.

Another participant in documents work is the head cataloger, who includes important documents titles in her work. She has most recently verified and corrected series tracings on hundreds of records for several documents titles. She makes decisions to work on such records based on the importance the title has for the curriculum, not on whether it is or is not a document. For instance, geology is a heavily used part of our collection. Because users are likely to approach our U.S. Geological Survey publications armed with a series citation, and since series headings in documents records have been less well controlled than most other access points, it seemed particularly appropriate to make these analyzed titles easily accessible through accurate series tracings. To that end, she has verified and corrected tracings for hundreds of records for *USGS Bulletins, USGS Circulars, USGS Open File Reports,* and *USGS Professional Papers.* Similarly important and heavily used documents titles on which she has worked are the *Bureau of Labor Statistics Bulletin* and the United States Women's Bureau *Bulletin.* In addition, she is available for consultation on cataloging issues whenever the senior documents assistant needs advice.

Finally, the serials cataloger meets as needed with the documents assistant to answer such questions pertaining to serials as holdings statement creation and maintenance, union list reporting, handling titles in more than one format or with multiple SuDoc numbers, managing duplicate records for serials, etc.

In addition, we are moving toward integrating the senior documents assistant into the mainstream of the cataloging department so that to the extent possible, standards for documents cataloging will conform to those for the regular collection. She has been included in cataloging meetings when pertinent topics were discussed, and we are considering the benefits of having her attend all cataloging meetings. There are at least two advantages: (1) to enhance her awareness of general cataloging issues, and (2) to help make the catalogers mindful of the existence of a documents unit which performs what must be considered cataloging and maintenance.

While the two units will doubtless always be physically separated, we can certainly work toward more interaction and sharing in order to enhance the quality of documents records in the catalog. We cannot hope for increased staff, professional or otherwise, in the documents unit or elsewhere in the library. Therefore, we must increasingly find ways to bring the work of documents beyond the documents workroom door.

A final element of shared expertise consists in the participation of reference librarians who work with the documents librarian to review and weed the documents collection in particular subject areas. They also handle all questions pertaining to documents, since the reference and documents collections are adjacent to each other.

CONCLUSION

As stated previously, in 1976 changes at GPO initiated what has now become nearly two decades of evolution in the way libraries handle documents. GPO personnel adopted AACR cataloging and eventually gained the status of official documents cataloging agency and full NACO participant. Over time, the agency has found ways to modify its practices in order to better balance the needs of libraries with the requirements of its own mission. Commercial vendors have learned how to enhance the GPO-produced and LC-distributed tapes with a view to providing libraries with services which GPO is unable to give. Libraries have begun to learn the impact of adding documents records to their public catalogs, impact not only on documents and technical services staff, but also on public services staff.

We are still in the midst of a large shift in our thinking about the place of documents in our collections and in our catalogs. We three–GPO, vendors, and libraries–still have much to do to accommodate our interdependent needs and limitations. It is a difficult challenge today and will likely remain so for some time to come. We cannot now, if ever, experience perfection.

Can the documents component of the catalog be good, however, without being perfect? Ideally, the tapeloaded records should match the quality standards to which the library catalog adheres. After the

LSU-Rice-Texas A&M cleanup project and with vendor-provided authority processing and other services, the GPO database comes much closer to meeting most libraries' standards than it did in the early years of tape production. Nevertheless, ongoing maintenance will be required to maintain the quality of the records. Libraries may find that a documents unit's small size or lack of expertise will make it impossible to carry out what are traditionally considered cataloging and maintenance functions. Cornwell and Kinney remind us of the importance of the "coordination of technical processing activities in documents with those of other units; [and] division of authority control and record maintenance responsibilities between documents and cataloging . . ."[28] The ultimate task and goal are "to *integrate* authority control procedures for GPO records into procedures for all other materials. Regardless of who does the work or how it is done, the outcome of work done on GPO records must be consistent with that done on other records." At Trinity, we believe that through our sharing of expertise across traditional lines we are achieving that goal.

NOTES

1. Judy E. Myers, "The Government Printing Office Cataloging Records: Opportunities and Problems," *Government Information Quarterly,* 2(1985): 29.

2. Sharon M. Edge, "Retrieval of United States Government Publications from Integrated Library Collections," *Kentucky Library Association Bulletin* 39, no. 4 (1975): 5.

3. Benjamin Shearer, "Federal Depository Libraries on the Campus: Practices and Prospects," *Government Publications Review,* 4(1977): 209.

4. Alice Harrison Bahr, "Cataloging U.S. Depository Materials: A Reevaluation," *College & Research Libraries* 47(1986): 587.

5. Paula Watson and Kathleen M. Heim, "Patterns of Access and Circulation in a Depository Document Collection Under Full Bibliographic Control," *Government Publications Review* 11(1984): 272.

6. Bernard M. Fry, "Government Publications and the Library: Implications for Change," *Government Publications Review* 4(1977): 113.

7. U.S. Congress, Office of Technology Assessment, *Informing the Nation: Federal Information Dissemination in an Electronic Age* (Washington, D.C.: USGPO, 1988), p. 145.

8. Bahr, "Cataloging U.S. Depository Materials," p. 587.

9. A. Mather, "Library of Congress: Acquiring and Cataloging Government Publications," *Government Publications Review* 1(1973): 222.

10. LeRoy C. Schwarzkopf, "The *Monthly Catalog* and Bibliographical Control of U.S. Government Publications," *Drexel Library Quarterly* 11(Jan./Apr. 1974): 95.

11. A. Mather, "Federal Documents and the Library of Congress," *Illinois Libraries* 56(April 1974): 316.

12. Judy E. Myers and Helen H. Britton, "Government Documents in the Public Card Catalog: The Iceberg Surfaces," *Government Publications Review* 5(1978): 311.

13. *Bowker Annual of Library & Book Trade Information* (New York: R. R. Bowker, 1975): pp. 95 ff.

14. Bahr, "Cataloging U.S. Depository Materials," p. 588.

15. Myrtle Smith Bolner and Barbara Kile, "Documents to the People: Access Through the Automated Catalog," *Government Publications Review* 18(1991): 53.

16. Myers, "The Government Printing Office Cataloging Records," pp. 27-56.

17. Jan Swanbeck, "Documents Librarianship: I, Federal Documents in the Online Catalog: Problems, Options, and the Future," *Government Information Quarterly* 2(1985): 187-192.

18. Bolner and Kile, "Documents to the People," p. 51-64.

19. Laura Tull, "Retrospective Conversion of Government Documents: Marcive GPO Tape Clean-up Project," *Technicalities* 9(August 1989): 4-7.

20. Bolner and Kile, "Documents to the People," p. 55.

21. Ibid.

22. Jan Swanbeck and Peter Hernon, eds., *Depository Library Use of Technology: A Practitioner's Perspective* (Norwood, N.J.: Ablex Publishing Corporation, 1993), p. 4.

23. Conversations with Jim Noel, Manager of GPO Services, Marcive, Inc. and with Jean Kahn, Manager of Tape Loading and Database Services, OCLC.

24. Fry, "Government Publications and the Library," p. 113.

25. Ben Amata acknowledged Jane Mackay's contribution in pioneering tape-loaded catalogs in the introduction to "Loading the GPO MARC Tapes: 1992 Preconference of ALA/Government Documents Round Table," *DTTP* (Documents to the People) 20(December 1992): 207.

26. Staffing includes two full-time library assistants and 60 hours per week of student work. The librarian responsible for the documents unit devotes about 20 hours weekly to documents, her principal duties being selection and maintenance decisions and monitoring the unit's general operations and special projects.

Participants in Documents Cataloging Project

Professionals:	Paraprofessionals:
Documents Librarian	Senior Documents Assistant
Head Cataloger	Copy Cataloging Supervisor
Serials Cataloger	Senior Copy Cataloger
Maintenance Cataloger	

27. Tull, "Retrospective Conversion of Government Documents," p. 6.

28. Gary Cornwell and Thomas Kinney, "Checklist for Loading GPO Cataloging Records into the Online Catalog" in *Depository Library Use of Technology,* eds. Jan Swanbeck and Peter Hernon, Norwood, N.J.: Ablex Publishing, 1993, p. 101.

29. "Loading the GPO MARC Tapes: 1992 Preconference of ALA/Government Documents Round Table," *DTTP* (Documents to the People) 20(December 1992): 217.

Automation:
The Bridge Between Technical Services and Government Documents

Darlene M. Pierce
Eileen Theodore-Shusta

SUMMARY. Olson Library included bibliographic records for government documents in its online catalog. Although preparing the initial profile and planning for the first computer tapeload were important and time-consuming projects, staff were somewhat unprepared for the impact the project would have on traditional staff functions. As the automation project evolved, procedures once performed in the Documents Unit were transferred to Technical Services. This article renders a case history of how Olson Library staff dealt with the impact of the first tapeload, re-structured work patterns to accommodate future tapeloads, and took advantage of the project to move forward toward a more fully automated environment. Additionally, it is evidence of how a project can bring together a staff who once viewed themselves as having related but separate missions.

Northern Michigan University's Olson Library has been a U.S. government publications depository since 1963. The librarian providing documents oversight has a half-time assignment in the unit; the librarian's remaining time is split between reference and other

---

Darlene M. Pierce is Government Documents and Maps Librarian at Northern Michigan University. Eileen Theodore-Shusta is Head of Cataloging, State University of New York-Binghamton.

[Haworth co-indexing entry note]: "Automation: The Bridge Between Technical Services and Government Documents," Pierce, Darlene M., and Eileen Theodore-Shusta. Co-published simultaneously in *Cataloging & Classification Quarterly* (The Haworth Press, Inc.) Vol. 18, No. 3/4, 1994, pp. 75-84; and: *Cataloging Government Publications Online* (ed: Carolyn C. Sherayko) The Haworth Press, Inc., 1994, pp. 75-84. Multiple copies of this article/chapter may be purchased from The Haworth Document Delivery Center [1-800-3-HAWORTH; 9:00 a.m. - 5:00 p.m. (EST)].

duties. Sixty hours per week of student help is assigned to documents. In the online environment, additional full-time library staff assist in managing the documents collection. Including documents in the Library's online catalog was the impetus for re-assigning various responsibilities to staff not in the documents unit. How and why these changes came to be is the focus of this article.

BRINGING DOCUMENTS ONLINE

Olson library had successfully implemented a NOTIS-based online catalog which included the majority of the library's holdings. The Library is a member of the Upper Peninsula Region of Library Cooperation (UPRLC) and shares it's database with special, public, and academic libraries in a multi-county region. The database is housed at Northern Michigan University and although all consortium libraries share a single online public access catalog, each library maintains its own records in the database. Because government documents had not been included in the card catalog, they were not included in the original conversion to an online system. Once the online catalog was functioning, government documents became one of the largest portions of Olson Library's collection not included in the database.

The Library administration's goal was to include all library materials in the online catalog. Grant funding to purchase bibliographic tapes from Marcive, Inc. was secured through the UPRLC and the documents librarian agreed to undertake the project of profiling the collection. On September 17, 1990, after months of preparation, the bibliographic records were loaded into the UPRLC's database.

A total of 129,218 government document bibliographic records were loaded from the first Marcive tape. These records reflected both current and retrospective item selections dating back to 1976 in a depository which routinely selected approximately 50 percent of the total Government Printing Office (GPO) items available. Technical services staff and the documents librarian basked briefly in a sense of accomplishment before the enormity of the project's impact on the database was fully realized. What had been done to the "pristine" database and just what was to be done next? Furthermore, who was going to do what?

Olson Library only six months earlier had brought its online public catalog to life. The circulation module was not yet in place, but plans for implementation were well under way. The great care taken to create a clean database was somewhat sabotaged with the introduction of government documents records.

The Documents Librarian recognized while profiling the collection that the further back in time the records extended, the greater the probability for error. Publications had been lost and weeded, the shelflist had been maintained by student assistants, some of whom did a good job and some of whom did not, and early documentation of the library's GPO item selections was missing or scanty. Errors in the database would include discrepancies between bibliographic records and actual holdings, and conflicts with location codes which had been assigned based on the document format (e.g., paper copy or microfiche). A potential error rate as high as ten percent was projected.

In the eyes of the Documents Librarian, well versed in the quirks of documents management, that error rate wasn't too bad: from Olson Library's tapeload there were, after all, nearly 116,300 good records providing access to the collection. So what about the potentially 12,922 erroneous records? The Technical Services Coordinator, who had so intently strived for database integrity, was somewhat appalled. And to make matters worse, in addition to the original tapeload, new records were to be introduced each month. Who would handle database management? There were two separate, albeit intertwined, problems. One challenge was retrospective in nature: database cleanup from the original tapeload.

The second challenge was future oriented: how were staff to handle newly arriving government documents? Would we create item records and apply barcodes for circulation purposes? Might we have to verify location designations in the cataloging tapes being loaded monthly? How would we make the corrections directed by GPO, especially when call numbers were involved? And who would be responsible for this work? Meetings intensified between the Documents Librarian and the Technical Services Coordinator. The existing method of processing new documents was mapped and those procedures were then compared to activities required in an automated system.

PROCESSING AND BIBLIOGRAPHIC CONTROL

In the pre-automation environment, documents could and did exist as a separate and discrete unit within the library. Physical processing of incoming publications was done in the documents work area rather than in technical services where all other materials were processed. The Documents Librarian would open shipments from GPO and remove publications which were to be routed to reference, the main stacks, or periodicals. Student assistants in documents performed all processing tasks: matching receipts to the shipping lists, labeling and property stamping new documents, and identifying missing publications for claiming. All statistics for documents received and discarded were maintained in the documents unit.

Also located in the documents work area was the shelflist. Student assistants maintained the documents shelflist, recording information on new, weeded, and lost publications. During planning for automation, it was agreed that manual shelflisting would cease after the database was functioning. By implication, the GPO shelflist requirement had to be met by the automated system.

Although most materials in Olson Library had been barcoded in anticipation of online circulation, the documents collection had not been barcoded, nor were new documents being barcoded upon receipt. The documents staff admittedly had no expertise with the technical services aspects of the NOTIS database, including applying barcodes and creating item records for circulation. In fact, documents staff didn't even have access to a NOTIS terminal.

Discussions about how to handle the circulation aspects of documents–barcodes and item records–led to a tentative conclusion to move the processing of new documents to the technical services unit. Although both the Technical Services Coordinator and the Documents Librarian had many reservations regarding such a move, there seemed to be no reasonable alternative. The logical conclusion was to let the staff most familiar with database management undertake for government documents the same tasks they were performing on all other library materials. Although unfamiliar with documents, the technical services staff had responsibility for and expertise in working with bibliographic records, performing database cleanup, creating item records, and processing library materials.

CONCERNS AND SOLUTIONS

Technical Services became involved with the documents cataloging project when the first Marcive bibliographic tape was loaded into the online catalog. Four major concerns were identified: the impact of the initial tapeload on the existing database; the need to develop means of communication between the Technical Services staff and the Documents Librarian; the probable necessity of integrating the physical processing of documents into the Technical Services workflow; and the need to prepare documents (both current receipts and the existing collection) for circulation in the automated system. Two of these four concerns, developing means of communication and assessing the impact of the initial tapeload, were of immediate importance. The latter two concerns evolved as work progressed and as the circulation module was implemented.

The need to develop a means of communication became obvious as the first tapeload was moved from the test database into production. Although the Technical Services Coordinator and the Documents Librarian had a good working relationship, it was clear that each spoke a somewhat different language. To remedy the situation, cross-training was undertaken. It was assumed that Technical Services staff who routinely interacted with the NOTIS system would also work with government documents. In an informal workshop, the Documents Librarian provided Technical Services staff with an introduction to documents. Most aspects of operating a depository were covered, including a brief history of government publishing, the Library's own depository history, GPO guidelines and regulations, SuDoc call numbers, publication selection by item number, shipping lists, corrections, and claims. In return, the Documents Librarian was given an introduction to NOTIS, including system architecture, MARC formats, and technical services language. It wasn't long before the Documents Librarian could speak some semblance of "tech services language" (e.g., series, serials, MARC fields) and the Technical Services staff could speak beginning "doc-ese."

Once both teams were sharing common language, the task of assessing the impact of the Marcive tapeload on the database was begun. Shipping lists had been retained and staff chose those dated eighteen months and three months back in time as test lists. Those time spans were chosen for specific reasons. Although in the documents community it was common knowledge that a time-lag existed between when a publication was shipped from GPO and when the bibliographic record appeared in the *Monthly Catalog* (and hence in the Marcive tapes and the Library's database), no one was quite sure of its duration. It was hoped that at three months, most records would appear and any corrections could be made to call numbers and locations. The eighteen month test was used to help determine how many publications received by the library had no bibliographic records in the database. That information would help answer the question of how long to wait before importing a bibliographic record from a national utility or performing original cataloging.

Receipts marked on the shipping lists were matched against the database to see how many records accurately appeared. As anticipated, this process of checking shipping lists enabled staff to detect call number errors, location designation errors, and titles for which no bibliographic record had been received. It was encouraging to find that most titles had records by the eighteenth month and that the incidence of errors in call number was relatively low. Errors in the location designation were more common because locations were based on format; for certain item numbers publications were not consistently arriving in one format or another (e.g., all titles from an item number arriving in microfiche).

Although answers to earlier questions of what needed to be done and by whom began to evolve, these seemingly simple database checks generated many questions. The Technical Services Coordinator began to evaluate a logical distribution of tasks and to prepare workflow analyses. Because policies and procedures for cataloging documents were non-existent, these manuals were drafted as work progressed. Communication became even more critical and both the Technical Services Coordinator and the Documents Librarian wanted input from staff members whose work lives were now changing to accommodate government publications. A documents staff group, a group comprised of Technical Services staff and the Documents Librarian from Public Services, was formed and monthly meetings were scheduled.

From these meetings solutions slowly emerged. Top priority was given to correcting errors in call numbers or locations and a staff member was assigned this task. The tests on shipping lists had shown that format errors could be quickly identified and that after three months few documents were without bibliographic records to correct. GPO correction notices were also given high priority. Corrections to call numbers online led to further questions about making these changes to the physical collection. It was clear that Technical Services staff made database corrections; it was less clear how changes to the documents themselves were to be made.

At the same time the documents group was grappling with the question of how to build a workflow bridge between database management and physical collection management, final preparations were being made to implement the online circulation system. All literature on the subject of having documents in the online catalog indicated a dramatic increase in use and circulation of documents. Circulation staff, not fond of documents to begin with, preferred not to barcode an increased flow of documents at the point of circulation. So, into the challenge of building a workflow bridge was pitched the element of barcodes. A suggestion that Technical Services adopt the physical processing of documents was tentatively put forward in the documents work group. Many reservations were verbalized, but discussion centered around that suggestion.

The Documents Librarian, legally responsible and accountable to GPO for depository management, voiced concerns about maintaining an adequate level of oversight. Because the Documents Librarian also had responsibility for collection development and outreach, it would be necessary to continuously review shipping lists and new publications. Communications from GPO vital to documents management, such as *Administrative Notes,* had to be routed in a timely manner to the Documents Librarian. So important were these concerns that the Documents Librarian indicated that should a comfortable level of oversight not be maintained, legal responsibility for documents management would be relinquished.

Technical Services staff presented their own concerns. Each person already had a full range of responsibilities. Funding was such that no additional staff positions could be created. It was unclear how much time would be consumed by the physical processing of documents. Physical processing was performed by student assistants in documents so there was no reason not to have student assistants do the same work in Technical Services, but from where would the student hours be drawn?

In spite of these concerns, the Technical Services Coordinator identified arguments which were difficult to refute. First, Technical Services was well suited, due to its mission, to handle physical processing of newly received library materials regardless of origin. Second, because the manual shelflist was closed, the receipt of documents ideally should be recorded in the online system to meet GPO's requirement for a shelflist. Recording receipts was typically handled by Technical Services. Although staffing might be problematic, the proposal to transfer processing tasks to Technical Services coincided with a lull in book buying which was driven by budgetary restraints, thus reducing other aspects of the Technical Services workload. Finally, circulation item records could be created at the point of physical processing.

This final argument was most compelling. Staff mapped the paths documents would take to accomplish the many facets of collection management in the automated environment. Shipments originally delivered by mail to the Technical Services area could continue to be routed unopened to documents for processing. To accommodate the circulation system and database maintenance, processed documents could then be routed to Technical Services to have barcodes attached and item records created. On the move again, barcoded publications would be shuttled back to the documents unit for shelving. Eventually, superseded and weeded documents could be shuttled back to Technical Services to be withdrawn from the database. Fewer shuttle trips would be required if Technical Services adopted physical processing.

The documents work group forged ahead, developing additional workflow charts, reviewing staff assignments, and preparing strategies to incorporate the various aspects of documents into the overall work patterns. Circulation staff agreed to barcode and create unlinked item records for older documents as they circulated. Technical services staff would take the documents upon return and link item records to bibliographic records before returning publications to Documents for shelving. A Technical Services staff member, under the guidance of the Documents Librarian, was assigned to train and supervise student assistants who would perform the processing tasks. The Documents Librarian also refined the list of titles routed to alternate locations (e.g., reference or periodicals) to aid staff with processing. As work progressed, solutions were developed for each new challenge.

OUTCOMES

Although initially the challenges created by including government documents in the online catalog seemed formidable, the outcomes of the project surpassed any anticipated results. The original goal to improve access to documents by having bibliographic records in the public catalog had been accomplished. The extent to which Technical Services would become involved had not been foreseen in the preliminary stages of planning. However, once the Technical Services staff began applying their expertise, bibliographic control of the collection improved greatly. As part of their vision of routine bibliographic control, projects were undertaken to include in the online system information such as volume holdings and retention notes. The circulation process was enhanced by the application of barcodes and creation of item records. Furthermore, as the online system became a more accurate reflection of holdings and receipts, the system became a more suitable replacement for the manual shelflist.

From the perspective of the Documents Librarian, these results surpassed any initial hopes. Detailed information about the collection was available more readily than ever before to more library users. Because the holdings were reflected in a shared online catalog, patrons in other consortium libraries could see which documents existed in Olson Library. Since Technical Services adopted the physical processing of new publications, student assistants in documents focused their attention on stack maintenance, special projects, and helping patrons use the collection. The daily routines surrounding processing were supervised by Technical Services, yet oversight had been maintained by routing completed shipments with shipping lists to the documents work area for review by the librarian prior to shelving. Communication between staff in Documents and Technical Services, recognized from the outset as a critical factor, had been successfully developed and sustained.

This element of communication is the key to one of the more pleasant and least anticipated outcomes: a merging of two units which often historically experience lines of separation. Documents had existed within public services as a distinct unit, able to function without much interaction with Technical Services. Inclusion of document bibliographic records in the online catalog could have been handled in many ways. Olson Library staff chose to integrate documents into the workflow using a more traditional yet somewhat holistic view. This choice was not made initially, but instead evolved slowly. The effect was to build a bridge between public and technical services. Through cooperation and communication, staff in units with differing perspectives and concerns came to realize just how parallel their missions really were. The documents automation project became the bridge that now links the technical services unit and the documents unit together.

SPECIAL ISSUES IN ONLINE ACCESS

Control of Government Document Serials in Local Electronic and Organizational Systems

Mary C. Bushing
Bonnie Johnson

SUMMARY. Current discussions concerning U.S. government documents center on attempts to mainstream these materials into technical and public service operations. Montana State University Libraries incorporated all document receipt, check-in, and cataloging functions into technical services operations. The goal is to treat documents, as far as possible, like other materials received by the library. A "decision tree" is utilized to organize document materials into logical groups for processing, using the OPAC and MicroLinx, a serial check-in system. Marcive GPO tapes provide records for monographs, while serials are handled locally. All records are placed in the OPAC, with holdings, to enhance patron search efficiency.

Mary C. Bushing is Head of Collection Development and Bonnie Johnson is Head of Collection Maintenance at Montana State University Libraries, Bozeman, MT 59717.

[Haworth co-indexing entry note]: "Control of Government Document Serials in Local Electronic and Organizational Systems," Bushing, Mary C., and Bonnie Johnson. Co-published simultaneously in *Cataloging & Classification Quarterly* (The Haworth Press, Inc.) Vol. 18, No. 3/4, 1994, pp. 85-95; and: *Cataloging Government Publications Online* (ed: Carolyn C. Sherayko) The Haworth Press, Inc., 1994, pp. 85-95. Multiple copies of this article/chapter may be purchased from The Haworth Document Delivery Center [1-800-3-HAWORTH; 9:00 a.m. - 5:00 p.m. (EST)].

The mainstreaming of government documents has been discussed periodically in library literature, but until recently, the discussion has been fairly theoretical. Documents librarians argued for the availability of documents to the general library patron, but with few specific or consistent recommendations concerning the "how" to treat documents at a level and in a manner consistent with other library materials. Practical management and processing techniques were presented with an emphasis upon the uniqueness of these materials. Explanations of the "special" procedures necessary to comply with depository regulations and to interact with the Government Printing Office (GPO) bureaucracy while providing access to government publications fill the literature. The special or unique nature of documents has been emphasized by the very existence of a separate body of literature about documents.[1]

Now that automated systems and GPO MARC records have made the theoretical concepts possible within the constraints of practical operations, librarians are looking for ways to truly mainstream documents in services and operations. The discussion has now moved away from the theoretical issues of the "why" or the importance of access to government documents in a democratic society, to the "how" to efficiently incorporate or mainstream documents in both technical and public service operations. By de-emphasizing the ways in which federal documents are different, and concentrating upon the ways in which documents are similar to other materials, it is possible to make them as accessible as the other items in the collection. Treating documents in a manner similar to other materials, achieves the ultimate goal of placing government information in the hands of citizens in a timely and efficient manner.

At the same time that the practical aspects are being examined, there are increased pressures on libraries to reorganize in order to operate as information organizations and not just as providers of information, and to streamline operations due to reduced resources. Reorganization has further moved the discussion of document integration to the forefront of technical service issues. As budgetary pressures, reorganization, and electronic sophistication increase, librarians are attempting to truly mainstream documents by integrating them into routine operations without isolating or discriminating against those published by the government. This move towards integration of document processing, cataloging, and access, has also served to de-mystify the government information realm by involving more people in the "knowledge" and by expanding the experience base from which decisions are made and the problems of integration solved.

REORGANIZATION

For Montana State University, an important change in the handling of documents occurred in 1990 when the technical service functions of The Libraries were reorganized into two units, Collection Development and Collection Maintenance. At the same time, all processing, ordering, and classifying of materials, regardless of format or publisher, were centralized and located within these units. Collection Development was given the responsibility for collection development, acquisition, receipt, budget, and initial check-in of all items including those purchased, received on deposit, through exchange or as donations. Collection Maintenance was given the responsibilities for cataloging, withdrawal, physical processing and systems-related functions for all items. Staff members who had previously only handled serial, monographs or document processing were brought into these units with other staff members who were accustomed to thinking about and doing things in a different manner. This meant that staff questioned the reasons for existing operations. They asked for clarification of purposes, and then rethought processes and wrote new procedures. A concerted effort to provide cross-training for staff within these units and to de-mystify documents and serials resulted in teams that approached problems with an optimistic and creative outlook. A consistency in approach and process rather than an emphasis on the uniqueness and the exceptions, has resulted in innovative and efficient means by which to accomplish the theoretical goal of mainstreaming documents.

This change in the organization enabled The Libraries to approach a true integration of documents into library operations by making documents more like everything else rather than emphasizing all the ways in which documents are different. An attempt is now made to acknowledge the differences and to accommodate those differences that matter, such as depository requirements, while minimizing those differences that hinder the real goal of placing information in the hands of those who need it. Not all of the wrinkles are out of the system, but there is constant improvement in the processes and clarification of the rationale for each decision. Further, there is a recognition that not only are procedures not written in stone, but that they are written in vanishing ink that disappears if not rewritten or updated periodically.

MONOGRAPH OR SERIAL?

The integration of state and Canadian documents was begun at the time of the reorganization. In order to accomplish this, it was determined that there would be two basic routes for materials entering the operations regardless of source or format. One stream of processing is for monographic items and one is for serial publications. Serial publications are further divided into those published annually or less often, and those with more frequent expected publication. The latter go through a traditional check-in process, while the former have an item record added to the OPAC and proceed to the collection immediately. Monographic series may have unique bibliographic records, but require check-in as a first step in order to track receipt of the series. Monographic items are sent through the usual review and faculty awareness processes, and then routed on for cataloging and physical processing. They then are routed to Collection Maintenance for processing for the shelf.

In the summer of 1991, federal document processing was also integrated into the regular technical services operations, but without the addition of staff positions in the department. This provided an ideal situation for revising the processing of federal depository materials. Those clerks who would handle these items were not documents personnel and did not have preconceived ideas about how things had to be done. They did, however, have apprehensions about the special nature of these documents based upon the mystique about the complicated nature of documents and the unique processes previously performed. At this point it became clear that the unwritten "decision tree" used to integrate other documents into the regular processes could be used here as well and would help to avoid the inclination to place, what seemed like 50 percent of the items, into a category of exceptions to the "rules" and processes. By thinking aloud, playing devil's advocate, and returning again and again to the concept of two basic processing routes, staff were gradually able to develop some consistency in determining how to integrate federal documents into existing operations.

The processing route for federal depository materials was determined regardless of format (fiche, paper, CD-ROM, map, or other), item number configuration, GPO designation, or other convention. The first questions for each item is: Is it monographic (one time publication, unique, individual bibliographic record) or is it serial in nature? If it is serial in nature or is questionable, it is routed through the serial processes where standard procedures are in place to deal with the serial exceptions that appear in the commercial world almost as often as in the world of federal documents. When truly problematical items are found, they are discussed and an attempt is made to identify similar publishing oddities in the commercial world so that the processing and cataloging paths of the documents can be parallel, if possible, to items of a similar nature. Such things include loose-leaf updating services, monographic series, paper that is later replaced by fiche. and special items such as census series that have multiple levels of serial identification. As few exceptions to the rules as possible are made because it is believed that the patrons are best served when items can be processed in a timely and correct manner and made available for use. The staff members in Collection Development and Collection Maintenance try to remember that the sole purpose for having materials is for patron use. Through creative problem-solving and flexibility, the staff have developed consistency in their decisions and find that there are few real exceptions. As changes occur in the depository program, an attempt is made to remain open to the need for change in response.

WORKFLOW

The basic process for depository items (state. federal and other) begins on the day of receipt with check-in accomplished by comparison against shipping lists, just as purchased items are compared to invoices and packing slips. At the same point, the necessary claim process and the maintenance of shipping lists files are completed. Documents are stamped as appropriate. SuDoc numbers are recorded directly onto federal items while the shipping list is in hand and problems can usually be resolved. Then items are routed into one of the basic work streams. They are handled at the same rate as other items with virtually no backlog in the processing, except those imposed by the depository program itself, for example, when shipping lists do not arrive. Serials are routinely handled in Collection Development and passed on to Collection Maintenance on the day of receipt. They are usually in the collection within two days of arrival. Binding operations for document serials are managed in the same manner as binding for other serials using the same principles to determine the appropriate titles for binding.

The Libraries' shelflist was closed in 1990 and the OPAC is used for inventory control and statistical reports. In addition, the serial check-in system, MicroLinx,[2] serves as an inventory record of all currently received serial items regardless of source. When the initial title record is entered into MicroLinx, coding fields are used to indicate the following classes of special serials: deposit federal document, non-deposit federal document, deposit Montana document, non-deposit Montana document, deposit Canadian document, non-deposit Canadian document, personal gifts, and publisher supplied free subscriptions. Reports using these fields can provide current lists of titles in any of these categories as needed for management purposes. The system makes it possible to profile titles for expected receipt of issues for claim reports. Depository titles can be included in this process as a means to alert staff to closed titles or other problems. The receipt profile for many document serials is done with a wide "window" so that delays by governmental agencies do not result in unnecessary work by the serial clerks.

ACCESS

At the time that documents were moved to Technical Services, manual check-in of serial documents was being done. The change to automated serial check-in took almost a year to complete because of the large number of document serial records that had been generated over many years and the number of serials being received. The process itself, however, was relatively simple. As serial documents arrived, the manual check-in card was retrieved, holdings verified against the collection, and a MicroLinx check-in record created. The issues were not delayed during the next steps, but were processed immediately and routed to the collection. Using the check-in records, the OPAC was then checked for a bibliographic record with current and complete information in agreement with both the serial check-in card and the verified stack holdings. If a bibliographic record was not available on the OPAC, the information was routed to Collection Maintenance so that the necessary cataloging could be completed and a bibliographic record with complete information could be provided.

Collection Maintenance enters the bibliographic records for the U.S. government document serials, as well as other serials, into the OPAC via the WLN bibliographic network. Therefore, the Libraries monograph as well as serial holdings information can be found in the online catalog, increasing patron and Public Service staff search efficiency. They need not go to a different or separate place to locate serials information. Once the bibliographic record is entered into the system, a separate "item record" is attached which shows call number, location, type of material, and availability. For serials, a "summary holdings statement" is listed directly after the call number and preceded by an asterisk. This statement tells patrons the volumes and/or years owned by the Libraries, as well as if it is currently being received. The following is an example of an open summary holdings statement as it appears on the screen:

CALL NUMBER	LOCATION	STATUS	MEDIA
A2.114: *1981-	DOCUMENT	AVAILABLE	PER

The complete item information (individual records for barcoded bound volumes), is available for patrons when they press the "Copies Avail?" key, but a short call number/location listing is also shown on the title screen, as illustrated by the example below.

```
Move selection bar with up/down keys.  For more entries, press PREV or NEXT.  For AVAILABILITY
add ADDITIONAL LOCATIONS, press COPIES AVAIL?

Title     Federal plan for meteorological ser


TITLE/AUTHOR                            CALL#            DATE   EDITION          LOCATION     NO.
------------------------------------    ---------------  ----   --------------   ---------    ---
Federal plan for clear air turbulence.                   1970                    STACKS
  United States.  Ofice of Federa       TL557.A5U52                                            1

The Federal plan of meteorological serv                  19uu                    DOCUMENT
  ---                                    C 55.16/2: *1967/68-1984                               9

A Federal plan for natural disaster warn                 1973                    STACKS
  United States.  Federal Committee     GB70.9.U54 1973                                        2

Federal policies affecting American work                 1986                    DOCUMENT
  Levitan, Sar A.                        Y 4.Ec 7/12:W 89                                       1
```

If a serial can be found in more than one location or format, a second "item" is created which provides that information.

```
    The Federal plan for meteorological serv...

    CALL NUMBER                   LOCATION    STATUS       MEDIA

    C 55.16/2: *1967/68-1984      DOCUMENT    AVAILABLE    PER
    C 55.16/2: *1985-             DOCUMENT    AVAILABLE    MICROFOR
```

The first item in the display is the one that will appear on the title screen. For U.S. government documents, the location appears as "DOCUMENT." When adding summary holdings to serials, the ones currently received were done first. We are now adding holdings to closed titles.

The Libraries subscribes to the Marcive GPO Tape Service which provides bibliographic records for the monographs cataloged by GPO and received on deposit. Serials are handled in-house to better ensure that the numerous title changes are accounted for and correct summary holdings attached. As Robert Alan recorded in a workshop conducted by Carol M. Foggin and Julia Gammon, "studies have indicated that government publications, serials published in the United States, and science and technology titles are the categories of serials that experience the highest rates of change."[3] Given the "high rate of change" for government document serials, the number of changes is taken into account before entering the serials into the OPAC. Generally, if there are more than three title changes, the latest entry only is used. The record is then adjusted in the local system by adding 247s (former title fields), changing the 362 field (dates), and adding appropriate corporate author fields. The "summary holdings" information for the entire run is thus attached to one record and makes it easier for patrons to locate serial records in the OPAC. Sharon Scott recorded in a workshop given by Bradley Carrington and Mary M. Case that in a user survey conducted at Northwestern University to determine user's ability to understand and interpret cataloging records, "user response demonstrated overwhelmingly that patrons understand latest entry better than successive entry records. Detailed holdings information is much easier to ascertain when held together by latest entry records."[4] And Jon R. Huffard proposed in his article on parts of bibliographic records most often used by reference staff, that "catalog and database use ought to play a part in the development of cataloging theory and practice . . ."[5]

Latest entry cataloging in our OPAC works well in part because the 247 and 246 fields are indexed by the system, in effect creating "see" references from earlier or alternate titles to later titles. Thus, if patrons have a citation that contains an earlier title, they will be directed to the latest title and can view the Libraries complete holdings for that serial run. In the full display, the 247 is listed as "former title." The 362 field is not displayed in the full display because patrons were confusing the Libraries' holdings with the official publication dates of the serial. Notes are added to the record as necessary to explain confusing details about numbering or title changes. A local (590) note is added with the code "MSU" which indicates that the record has been locally altered for patron convenience.

As yet, there is no official policy as to when a serial will be entered under latest versus successive entry cataloging, but several factors are considered. If the title has merged or split, if it has only changed title two or three times, or if the numbering has changed to the extent that latest entry records would be more confusing than successive, the serials are generally not considered candidates for latest entry cataloging. By not having a "strict" policy, catalogers are able to use their own judgment, or to respond to requests from Public Service staff, as to when to adopt latest entry cataloging. For those records which are cataloged under successive entry, the linking 780 and 785 fields appear in the full display preceded by "formerly:" and "continued by:." Although there exists a mixture of successive and latest entry cataloging records in the OPAC, patrons are better served when the best method for each serial is employed. As Jim Cole states in his article on the entry of serials, "we as catalogers cannot serve both the catalog user and the theoretician unless the theoretical principles espoused have true regard for the needs of the user."[6]

CONCLUSION

Mainstreaming government documents into the regular work processes not only provides "for the needs of the user," but also simplifies the flow of materials through the Departments. This simplification provides an added degree of efficiency and makes the materials available in a more timely manner. Full bibliographic records that accurately reflect call number, location, and format for all materials in the collection, including documents, means that patrons will easily locate needed materials. The question of "how" to mainstream documents into the local system can now be answered. Patrons can locate a variety of materials, even government documents, using one tool, the Libraries' OPAC.

NOTES

1. In addition to separate journal literature, there is a large body of monographic literature about the management and unique processing of federal documents. One of the best known of these is Rebekah M. Harleston and Carla J. Stoffle's *Administration of Government Documents Collections.* (Littleton, CO: Libraries Unlimited, 1974.) Such information was invaluable in assisting libraries during a time when documents truly did require unique handling.

2. MicroLinx is a Faxon supported PC-based serial check-in system. It has been used by The Libraries since 1988. Two stations have been implemented with two-thirds of the title records, A-L, on a 486 PC, and with one-third of the title records, M-Z, still on an older and much slower machine.

3. "Title Changes: A Practical and Theoretical View." Carol M. Foggin, Julia Gammon, workshop leaders; Robert Alan, recorder. *Serials Librarian* 19 (1991): 173-75.

4. "Latest Entry Cataloging as an Option." Bradley Carrington, Mary M. Case, workshop leaders; Sharon Scott, recorder. *Serials Librarian* 17 (1990): 155-57.

5. Jon R. Hufford, "Elements of the Bibliographic Record Used by Reference Staff Members at Three Academic Libraries." *College & Research Libraries* 52 (Jan. 1991): 54-64.

6. Jim E. Cole, "Final Thoughts on the Entry of Serials; or, Reaching a Logical Conclusion." *Serials Librarian* 20 (1991): 1-24.

Cataloging Challenges:
Providing Bibliographic Access to Florida's
Full-Text Electronic State Documents

Mae M. Clark
Michael D. Esman
Claudia V. Weston

SUMMARY. Researchers at the University of Florida Institute of Food and Agricultural Sciences have produced a series of CD-ROMs, entitled FAIRS (Florida Agricultural Information Retrieval System), containing many of the state document publications used by agricultural extension agents when assisting the public. FAIRS discs contain full-text information, decision making aids, a database, color graphics, and line drawings. Discs are issued sequentially with later discs superseding earlier ones. They were developed to resolve some of the difficulties of maintaining and controlling print publications faced by agricultural extension agents. This article discusses the development of the FAIRS CD-ROM product, cataloging issues raised by this use of full-text information on a disc, and two proposed electronic solutions to more easily catalog documents on this CD-ROM product. One of these solutions can be implemented currently, the other is still in the planning process.

Mae M. Clark is Associate University Librarian and Agricultural Documents Cataloger at the University of Florida. Michael D. Esman is Head, Special Materials Section, Cataloging Branch, National Agricultural Library. Claudia V. Weston is Library System Coordinator, National Agricultural Library.

[Haworth co-indexing entry note]: "Cataloging Challenges: Providing Bibliographic Access to Florida's Full-Text Electronic State Documents," Clark, Mae M., Michael D. Esman, and Claudia V. Weston. Co-published simultaneously in *Cataloging & Classification Quarterly* (The Haworth Press, Inc.) Vol. 18, No. 3/4, 1994, pp. 97-119; and: *Cataloging Government Publications Online* (ed: Carolyn C. Sherayko) The Haworth Press, Inc., 1994, pp. 97-119. Multiple copies of this article/chapter may be purchased from The Haworth Document Delivery Center [1-800-3-HAWORTH; 9:00 a.m. - 5:00 p.m. (EST)].

97

INTRODUCTION

The University of Florida Institute of Food and Agricultural Sciences (IFAS) publishes information on a broad range of topics related to agriculture, the second largest industry in the state. Although an exact count of the publications issued per year is not available, an estimate of their number would be several hundred. Because agricultural literature is so interdisciplinary in nature, articles published encompass the life sciences, social sciences (especially economics), physical sciences, and engineering. These state documents report on topics such as new crop varieties that have been developed for Florida, the economic impact that implementation of the NAFTA treaty (North American Free Trade Agreement) will have on Florida agriculture, and safe methods for disposing of hazardous chemicals in the home. Sea Grant publications are also issued by the University. These publications, many of which are only a few pages long, are distributed primarily to the agricultural extension agents in Florida's sixty-seven counties and to a limited number of libraries. They are also used to some extent by the University of Florida Libraries for exchange.

HISTORY OF AGRICULTURAL PRINT PUBLICATIONS IN FLORIDA

Although Florida is the fourth most populous state, there are still some rural counties where the extension agent is one of the primary sources for current agricultural information. In these areas there are no large public or university libraries where patrons can go for information. For the latest information about agriculture the agricultural extension agents and the public are thus dependent on these publications which are supplied through a central distribution point at the University.

While the agent receives documents from the University and avoids many of the problems that libraries have in acquiring state documents (Thomas 1988), other difficulties remain. With many publications being issued every year, some are more in demand than others. When an extension agent's supply of a print publication is exhausted, a request is sent to the University for additional copies. The order is filled quickly if the requested copy is in stock. However, it could be months before the needed copies are supplied if the publication is out of print. The opposite situation also presents difficulties for the extension agent. Publications that are less frequently needed accumulate and occupy valuable storage space. Without a well-defined method for arranging publications, extension agents often have had trouble locating the information they have needed quickly (Jones 1990).

DEVELOPMENT OF THE FAIRS CD-ROM

In an effort to solve some of the problems faced by the agricultural extension agents in maintaining, organizing and controlling publications, the CD-ROM Implementation Group was formed within the University of Florida's Institute of Food and Agricultural Sciences (IFAS). This ad-hoc group developed document formatting and tagging conventions, retrieval software, and a document tracking system. Additional support for the dissemination of agricultural publications in electronic format was provided by the Florida Legislature in the 1980's when they authorized the purchase of identical equipment (PC, modem, CD-ROM player and printer) for each of the agricultural extension offices. These developments ultimately led to the creation of the FAIRS (Florida Agricultural Information Retrieval System) series of CD-ROMs. Each FAIRS disc contains hundreds of publications, many of which will no longer be available in print. Within a few years it is expected that Florida state agricultural publications will be available only on CD-ROM.

Discs containing publications used most heavily by the county agricultural extension agents are in the FAIRS series and are the ones which will be discussed in this paper. Because the intended primary users were agricultural extension agents in Florida's counties, the CD-ROM was developed without advice from the University of Florida Libraries. It was not until Summer 1992, when five discs had been produced, that discussions were held between the developers and library personnel. At that time some of the library's concerns about the effect this format would have on exchange partners, the importance of archiving the information on the CD-ROMs, and an easily accessible author/title index to the articles on the discs were discussed. Since then, the developers and library personnel have been working together to address these concerns.

FLORIDA AGRICULTURAL INFORMATION RETRIEVAL SYSTEM (FAIRS)

Agricultural extension personnel are primarily concerned with the most current information. Therefore, the FAIRS CD-ROMs have been developed so that the latest disc in the series supersedes earlier ones. Each disc in the series contains new publications, revised versions of earlier publications, and unchanged publications issued on previous discs. Disc 4, which contains plant selection choices, is an exception to this replacement policy because it has not been superseded by a later disc.

In order to use the FAIRS CD-ROMs the following computer equipment is required: an IBM-compatible microcomputer (preferably an 80386 or 80486), a hard disk, a floppy disk drive, and a CD-ROM drive. A super VGA color video system (video card and monitor) is recommended so that the user can view color images of plants and pests on the discs. A laser printer is also desirable so that copies of documents on the discs can be printed on demand. A mouse is optional but recommended for easier access (Cilley 1992). For more detailed information about the FAIRS system, contact the IFAS Software Support Office at (904) 392-7853. The retrieval software for currently issued FAIRS CD-ROMs is a proprietary software package developed by the Institute for Food and Agricultural Sciences at the University of Florida. This software is contained on each disc. For the user, access to the articles and information stored on the CD-ROM is through a menu system (Figure 1). At present, there is no easily accessible author/title index for the full-text documents or key word search facility that searches the entire contents.

A variety of information is provided on the FAIRS discs. The *Extension Handbooks* contain most of the full-text documents on agricultural and extension topics. These electronic documents will be the focus of the discussion on cataloging issues in this article. Other full-text documents are found in the *Pest Control Guides* section of each disc. The *1992 Faculty Directory* for the Institute of

FIGURE 1

```
┌──────────────────────────────────────────────────────────────┐
│     HIDE              MOVE              CLOSE                 │
├──────────────────────────────────────────────────────────────┤
│                  │FAIRS CD–ROM MENU│                          │
│                                                              │
│  ┌───────────────────────┐                                   │
│  │Extension Handbooks    │                                   │
│  Pest Control Guides                                         │
│  Citrus Selector                                             │
│  Plans Service                                               │
│  Landscape/Plant Selector                                    │
│  1992 Faculty Directory                                      │
│  DOS Command Line                                            │
│  HELP!!(F1)                                                  │
│  Exit Program                                                │
│                                                              │
│                      About                                   │
│                                                              │
└──────────────────────────────────────────────────────────────┘
```

Simulated menu screen   FAIRS disc 6
Menu selected for viewing is outlined

Food and Agricultural Sciences is a database containing pertinent faculty information. The *Plans Service* includes graphics of agricultural building plans which can be viewed on the monitor or printed. Standard features such as "Help," "Exit" and "About," have also been incorporated on each disc.

Examples of decision making aids are the *Citrus Selector* and the *Landscape/Plant Selector.* These are not document databases but instead contain selection options that assist the user in plant selection. The *Citrus Selector,* for example, offers two choices: Cultivars, which presents information about a specific variety from an alphabetical listing; or Selector, which identifies cultivars meeting specific needs identified by the user. The Selector allows the user to choose specific characteristics such as citrus type, cold hardiness, or seediness. Possible characteristics appear for each of these choices such as grapefruit, lemon or tangelo; moderate, good or very good cold hardiness, and low or moderate seediness. After the possible characteristics for the list have been chosen, the software searches for citrus varieties matching the selected attributes. A list of the varieties meeting these qualities then appears and color graphics of the selection can be viewed.

There are two different methods of accessing information contained on the FAIRS disc. The first access method takes advantage of the FAIRS software and uses the menu illustrated in Figure 1. The second method provides access to the WordPerfect files through the DOS command line. The information displayed to the user is almost identical but there are differences in layout and text. Accessing the information through the FAIRS software enables the user to print entire articles and navigate via hypermedia links to related information such as tables, color graphics, and information about the authors. However, if the user wishes to manipulate the information in any way, then the WordPerfect files must be accessed and downloaded or printed. Because of the need to manipulate and print selected portions of the files, access for cataloging purposes was achieved via the DOS command line.

THE CATALOGING ENVIRONMENT

Presently at the University of Florida, one cataloger with support from a senior technician, is dedicated to the original cataloging of Florida state agricultural monographs. Typically, cataloging records are created for original monographic materials via the OCLC Cataloging Microenhancer Plus (CATME Plus). Records are uploaded to OCLC, downloaded to disk, and then uploaded into LUIS (Library User Information Service), the University of Florida's NOTIS-based integrated library system.

Within the last few years, an effort has been made to increase the number of Florida state agricultural publications receiving full level cataloging. This cataloging includes the assignment of Library of Congress subject headings (LCSH) and the creation of personal and corporate authority records that are submitted to NACO (National Coordinated Cataloging Operations). Additional AGRICOLA-specific information is assigned for those items found in-scope for the National Agricultural Cooperative Cataloging Program.

The National Agricultural Cooperative Cataloging Program is an OCLC-based network coordinated by the National Agricultural Library (NAL). Through this network, cooperating institutions submit unique citations to the AGRICOLA database, which with CAB

Abstracts and AGRIS, is one of the three major agricultural data-bases in the world. The University of Florida has been contributing records to AGRICOLA since 1991 (Collins 1992).

In addition to participating in the National Agricultural Cataloging Network, the University of Florida is an active participant in the NAL Land-Grant State Publication Program. The focus of this program is to systematically identify, collect, and provide access to state agricultural experiment station, cooperative extension service, and other state-produced agricultural publications.

It is within the framework of these two national programs that the University of Florida and the NAL began to discuss how to continue to provide bibliographic access to electronic documents stored on the FAIRS CD-ROM. Unless a method is found, this information will not be disseminated through existing bibliographic databases. This would result in the loss of University of Florida's faculty members' research to patrons that were not fortunate enough to be served by county agents in the Florida Cooperative Extension Service.

THE CATALOGING PROCESS

The Extension Handbooks section of the FAIRS CD-ROM contains over 200 documents produced by the Florida Cooperative Extension Service. If these publications had been received in print, full level original cataloging would have been performed. At both the University of Florida and the NAL, a cataloger spends on the average one hour creating a full level original cataloging record. This translates into an estimated 200 hours of cataloging staff time to process all the print documents.

The arrival of the print publications, however, would have been staggered. By coming at different times, it was easier to absorb the work into the routine processing flow. By receiving all the documents at once via CD-ROM, a hidden backlog was immediately created. As with any other type of backlog, this in turn reduced the availability of the documents to other staff and patrons. It quickly became apparent that some reorganization of current cataloging procedures was necessary to expedite the processing of the electronic documents.

Level of Cataloging

The level of cataloging performed on the individual documents stored within the CD-ROM was one of the first areas examined. It was decided that a minimal-level cataloging record with no subject headings, but at least one author entry would be created. With so many OPACs offering keyword search capability and the relatively explicit nature of titles on agricultural publications, a consensus was reached that the assignment of subject headings was a luxury which could not be afforded because of the time constraints. However, due to the repetitive appearance of authors, it was felt that performing authority control on the authors' names and submitting them to NACO would ultimately save time in processing and maintenance. The move from full level cataloging for the print to minimal level cataloging for the electronic was the first concession made to expedite the processing of the CD-ROM.

Constant Data Record

To save additional time, it was decided that a constant data record would be created. This record would contain default information which would be replicated from one bibliographic record to another (Figure 2). While creating this record, attempts were made to take into consideration the present cataloging environment as well as future developments. On many cataloging points, compromises were made between bibliographic accuracy and speed in order to automate various manual processes.

Unique Data

At the same time that the constant data record was being established, discussions were underway with the FAIRS programming staff. This staff was in the process of developing a tracking database which would indicate publication status for all document submissions. The objectives of these discussions were to identify unique document information necessary for the creation of a bibliographic record and eventually to develop procedures for electronically extracting this information and mapping it into appropriate areas of

FIGURE 2

```
Entered:     19930330      Replaced:     19330330
Type:      m        Bib lvl: b        Source:  d      Lang:    eng
File:      u        Enc lvl: K        Govt pub: s     Ctry:    flu
Audience:  f        Mod rec:          Frequn:  n      Reglr:
Desc:      a                          Dat tp:  s      Dates:   1992, ¶
▲ 1  070 0   NAL call number ¶
▲ 2  072 0   AGRICOLA subject category code ¶
▲ 3  090     U. of Florida call number ¶
▲ 4  049     AGLL ¶
▲ 5  245 00  Title ǂh computer file / [authorship statement]. ¶
▲ 6  250     Edition statement. ¶
▲ 7  300     on 1 computer laser optical disk ; ǂc 4 3/4 in. ¶
▲ 8  538     System requirements: IBM-PC or compatible; 640K RAM; DOS 3.3 or
higher; CD-ROM Extensions; CD-ROM drive; super VGA color video system; mouse
(optional); laser printer with 2.5MB (optional). ¶
▲ 9  500     Title from WordPerfect file. ¶
▲ 10 500     Responsibility dispersed among various authors, programmers
and others. ¶
▲ 11 500     Printed out version varies from the on-screen text. ¶
▲ 12 500     A unit found within the CD-ROM under the menu title: ¶
▲ 13 500     Directory/file name: ¶
▲ 14 500     Series/stock number: ¶
▲ 15 504     Includes bibliographical references. ¶
▲ 16 700 10  Personal author(s)the 245 fields ¶
▲ 17 773 0   ǂ7 nnas ǂt FAIRS. ǂd Gainesville, FL : Florida Cooperative
Extension Service, Institute of Food and Agricultural Sciences, University of
Florida, ǂe c1992. ǂw (OCoLC)1234567 ¶
```

Constant data record

the MARC constant data record. This activity remains in preliminary stages and until finalized, other methods were identified through which unique bibliographic data could be entered.

The two methods identified were: (1) manually keying the data and (2) copying/pasting the information. Using a split screen environment by activating two windows in a Windows session, the cataloger and/or cataloging paraprofessional would view both the electronic document and the constant data record. Depending on the length of the title, either method could be used for data entry. In the case of brief titles, direct keying appeared to be faster, but with a greater potential for error.

THE CATALOGING RECORD

As mentioned earlier in the paper, in order to manipulate data contained in the FAIRS CD-ROM, the WordPerfect files had to be the source of information accessed. The layout and content of these files differ from what is viewed by the user when accessing the information via the FAIRS software. The use of the WordPerfect files as the source of the cataloging record was a decision that in itself was a source of great discussion and a major compromise.

One of the first questions addressed was whether two versions of the same publication exist, or one version with a printout. While the printed out version is generated from internal sources within the CD-ROM, it is formatted to appear as a traditional paper document published by the Florida Cooperative Extension Service lacking, however, the color illustrations of separately issued print publications. If viewed as electronic desktop publishing, the printed out document could be treated as a unique version. The University of Florida and NAL will likely catalog only one version and note the availability of the second in a 500 note.

For the purpose of illustrating how an individual publication would be cataloged using bibliographic data from the WordPerfect file, one example from the FAIRS disc will be highlighted. Many of the cataloging decisions that were made for *Beneficial Insects* (Figures 3 and 4), are indicative of those that needed to be made for many of the other documents. On a field by field basis, peculiarities, special features, and/or special decisions concerning that field will

FIGURE 3

HIDE	MOVE	CLOSE

Beneficial Insects

The Beneficial Insect handbook was produced with the help of a grant from:

Energy Extension Service
Institute of Food and Agricultural Sciences
University of Florida

Credits

James Castner, Scientific Photographer
Department of Entomology and Nematology
(All photographs in this program and in the printed document
were taken by James Castner)

Don Short, Extension Entomologist
Department of Entomology and Nemotology

Sydney Park Brown, Extension Agent
Enviromental Horticulture
Hillsborough County Cooperative Extension Service

Geri Cashion, Extension Agent
Ornamental Production
Manatee County Cooperative Extension Service

Selecting "print" will print a document including these credits,
information on energy use and pesticides,
and definitions of predators and parasites

Print	WP−file

Simulated screen   FAIRS disc 6

be discussed. Comparisons also will be made between this record
(Figure 5) and a standard AACR2 record. Please note that a one to
one correlation between the screen display and the resulting bibliographic record was not and will not be achieved. In the areas where
differences exist, a brief overview of the decision making process

FIGURE 4

**Florida
Energy
Extension
Service**

Beneficial Insects[1]

Don E. Short and Jim Castner[2]

Wise pesticide management pays off in many ways:

* protects natural enemies and the environment.
* reduces pest resistance and keeps useful pesticides on the market.
* saves energy dollars associated with the production and use of pesticides

Few people realize the energy inputs and environmental impacts resulting from the production, formulation, packaging and transportation of pesticides. For example: For every

PREDATOR - DEFINITION

A predator is an insect, mite or spider that attacks and feeds on its prey, which is usually smaller. The prey is usually killed and eaten and many individuals are consumed by each predator.

PARASITE - DEFINITION

A parasite is an organism that lives in or on the body of its host, at least during part of its life cycle, or a relatively long time. It consumes all or most of the host's tissues and eventually kills it.

acre of lawn or commercial turf sprayed with 25% Diazinon or 80% SEVIN (respectively), the energy used is equal to about 5 gallons of gasoline. The environmental consequences of this energy consumption include about 100 pounds of CO_2 (global warming) and 0.6 pounds of sulfur dioxide (acid rain).

Even more energy is consumed when pesticides are applied. However, when IPM approaches like scouting and spot treatment replace routine, blanket sprays, smaller spray (check this) and transportation equipment can be used. Therefore, less pesticide use and lower operational costs are possible.

"Spray smart. It's easy on energy and the environment."

CREDITS

Energy Extension Service
IFAS / University of Florida

James Castner, *Scientific Photographer*
Department of Entomology and Nematology

Don Short, *Extension Entomologist*
Department of Entomology and Nematology

Sydney Park Brown, *Extension Agent,*
Environmental Horticulture
Hillsborough County Extension Service

Geri Cashion, *Extension Agent,*
Ornamental Production
Manatee County Extension Service

1. This document was published 8/92 as part of the Beneficial Insects Handbook, Florida Cooperative Extension Service. For more information, contact your county Cooperative Extension Service office.

2. Professor and Scientific Photographer, Department of Entomology and Nematology, Institute of Food and Agricultural Sciences, University of Florida, Gainesville.

The Florida Energy Extension Service receives funding from the Florida Energy Office, Department of Community Affairs and is operated by the University of Florida's Institute of Food and Agricultural Sciences through the Cooperative Extension Service. The information contained herein is the product of the Florida Energy Extension Service and does not necessarily reflect the views of the Florida Energy Office.

FIGURE 5

```
Entered:    19930128      Replaced:    19930728
Type:    m       Bib lvl: b        Source:  d       Lang:    eng
File:    u       Enc lvl: K        Govt pub: s      Ctry:    flu
Audience:        Mod rec:          Frequn:  n       Regulr:
Desc:    a                         Dat tp:  s       Dates:   1992,  ¶

▲  1  070  0    S49.F34 ǂb DISC 6 ¶
▲  2  070       ǂb ■ ¶
▲  3  072  0    F700 ǂa L001 ¶
▲  4  090       S49 ǂb .F34 DISC 6 ¶
▲  5  049       FLGE ¶
▲  6  245  00   Beneficial insects ǂh computer file / ǂc Don E. Short and
Jim Castner. ¶
▲  7  300       on 1 computer laser optical disk ; ǂc 4 3/4 in. ¶
▲  8  538       System requirements: IBM-PC or compatible; 640K RAM; DOS 3.3
higher; CD-ROM Extensions; CD-ROM drive; super VGA color video system; mouse
(optional); laser printer with 2.5 MB (optional). ¶
▲  9  500       Title from WordPerfect file. ¶
▲ 10  500       Responsibility dispersed among various authors, programmers
and others. ¶
▲ 11  500       Printed out version varies from on-screen text. ¶
▲ 12  500       A unit found within the CD-ROM under the menu title:
Extension handbooks. ¶
▲ 13  500       Directory/file name: L:\handbook\bi ¶
▲ 14  504       Includes bibliographic references.¶
▲ 15  700  10   Short, Donald E. ¶
▲ 16  700  10   Castner, James L. ¶
▲ 17  773  0    ǂ7 nnas ǂt FAIRS. ǂd Gainesville, FL ; Florida Cooperative
Extension Service, Institute of Food and Agricultural Sciences,
University of Florida, c1992. ǂw (OCoLC)12345678 ¶
▲ 17  753       IBM-PC. ¶
```

Completed cataloging record

will be outlined. Fields that were not used for the *Beneficial Insects* record, but which may apply to other records on the FAIRS disc, are indicated by angle brackets < >.

Fixed Fields

Fixed field information has been incorporated into the constant data record and does not vary from one CD-ROM analytic record to another. This information for the fixed fields was based on defaults made within the body of the record. One assumption was made, however, and this was that each document would be English language.

Call Numbers

090 Locally assigned LC call number
070 National Agricultural Library call number

A general call number, either LC or an NAL-one based on the LC classification scheme, has been assigned to the serial title. The University of Florida will assign LC call numbers to the 090 and will input NAL's call number, an AGRICOLA specific field, in the 070. Each analytical title will receive the base call number plus the disc number reflecting the first time that particular article appeared on a disc. If the title is reissued without changes, it will not be recataloged, and no note will be added to the existing cataloging record indicating that a title appears on a later disc. When a revised edition of an article is issued on a later disc, it will be cataloged at that time and a new call number assigned.

1XX/245 Main Entry

Deciding on the main entry was difficult because for years similar print publications have been treated as monographs with author main entries usually being assigned. In the case of the FAIRS CD-ROM publications, most documents will be entered under title. This is necessary because responsibility for the intellectual and artistic content, as well as programming features, is dispersed. The elaborate color illustrations in many of the documents and the complex programming required to display these articles clearly indicates the collaborative effort of a number of individuals.

245 00 Beneficial insects #h computer file / #c by Don E. Short and Jim Castner

The title proper appears exactly as it is presented on both the screen and WordPerfect versions. Although not present for this particular title, it was noted that subtitle information for other documents would need reformatting to conform with standard AACR2 practice. In some instances, punctuation, capitalization, and layout would need to be modified.

Bibliographic data in the statement of responsibility based on the WordPerfect file may vary significantly from the information presented on the title screen. See Figures 3 and 5. Seeing the statement of responsibility transcribed in this manner might indicate that the main entry should be under author. In the printed out version of the WordPerfect file, the individuals primarily responsible for this document, Don Short and James Castner, are clearly credited below the title as being the chief authors.

Looking at the screen version of the document, however, one sees a lengthy list of credits that does not indicate the role the individuals played in the creation of the publication. It notes only the professional titles of the contributors. The statement of responsibility for the screen version would have been transcribed as follows: / #c [photographer] James Castner ; [authors] Don Short, Sydney Park Brown, Geri Cashion with the assumption being that Don Short et al. are authors.

<250 No edition statement on this cataloging record>

Although this cataloging record does not contain an edition statement, one of the issues that has been under discussion between IFAS and library staff is how to indicate that an article on one of the later FAIRS discs is a reissue or revision of a document on a previous disc. On some CD-ROM articles, reprint and edition statements are hidden in hypertext attached to the title, and may not be found by a cataloger. This information needs to be made clearly available so that unnecessary recataloging of previously issued articles is avoided. If the information remains hidden in an article, cataloging staff would expend considerable effort determining which titles are new publications, which are revisions, and which are simply reissued publications.

<260 Imprint statement not used on "In" analytic records>

A fundamental difference between the cataloging of print and electronic texts on a CD-ROM is the treatment of the imprint information. Because documents on CD-ROMs are treated as "in" analytics, imprint information is given only in the 773 field for the serial title. No information is provided in the 260 field.

300: 1 computer laser optical disk ; #c 4 3/4 in.

Collation information is one of the few straightforward descriptive elements within this cataloging record. There are two possible ways to describe the CD-ROM. AACR2 states the form should be "on 1 computer laser optical disk" (AACR2 1988). Nancy Olson recommends that "on 1 computer disk" be used (Olson 1992), because the only computer disc manufactured in 4 3/4 in. dimensions, is in a laser optical format.

In addition to the extent and dimensions, another element of the 300 field that can be noted is whether the displays are in one or more colors. Within this CD-ROM some documents appear in multiple colors and others in only one color. In order to maintain this field on the constant data record, this element has been excluded.

538 System requirements: IBM-PC or compatible; 640K RAM; DOS 3.3 or higher; CD-ROM Extensions; CD-ROM drive; Super VGA color video system; mouse (optional); laser printer with 2.5 MB (optional)

The "System Requirements" field on an I-level cataloging record should be a required field on all records. On a K-level analytic, many catalogers might decide optionally not to include it. This point was debated among the authors. The argument against including this nonessential information on each record, is that the parent serial record contains this information, and staff and users should refer to the main record. The reason for including this data on each record is that if this information is already supplied on a constant data record and does not need to be manually typed on each new cataloging record, there is little reason for not automatically including this field as a service to the user. It is also unreasonable to assume that patrons, as well as library staff, will know to check the parent record for "system requirements" information.

500 Title from the WordPerfect file.

AACR2 rule 9.1 requires that the source of the title used on the cataloging record be identified. The title and statement of responsibility information used in creating the bibliographic record originated from the WordPerfect file. Even though the title, in most cases, will be identical on the screen version, the true source of the title proper should be identified. Hopefully, programming adjustments can be made in the future by the CD-ROM developers so the information displayed on the screen and WordPerfect file is the same.

500 Responsibility dispersed among various authors, programmers and others.

The statement of responsibility in the 245 field is transcribed as it appears in the WordPerfect file. In many instances this results in individuals who should be noted for their contributions being overlooked. A 500 note is included on the constant data cataloging record to indicate to the user that several people assisted in the creation of the electronic document although their names have not been explicitly stated on the cataloging record.

500 Printed out version differs from the screen version.

This is a standard note that alerts the patron to the existence of the printed-out version. Besides discrepancies in the organization of the print and screen texts, there will be illustrations that appear in the electronic versions but not on the paper printouts. This is in addition to the already mentioned differences in the statement of responsibility.

500 A unit found within the CD-ROM under the menu title: Extension handbooks.

One of the primary concerns of public services staff is the ability to find a particular document on a CD-ROM. Because FAIRS CD-ROMs have only a very general menu structure within the FAIRS software, it is important to indicate to both patrons and library staff under which menu item this document can be retrieved. By including this information on the cataloging record, document retrieval can be expedited.

504 Includes bibliographical references.

Many of the publications in FAIRS have accompanying bibliographical references. This note has been incorporated on the constant data record but can easily be deleted if not needed.

<520 Summary>

Summary notes generally apply to an entire software package, not to its analytical contents. For that reason, creating a summary for this type of record is not necessary. The cost of including summaries would be prohibitive unless supplied by the document itself. If the summaries were provided with or as a part of the document, however, it would be fairly straightforward to add them to the bibliographic record.

500 Series/stock no.

Historically, the series title/stock number problem has posed a dilemma for the cataloger. In her 1985 article "Fugitive U.S. Government Publications" Nora S. Copeland states, "Series statements were not consistently presented. Additionally, many items contained combinations of letters and numbers that were assigned by the publisher for internal control purposes but were not "true" series. However, unlike similar numbers assigned to commercial publications, these alphanumeric combinations often are important access points for government documents" (Copeland et al. 1985). This has also been the case for land-grant agricultural publications where, for example, "HO-2111" is the two thousand one hundred eleventh publication issued by an institution and the subject matter is horticulture.

This situation is further compounded on the FAIRS disc when the series/stock number does not appear on the screen version but does appear on the WordPerfect version, or vice versa. A print only index (Figure 6) is available in a WordPerfect file and it provides a listing of series/stock numbers and associated authors and titles. This index cannot be used for automated access to the individual documents. Due to the limited utility and irregular and inconsistent display of the pseudoseries on the CD-ROM, a decision was made to place this information in the note area. This decision was strengthened by the current trend of separately issued University of Florida agricultural print publications to be assigned stock numbers. According to the IFAS Editorial Office, many of the series titles are being eliminated.

500 File/Directory name: L: handbook\bi

At this time there is no MARC tag specifically designated for identifying file names associated with a particular title. The 856 field identifies file names in remote databases but there is no similar MARC tag for CD-ROMs and other computer files. This field would be particularly helpful to document delivery staff who need to rapidly locate and copy a specific file for downloading or printing.

700 10 Personal name tracing: Short, Donald E., Castner, James L.

Individuals primarily responsible for the overall content of a publication whether print or electronic should be traced as added entries. In the case of *Beneficial Insects,* Don Short and James Castner were cited on the WordPerfect version as chiefly responsi-

FIGURE 6

```
┌──────────────────────────────────────────────────────────────┐
│ 1. 1992 FLORIDA CITRUS SPRAY GUIDE (\handbood\cg)  (TIM APPELBOOM) │
│                                                                │
│ CG015  AGR-17   -Submersed Aquatic Weeds  Judy Rogers  Vandiver, Jr., V.V. │
│ CG016  AGR-18   -Emergent Aquatic Weeds   Judy Rogers  Vandiver, Jr., V.V. │
│ CG001  ENY-600  -Pesticide Regulations    Judy Rogers  Knapp, J.L. │
│ CD017  ENY-601  -Registered Pesticides    Judy Rogers  Knapp, J.L. │
│ CD003  ENY-602  -Spider Mites             Judy Rogers  Bullock, R.C. et al. │
└──────────────────────────────────────────────────────────────┘
```

PRINT ONLY INDEX

ble for the creation of the publication and included in the statement of responsibility. The added entries for Short and Castner have been created in accordance with AACR2 and submitted to NACO.

The number of entries traced on K-level records is determined by each library's guidelines and depends on the item being cataloged. For instance, in most situations at the University of Florida and the National Agricultural Library, only one 7XX heading is traced on a K-level record. However, for documents within FAIRS, if more than one person has been included in the statement of responsibility, cataloging staff will create an added entry for each one identified.

773 0 #7 nnas #t FAIRS. #d Gainesville, FL : Florida Cooperative Extension Service, Institute of Food and Agricultural Sciences, University of Florida, c1992 #w (OCoLC)12345678

The 773 tag is coded for "In Analytics." Publication information for the entire CD-ROM is presented in this field. Access to the OCLC number for the parent record is available in the subfield "w". Use of the 773 field instead of the 260 for electronic publications creates a situation where a simultaneously published monograph may have a different imprint statement in the 260 field than does the electronic version in the 773 field.

753 Technical Details Access: IBM-PC

IBM-PC will be a constant data element on each analytical record.

CONCLUSION

In this paper, we have touched upon some of the compromises, techniques, and decisions made by the University of Florida and NAL to provide access to full-text documents stored within the FAIRS CD-ROM. The creation of bibliographic records for only one version of the document, minimum-level cataloging without the assignment of subject headings but with the creation of NACO headings for the authors, and the use of constant data records were some of the key decisions made to expedite the processing of these items. The techniques that were explored for entering unique data included keying, copying and pasting, and in the near future mapping from either a tracking database or the actual documents. Throughout the cataloging process, compromises were made in the application of cataloging procedures and guidelines. Those compromises, techniques, and decisions which were discussed in this paper are only the tip of the iceberg in the issues surrounding providing access to electronic documents. Many more remain. Throughout the library, equipment, staff capabilities, training, and policies and procedures need to be evaluated to determine how electronic documents fit within the existing framework of document selection, collection, control, access, and dissemination and what needs to be changed. Fiscal constraints, human resources, user capabilities, and automation trends will and should also play a role in this decision making process.

REFERENCES

Anglo-American Cataloguing Rules. 2nd ed. 1988 revision. Chicago: American Library Association, p. 232.

Cilley, Mary L. et al. 1992. *FAIRS CD-ROM User's Manual: Disc 6.* Gainesville, Fla.: University of Florida, p. 1-2.

Collins, Donna S. 1992. National Agricultural Cooperative Cataloging Program. *Agricultural Libraries Information Notes* 18(1/2):1-3.

Copeland, Nora S., Fred C. Schmidt, and James Stickman. 1985. Fugitive U.S. government publications: elements of procurement and bibliographic control. *Government Publications Review* 12:227-237.

Jones, Pierce. 1990. Producing a CD-ROM: preparation of extension publications. *CD-ROM EndUser* 2(3):14-16.

Olson, Nancy. 1992. *Cataloging computer files.* Lake Crystal, Minn.: Soldier Creek Press, p. 9.

Thomas, Sarah E. 1988. A coordinated program for state agricultural publications. *College & Research Libraries News* 49:425-430.

F.B.I.
(Fugitive Bibliographic Information)

Kathleen Keating

SUMMARY. Technology has made government information more accessible to the public through loading of the Government Printing Office's GPO *Monthly Catalog* MARC records onto local online catalogs. This study examines and identifies documents received against the matching bibliographic records on the GPO *Monthly Catalog* tapes. Also compared are the GPO cataloging priorities and the priorities of a high use/high demand government publications reference department in a large academic library.

INTRODUCTION AND BACKGROUND

In mid-1976 the U.S. Government Printing Office (GPO) began producing MARC cataloging records through the bibliographic utility, OCLC. This development made bibliographic access to government information more available to the public as tapes of these records were loaded onto local online public access catalogs (OPACs). Private vendors such as Brodart, Inc. and Marcive, Inc. were early providers of subscription services tailored to item number selection profiles enabling libraries to match records with their collections. As a Regional depository the University of New Mexi-

Kathleen Keating, Assistant Professor of Librarianship, Government Information Department, University of New Mexico General Library, Albuquerque, NM 87131

[Haworth co-indexing entry note]: "F.B.I. (Fugitive Bibliographic Information)," Keating, Kathleen. Co-published simultaneously in *Cataloging & Classification Quarterly* (The Haworth Press, Inc.) Vol. 18, No. 3/4, 1994, pp. 121-130; and: *Cataloging Government Publications Online* (ed: Carolyn C. Sherayko) The Haworth Press, Inc., 1994, pp. 121-130. Multiple copies of this article/chapter may be purchased from The Haworth Document Delivery Center [1-800-3-HAWORTH; 9:00 a.m. - 5:00 p.m. (EST)].

121

co (UNM) receives and retains all publications available through the depository system. Therefore, UNM decided to load all of the GPO tapes on the overall assumption that all depository documents received had been cataloged and would have a MARC record available on the tapes.

In March 1988 GPO's Library Programs Service adopted a set of cataloging priorities for incoming materials. This "priority system for the cataloging operation within the Library Programs Service is being implemented to effectively manage the Cataloging and Indexing Program for federal documents."[1] The cataloging priorities implemented are: "(1) congressional documents; (2) documents mentioned in the news media; (3) documents sold by GPO; (4) presidential documents; (5) legislative branch documents, except technical reports; (6) executive and judicial branch reports, serials, maps, and audiovisuals, except technical reports; (7) technical reports; and (8) documents not distributed to depository libraries."[2]

In 1983 Margaret T. Mooney began conducting a study of GPO cataloging activity in an effort to identify the time lag between receipt of a document by a depository and the appearance of its bibliographic record in the *Monthly Catalog of United States Government Publications.* One of her categories contained titles not listed in the *Monthly Catalog* twenty-four months after depository distribution. She found that thirty-seven out of 1800 titles or 2.1% had not received a bibliographic record in the *Monthly Catalog* after two years.[3]

QUESTIONS AND ASSUMPTIONS

Many more libraries have now loaded GPO cataloging records since Ms. Mooney's study identified this potential problem, leading practitioners to ask several questions. Has the pattern of non-cataloged records changed in the years since the GPO cataloging priorities were established in 1988? Is the percentage of non-cataloged items as found by Mooney characteristic of the entire database from 1976 to date? Are there any historical patterns which could identify the problem areas? Can specific government issuing agencies or Superintendent of Documents (SuDoc) call number ranges be identified as lacking in bibliographic control? Are cataloging records available for the non-cataloged items from other sources, such as member contributions in OCLC?

In order to try to answer these questions the present study made three assumptions: (1) that as a Regional depository library, the University of New Mexico Library receives all documents distributed by GPO through the depository system, (2) that there is a matching MARC record on the vendor supplied tapes for each document received from 1976 to the present, and (3) that the current priorities for GPO cataloging will match those of a high use and high demand university reference collection. The goals of the project described below were to identify depository documents for which no bibliographic records were received on tape and to set the holdings location for the University of New Mexico General Library's Government Publications Department (UNM GPD) reference collection.

REFERENCE COLLECTION DESCRIPTION

The University of New Mexico General Library's Government Publications Department (UNM GPD) reference collection includes 4309 depository titles published from 1976 to the present. Reference documents are selected for their high use and include those documents considered timely and current. For high use titles, the reference copy is designated for "in library use only" and a second, circulating copy is added to the general documents collection. For many serial titles, UNM GPD places the most recent edition in the reference collection, with older editions housed in the stacks.

DATABASE DESCRIPTION

The University of New Mexico General Library's online catalog, called LIBROS, runs on Innovative Interfaces, Inc. software. The following vendor supplied GPO *Monthly Catalog* tapes have been loaded:

     1976 to 1980   (Marcive, Inc.)
     1981 to 1986   (Brodart, Inc.)
     1987 to date   (Marcive, Inc.)

The retrospective and currently monthly GPO tapes are loaded onto LIBROS and the records interfiled with those of the UNM General Library's Library of Congress classified collection. At this time, GPO records make up one-third of the LIBROS database and number 271,453 records dating from 1976 to February 1993.

The majority of the documents collection is located and serviced in Zimmerman Library with some scientific and technical publications housed in the Centennial Science and Engineering Library (CSEL). Specification of holdings locations for individual SuDoc classifications is done through the profiling process with Marcive so that records display proper holdings locations for Zimmerman and CSEL. However, holdings locations for documents placed in reference must be added manually at the time documents are selected for addition to the reference collection.

DATA COLLECTION AND METHODOLOGY

This study evaluates and compares the bibliographic records distributed on the GPO cataloging tapes from July 1976 to February 1993 with the UNM GPD's reference collection. Its purpose is to identify any patterns of publications which do not have bibliographic records on the Monthly Catalog tapes.

Selection of Sample Titles

The UNM GPD's reference collection was examined by matching the 4309 U.S. depository titles against the LIBROS database. In selecting titles for the study, each document had to be marked with a Regional depository identification stamp, thereby excluding non-depository materials. Both serials and monographs were included if they met this basic test. The study did not include titles received before July 1976 or documents issued in microfiche format.

Data Sheets

Each title selected matching the above criteria was entered on data collection sheets by SuDoc call number and title. Both elements were searched in LIBROS to assure identification of a correctly matching bibliographic record. In addition, the following information was recorded for the titles: (1) a matching SuDoc number and title had a bibliographic record on LIBROS, or (2) no matching record was found on LIBROS; (3) the fixed field identified the document as a monograph, or (4) the fixed field identified the document as a serial; (5) the holdings location in LIBROS properly reflected the reference location. For those documents not found on LIBROS, either by title or SuDoc call number, a further search was conducted on OCLC to identify a matching bibliographic record.

FINDINGS

Of the 4309 depository titles searched, bibliographic records were found for 4256 titles (98.8%). Fifty-three (1.2%) did not have records in the *Monthly Catalog* database on LIBROS. This is half that found by Mooney (2.1%) that had no records on the tapes. Nineteen of the thirty-eight U.S. government agencies represented by publications in the UNM GPD's reference collection had bibliographic records for all the items searched (i.e., 100% coverage) (Table 1). Publications of the other nineteen agencies represented in the reference collection did not have records for all the titles. A few agencies identified with high percentages of non-cataloged titles were the Labor Department (15.1%), the Treasury Department (10.6%), the Transportation Department (10%), and the Defense Department (6.8%).

When the fifty-three titles with no records on LIBROS were searched on OCLC, thirty-four were found (Table 2). Twenty-eight were monographs and six were serial titles. Six had been cataloged by GPO, five had been cataloged by the Library of Congress, two had been cataloged by the General Accounting Office, and the remaining twenty-one records had been cataloged by OCLC member libraries other than GPO, leaving nineteen titles still unaccounted for at the time of this search. Table 2 also identifies the documents by agency. When compared to GPO's cataloging priorities adopted in 1988, the table identifies that even the highest priority documents, being congressional, are unaccessible because no bibliographic record exists. One also wonders, especially, why the

TABLE 1. Description of Reference Collection

Agency	SuDoc class number	Number of titles	% on LIBROS	% on Mono-graph	% Serials	% No Bib record
All titles		4309	98.8	92.0	8.0	1.2
Agriculture	A	40	97.5	75.0	25.0	2.5
Arms Control	AC	3	100.0	100.0	0.0	0.0
National Archives	AE	43	97.6	72.0	28.0	2.4
Commerce Department	C	3511	99.5	98.6	1.4	0.5
Federal Communications Commission	CC	8	100.0	12.5	87.5	0.0
Civil Rights Commission	CR	1	100.0	100.0	0.0	0.0
Defense Department	D	44	93.2	59.0	41.0	6.8
Energy Department	E	43	97.7	42.0	58.0	2.3
Education Department	ED	58	98.3	51.7	48.3	1.7
Environmental Protection Agency	EP	14	100.0	92.8	7.2	0.0
Federal Insurance Administration	FEM	4	100.0	100.0	0.0	0.0
Federal Reserve System	FR	4	100.0	25.0	75.0	0.0
General Accounting Office	GA	6	100.0	66.7	33.3	0.0
Government Printing Office	GP	16	100.0	43.7	56.3	0.0
General Services Administration	GS	42	97.6	85.7	14.3	2.4
Health and Human Services	HE	73	98.6	52.0	48.0	1.4
Interior Department	I	51	98.0	82.4	17.6	2.0
U.S. Information Agency	IA	2	50.0	100.0	0.0	50.0
International Trade Commission	ITC	1	100.0	0.0	100.0	0.0
Justice Department	J	26	96.0	61.5	38.5	4.0
Judiciary	JU	7	100.0	28.6	71.4	0.0
Labor Department	L	53	84.9	56.6	43.4	15.1
Library of Congress	LC	17	100.0	53.0	47.0	0.0
National Aeronautics and Space Administration	NAS	2	100.0	100.0	0.0	0.0
National Science Foundation	NS	6	100.0	50.0	50.0	0.0
Personnel Management Office	PM	15	100.0	53.3	46.7	0.0
President of the United States	PR	14	100.0	100.0	0.0	0.0
Executive Office of the President	PrEx	23	87.0	45.0	55.0	13.0
State Department	S	24	92.0	37.5	62.5	8.0
Small Business Administration	SBA	16	100.0	81.2	18.8	0.0
Securities and Exchange Commission	SE	1	100.0	0.0	100.0	0.0
Smithsonian Institution	SI	8	100.0	100.0	0.0	0.0
Treasury Department	T	19	89.4	68.4	31.6	10.6
Transportation Department	TD	10	90.0	20.0	80.0	10.0
Veterans Affairs Department	VA	5	100.0	20.0	80.0	0.0
Congress Reports/Documents	Y1.	40	97.5	85.0	15.0	2.5
Commissions, Committees and Boards	Y3.	29	86.2	76.0	24.0	13.8
Congress Hearings/Prints	Y4.	30	97.0	70.0	30.0	3.0

TABLE 2. Bibliographic Titles Not Found on LIBROS but Searched on OCLC

SuDoc	Titles	On OCLC	Not on OCLC
A	1		1
AE	1		1
C	19	14	5
D	3	2	1
E	1	1	
ED	1		1
GS	1	1	
HE	1		1
I	1		1
IA	1	1	
J	1		1
L	8	7	1
PrEx	3	3	
S	2	1	1
T	2		2
TD	1	1	
Y1.	1		1
Y3.	4	2	2
Y4.	1	1	
TOTAL	**53**	**34**	**19**

six records cataloged by GPO were not included on the tapes. Could GPO develop a mechanism to capture depository bibliographic records contributed by other governmental agencies or member libraries for inclusion in the *Monthly Catalog* tapes? As for the nineteen remaining records, what will be the likely time lag before some library catalogs these high use/high demand documents?

The nineteen non-cataloged titles included eight monographs and eight serials. The Commerce Department had five uncataloged titles and Congressional publications three. There were no distinct patterns found for the year of publication. Two titles were published in 1991 and 1992 while the other seventeen were distributed between 1984 and 1989. For these nineteen non-cataloged titles, the

University of New Mexico plans to catalog the titles and make them accessible on OCLC. The nature of these titles categorizes them as high priority documents. None of the titles were technical reports or non-depository items.

CONCLUSIONS

If the present rate of 1.2% of all depository reference documents received having no bibliographic records on the *Monthly Catalog* tapes, extends to the non-reference items and regional libraries continue to receive approximately 20,000 monographic and serial titles per year, then within ten years 2,400 documents will not be accessible to the public because of fugitive bibliographic records. (Comparison with Mooney's findings tend to support this assertion. See Table 3.)

The assumptions made at the beginning of this study have been found to be false. There is not a matching MARC record for each document received from 1976 to the present and the current GPO

TABLE 3. Comparison of Mooney's Agencies with No Record After 24 Months and UNM's Reference Collection of Agencies with No Bibliographic Record

	SuDoc class number	Number of titles	Mooney's Titles Not Listed 24 Months After Receipt		Number of titles	UNM's Titles Not Listed on LIBROS	
			Number	%		Number	%
All titles		1800	37	2.1	4309	53	1.2
Agriculture Department	A	305	7	2.3	40	1	2.3
Commerce Department	C	170	1	0.6	3511	19	0.5
Defense Department	D	162	1	0.6	44	3	6.8
Health and Human Services Department	HE	130	2	1.5	73	1	1.4
Executive Office of the President	PrEx	26	6	23.0	23	3	13.0
Congress Hearings/Prints	Y4.	151	2	1.3	30	1	3.0
Energy Department	E	165	17	10.3	43	1	2.3

cataloging priorities do not match that of a high use high demand university reference collection.

THE FUTURE

The Government Printing Office continues to try to improve its policies on bibliographic access. In order to increase the effectiveness of its cataloging, GPO adopted a policy outlining abridged cataloging in August 1992. This policy states, "Abridged cataloging will be employed by GPO to catalog the following regardless of class: (1) Technical reports, (2) Dept. of Defense technical manuals and bulletins, (3) EPA summaries, (4) ERIC documents, (5) Fatalgram[s], (6) Flood insurance studies, (7) Juvenile activity and coloring books, (8) Publications consisting of only one sheet 8.5 × 11 or 8.5 × 14 or smaller, (9) Open file reports/U.S. Geological Survey open-file reports, (10) Items selected by less than 100 depository libraries, and (11) Publications which are NOT distributed to depository libraries."[4] This policy to use abridged cataloging is intended to: "(1) Provide a measure of bibliographic control for publications which would otherwise not be cataloged, (2) Increase the number of publications which are cataloged by GPO, and (3) Improve the timeliness of cataloging for the items cataloged."[5]

Thomas A. Downing, Chief, Cataloging Branch of the GPO Library Program Service recently stated the objectives and initial initiatives of the Cataloging Branch during the Spring 1993 Federal Depository Conference. Two objectives mentioned were "to publish some form of acceptable bibliographic record to represent each title that has been received within the Branch during the preceding month [and a] long-term objective to eliminate approximately 20,000 titles that are in the backlog."[6]

The cataloging initiatives include:

1. To create a work environment that emphasizes production and recognizes catalogers for their initiative, hard work, and ability to balance their cataloging decisions with production requirements.
2. Determine the materials that absolutely must be cataloged at full level.

3. Expand the categories of materials to be cataloged at less than full level.
4. Determine how information can be shared more efficiently within LPS.
5. Determine how relevant records from outside sources can be migrated to the *Monthly Catalog* via electronic transfer.
6. Publish editions of *Monthly Catalog* that contain significant numbers of records with data that are not equivalent to data within OCLC.[7]

These initiatives are preliminary. This study and Mooney's reinforce the need to take action to reduce the number of records for document titles that are late or never created to ensure access to the government information received by depository libraries. Libraries subscribing to the *Monthly Catalog* tapes must not rely on this database as the only source. Other alternatives such as searching OCLC and other national and governmental databases will be necessary until the above GPO cataloging initiatives can be implemented to eliminate fugitive bibliographic information.

NOTES

1. *GPO Cataloging Guidelines* (Washington, D.C. : U.S. Government Printing Office, 1988) p. 1.

2. Ibid.

3. Margaret T. Mooney, "GPO Cataloging: Is It a Viable Current Access Tool for U.S. Documents?" *Government Publications Review* 16 (1989): 259-270.

4. *GPO Cataloging Guidelines* (Washington, D.C.: U.S. Government Printing Office, 1992) p. 2.

5. Ibid.

6. Thomas A. Downing, "Remarks," *Administrative Notes* 14 (May 15, 1993): 20.

7. Ibid. p. 20-21.

Life After the "Earthquake": The Myths and Realities of Cataloging U.S. Government Depository CD-ROM Documents

Lynne M. Martin
Catherine M. Dwyer

SUMMARY. This study identifies issues and problems associated with the cataloging of depository CD-ROM titles. MARC cataloging records in both the RLIN and OCLC databases for depository CD-ROM document titles, distributed to depository libraries from July 1989 to December 1991, were analyzed to determine specific problems, problem areas, and issues including: selection of MARC formats, title entries, presence or absence of SuDoc numbers, use of technical notes fields, etc. This study, while specific to the cataloging of depository CD-ROM document titles, suggests a broader application to the cataloging of non-depository CD-ROM titles.

The depository CD-ROM document "earthquake" rocked the United States depository library world in July 1989 when the Gov-

---

Lynne M. Martin is Cataloger, College of Agriculture and Technology, State University of New York–Cobleskill, Cobleskill, NY 12043. Catherine M. Dwyer is Government Documents Librarian/Senior Assistant Librarian, University Libraries (ULB35A), State University of New York–Albany, 1400 Washington Avenue, Albany, NY 12222.

[Haworth co-indexing entry note]: "Life After the "Earthquake": The Myths and Realities of Cataloging U.S. Government Depository CD-ROM Documents," Martin, Lynne M., and Catherine M. Dwyer. Co-published simultaneously in *Cataloging & Classification Quarterly* (The Haworth Press, Inc.) Vol. 18, No. 3/4, 1994, pp. 131-153; and: *Cataloging Government Publications Online* (ed: Carolyn C. Sherayko) The Haworth Press, Inc., 1994, pp. 131-153. Multiple copies of this article/chapter may be purchased from The Haworth Document Delivery Center [1-800-3-HAWORTH; 9:00 a.m. - 5:00 p.m. (EST)].

emment Printing Office (GPO) distributed the first United States Government documents in CD-ROM format to depository libraries. By December 1991 (a little more than two years after the distribution of the first depository CD-ROM documents), over 100 CD-ROM disks, representing more than a dozen depository CD-ROM document titles, had been distributed to depository libraries. The first documents were issued with the promise of many more to follow, with increasing frequency.

The depository CD-ROM document "earthquake" did not strike without warning, however. In 1988, the Government Printing Office announced a pilot project which would distribute a test *Census* CD-ROM disk to 143 depository libraries. The 143 libraries served as resource libraries during the subsequent distributions.[1] After months of announcement and discussion regarding the impending distribution of the depository CD-ROM documents, many documents and cataloging librarians were shocked by the physical reality of merely receiving the CD-ROM disks, not to mention the prospects of grappling with the perceived myths and hard realities of providing access to the CD-ROM documents in online databases (such as RLIN and OCLC) and in local or shared automated catalogs, the logistics and technicalities of loading the disks and software into computers and the ramifications of disk storage. The perceived myths and hard realities regarding the provision of public service, including access and bibliographic instruction also gave many librarians pause.

The depository CD-ROM document "earthquake," did not bode only evil, however, as a whole new world of information and light-speed access to that information had suddenly opened up to the depository library world. Depository libraries would never be the same following the distribution of the depository CD-ROM documents; on the whole, the prospects were simultaneously exciting and frightening.

LITERATURE REVIEW

The distribution of the depository CD-ROM documents is a new phenomenon, and, at the time of this writing (February 1992), very little has been published about the documents, in any aspect. A literature search revealed few pertinent articles.

A number of articles describe specific depository CD-ROM document titles, including: Mason's "Planning the National Agriculture Library's Multimedia CD-ROM *Ornamental Horticulture*"[2] and Jackson's "CD-ROM Databases from the U.S. Government: Some with Minimal Software."[3] These two articles, while accurately describing the content and use of the specific depository CD-ROM document titles and the information contained in the documents themselves, do not discuss cataloging the document titles.

Two other articles cover much more ground, including discussions of accessibility, durability and standards related to the depository CD-ROM documents: Sanchez's "Dissemination of United States Federal Government Information of CD-ROM: An Issues Primer"[4] and Dossett's "For Those Few of You Who Still Aren't Confused: An Introduction to Government Information and CD-ROM."[5] Like Mason's and Jackson's article, these two articles also do not discuss cataloging the depository CD-ROM documents. Unfortunately, as of February 1992, no articles have been published specifically dealing with the cataloging of depository CD-ROM titles.

To complicate matters even further, few articles have been published regarding the cataloging of any item issued in CD-ROM format. The most notable articles are: Wang's, "The Challenge of Cataloging Computer Files"[6] and Vanderberg's "CD-ROMs and Seriality."[7] Both Wang and Vanderberg, while primarily discussing the cataloging of computer files, devote several pages to the cataloging of items issued in CD-ROM format. Neither author specifically discusses the cataloging of depository CD-ROM documents.

Two benchmark books also examine the cataloging of computer files: Dodd and Sandberg-Fox's *Cataloging Microcomputer Files: A Manual of Interpretation for AACR2*[8] and Olson's *Cataloging Microcomputer Software: A Manual to Accompany AACR2 Chapter 9, Computer Files.*[9] Olson does include a small section on cataloging materials in CD-ROM format, but Dodd and Sandberg-Fox do not. Neither book includes specific information on cataloging depository CD-ROM documents. Specific information regarding the cataloging of the depository CD-ROM documents (and other materials issued in CD-ROM format) in MARC format, must, instead, be derived from the primary cataloging sources. The primary sources available from the Government Printing Office do not, however, specifically deal with items in CD-ROM format.[10]

The lack of published discussion regarding the cataloging of depository CD-ROM documents (and other materials issued in CD-ROM format) is regrettable and has created some confusion about cataloging such materials. In addition, the relative newness of the materials themselves has hampered the "post-earthquake" recovery following the distribution of the depository CD-ROM documents, creating a "mixed-bag" of cataloging records (i.e., records entered in various MARC formats and varying levels of accuracy and consistency) in both the RLIN and OCLC databases.

This paper will examine and discuss the extent to which the depository CD-ROM documents have been cataloged, by studying the cataloging records entered for depository CD-ROM documents from July 1989 to December 1991 in both the RLIN and OCLC databases. In addition, recommendations will be made regarding the enhancement of cataloging records to provide improved access to the depository CD-ROM documents.

This information is important to depository and non-depository libraries alike, since many non-depository libraries also hold specific CD-ROM document titles. Further, much of the information and recommendations are also applicable to other, non-depository CD-ROM titles.

METHODOLOGY

Seventeen depository CD-ROM document titles were identified via the "Electronic Shipping Lists" distributed by the Government Printing Office through December 1991. The seventeen depository CD-ROM document titles thus identified included general titles (such as the *Congressional Record*) and specialized documents titles (such as the *Aeronautical Charting Sample*).

Following the identification of the titles from the "Electronic Shipping Lists," exact titles for each of the seventeen depository CD-ROM documents were determined, by applying *AACR2R* Rule 9.0B1: "*Chief source of information. The chief source of informa-*

tion for computer files is the title screen(s). If there is no title screen, take the information from other formally presented internal evidence (e.g., main menus, program statements). If the information required is not available from internal sources, take it from the following sources in this order of preference: the physical carrier or its label; information issued by the publisher, creator, etc., with the file (sometimes called 'documentation'); information printed on the container issued by the publisher, distributor, etc."[11] In most cases, the title could be determined from the title screen(s) or other internal source(s).

The seventeen CD-ROM document titles (followed by SuDoc classification number or stem), garnered from the "Electronic Shipping Lists" are:

1. *Aeronautical Charting* (C55.402:AE8/5/CD).
2. *Census of Agriculture* (C3.277:AG8/987/CD).
3A. *Census of Population and Housing: [Full Series]* (C3.281:).
3B. *Census of Population and Housing: [State by State Listing]* (C3.281:).
4. *Congressional Record: Proceedings and Debates of the 99th Congress, 1st Session* (X.99/1:).
5. *County & City Databook* (C3.134/2:C93/2).
6. *County Business Patterns, 1987* (C3.204/4:).
7. *1988 DOD Hazardous Materials* (D7.32:).
8. *Dress Rehearsal Census* (C3.275:D81).
9. *Economic Census* (C3.277:EC7).
10. *FIRMR* (GS12.15/2:).
11. *1987 National Health Interview* (H20.6209/4-3:10/).
12. *National Trade Databank* (C1.88:).
13A. *Tiger/Line Files: [Full Series]* (C3.79).
13B. *Tiger/Line Files: [State by State Listing]* (C3.79).
14. *1987 Toxic Chemical Release Inventory* (EP5.22:T65).
15. *U.S. Exports of Merchandise* (C3.278.EX7/).
16. *1:2,000,000–Scale Digital Line Graph (DLG) Data* (I19.120: D56/CD) Note: Title on disk is *U.S. Geodata.*
17. *U.S. Imports of Merchandise* (C3.278.IM7/).

Previous experiences with cataloging non-document CD-ROM titles (including a range of index/abstract databases and other reference sources such as CD-ROM encyclopedias, maps and interactive media packages) and other computer files, led to the development of a list of nine assumptions, regarding the cataloging of depository CD-ROM documents. Some of the nine assumptions turned out to be myths, some realities.

The nine assumptions are:

1. No cataloging records will be found in books format.
2. Approximately half (or less) of the document titles will have cataloging records.
3. Some (approximately 25%-30%) of the cataloging records will be in the MARC computer files format.
4. Of the approximately 25%-30% in the computer file format, approximately half will be entered as computer file monographs (with a very few entered as open entry monographs), and approximately half will be entered as computer file serials.
5. The majority (approximately 60-75%) of the cataloging records will be in the MARC serials format.
6. Most of the document titles with cataloging records will be cataloged by the Library of Congress and/or the Government Printing Office.
7. Titles cataloged by the Library of Congress will be cataloged in the MARC serial format.
8. Titles cataloged by either the Library of Congress or the Government Printing Office will have the largest number of holdings or attached cataloging records.
9. As with other computer file materials, title entries found in the cataloging records will vary.

Each of the seventeen depository CD-ROM document titles was searched in both the RLIN and OCLC databases by SuDoc (Superintendent of Documents) classification number and by title in the MARC books, computer file, and serials formats. For document titles found in the RLIN database, each cluster record and each individual cataloging record comprising each cluster was examined; for titles found in the OCLC database, each master cataloging record and the comprehensive holdings screen was examined.

Because of the cataloging and database differences, data regarding the RLIN and OCLC cataloging practices were kept and tabulated separately. Two tables, one for cataloging records found in the RLIN database (Table 1) and one for cataloging records found in the OCLC database (Table 2) were devised, recording cataloging information for each title, with particular attention paid to:

1. The date that the cataloging record was first entered into the database (USMARC field 008, character positions 00-05– "AD" in the RLIN MARC fixed field and "ENTERED" in the OCLC MARC fixed fields.
2. The cataloging format or bibliographic level (USMARC leader character positions 06-07; "BLT" in the RLIN MARC fixed field and "BIB LVL" in the OCLC MARC fixed field.
3. The initial cataloging library (MARC field 040, delimiters "a" and "c," in both RLIN and OCLC MARC variable fields).
4. The presence or absence of a record entered by the Library of Congress and/or the Government Printing Office (MARC field 040 in both RLIN and OCLC variable fields).
5. Title access (primarily MARC fields 245, 246, 247 and 740 in both RLIN and OCLC variable fields).
6. The presence or absence of a Sudoc number (MARC field 086 in both the RLIN and OCLC variable fields).

Due to spatial limitations, documents titles listed on the two tables were shortened either to the common title or to a mnemonically relevant abbreviated title, with date designations removed. SuDoc numbers or stems are given on both tables. The two tables record the presence or absence of both Library of Congress and the Government Printing Office cataloging record, and the format of the record. The two tables go on to record the number of records found in each database for each title, including the format of the record.

Again, due to spatial limitations, the three computer file cataloging format variations have been abbreviated on the two tables to: CF/M (Computer File/Monograph), CF/MOE (Computer File/Monograph, Open Entry or monographic set); CF/S (Computer File/Serial). Separate columns are included for the number of clusters (in the RLIN database) and master records (in the OCLC database), as well as the number of holdings.

TABLE 1. RLIN CD-ROM Records

	SUDOC NUMBER	LC RECORD FORMAT	GPO RECORD FORMAT	CF/M CLUST.	CF/M HOLDS
Aeronautical Charting	C55.402:AE8/5/CD	No Record	No Record	1	1
Census of Agriculture	C3.277:AG8/987/CD	No Record	No Record	3	3
Census of Population	C3.281:	No Record	No Record	2	2
Census By State Group	C3.281:	No Record	No Record	0	0
Congressional Record	X.99/1:	Serial	No Record	0	0
County & City Databook	C3.134/2:C83/2/	No Record	No Record	1	1
County Business Patterns	C3.204/4:	Serial	Serial	0	0
DOD Hazardous Materials	D7.32:	No Record	Serial	0	0
Economic Census	C3.277:EC7	No Record	No Record	0	0
Dress Rehearsal Census	C3.275:D81	No Record	No Record	2	2
FIRMR	GS12.15/2:	No Record	No Record	0	0
National Health Interview	HE20.6209/4-3:10/	No Record	Serial	1	1
National Trade Databank	C1.88:	No Record	No Record	0	0
Tiger/Line (State)	C3.279:	No Record	No Record	20	20
Tiger/Line (All)	C3.279:	No Record	No Record	0	0
Toxic Chemical Release	EP5.22:T65	No Record	No Record	2	2
US Exports	C3.278:EX7/	No Record	Serial	0	0
US Geodata	I19.120:D56/CD	No Record	No Record	1	1
US Imports	C3.278:IM7/	No Record	Serial	0	0
TOTALS				**24**	**24**

CF/MOE CLUST.	CF/MOE HOLDS	CF/S CLUST.	CF/S HOLDS	SERIAL CLUST.	SERIAL HOLDS	TOTAL CLUST.	TOTAL HOLDS
0	0	0	0	0	0	1	1
0	0	0	0	0	0	3	3
1	1	0	0	1	2	4	4
0	0	0	0	0	0	0	0
0	0	2	2	1	2	3	4
0	0	0	0	0	0	1	1
0	0	2	2	2	6	4	8
0	0	3	3	1	2	4	5
6	6	0	0	1	1	7	7
0	0	0	0	0	0	2	2
0	0	1	1	2	2	3	3
0	0	2	2	1	5	4	8
0	0	2	2	3	3	5	5
0	0	0	0	0	0	20	20
1	1	0	0	0	0	1	1
0	0	1	1	1	4	7	1
0	0	3	3	2	6	5	9
0	0	0	0	0	0	1	1
0	0	3	3	3	6	6	9
1	1	12	12	12	26	52	88

TABLE 2. OCLC CD-ROM Records

	SUDOC NUMBER	LC RECORD FORMAT	GPO RECORD FORMAT	CF/M MASTER	CF/M HOLDS
Aeronautical Charting	C55.402:AE8/5/CD	No Record	No Record	1	10
Census of Agriculture	C3.277:AG8/987/CD	No Record	No Record	0	0
Census of Population	C3.281:	No Record	No Record	0	0
Census By State Group	C3.281:	No Record	No Record	0	0
Congressional Record	X.99/1:	No Record	Serial	0	0
County & City Databook	C3.134/2:C83/2/	No Record	CF/S	0	0
County Business Patterns	C3.204/4:	No Record	Serial	0	0
DOD Hazardous Materials	D7.32:	No Record	Serial	0	0
Economic Census	C3.277:EC7	No Record	CF/S	1	4
Dress Rehearsal Census	C3.275:D81	No Record	CF/S	0	0
FIRMR	GS12.15/2:	No Record	No Record	0	0
National Health Interview	HE20.6209/4-3:10/	No Record	Serial	0	0
National Trade Databank	C1.88:	No Record	Serial	0	0
Tiger/Line (State)	C3.279:	No Record	No Record	0	0
Tiger/Line (All)	C3.279:	No Record	No Record	35	90
Toxic Chemical Release	EP5.22:T65	No Record	CF/S	0	0
US Exports	C3.278:EX7/	Serial	CF/S	0	0
US Geodata	I19.120:D56/CD	No Record	No Record	1	27
US Imports	C3.278:IM7/	Serial	CF/S	0	0
TOTALS				**37**	**121**

CF/MOE MASTER	CF/MOE HOLDS	CF/S MASTER	CF/S HOLDS	SERIAL MASTER	SERIAL HOLDS	TOTAL MASTER	TOTAL HOLDS
0	0	0	0	0	0	1	10
0	0	2	33	0	0	2	33
0	0	0	0	1	4	1	4
0	0	12	189	0	0	12	189
0	0	1	27	1	94	2	121
0	0	1	85	0	0	1	86
0	0	1	29	1	29	2	58
0	0	1	5	1	37	2	42
0	0	2	124	0	0	3	128
0	0	1	83	0	0	1	83
0	0	1	11	0	0	1	11
0	0	1	5	1	32	2	37
0	0	0	0	2	81	2	81
0	0	1	15	0	0	1	15
0	0	2	0	0	0	35	90
0	0	1	95	0	0	1	94
0	0	1	82	1	13	2	95
0	0	2	0	0	0	1	27
0	0	12	82	1	3	2	85
0	0	26	531	7	195	55	880

Because the lag-time between the distribution dates and catalog-ing dates (i.e., dates of entry into the RLIN and/or OCLC) of each title was always short (at least two to three days and at most two to three weeks), cataloging date information was omitted from the two tables. Also, because RLIN or OCLC member libraries (rather than the Library of Congress or the Government Printing Office) were more consistently (in 95% of the cases) the first library or catalog-ing agency to enter a record in the respective database, information about the first library to catalog a title was also omitted from the two tables.

It must be noted that two of the titles, *Census of Population and Housing* (3A and 3B above) and *Tiger/Line Files* (13A and 13B above), are issued on multiple CD-ROM disks and contain file sets for individual states, as well as file sets for groups of states. The file sets for individual states and the files sets for groups of states were cataloged as one group (or serial) title and also as separate titles on RLIN and OCLC, giving the false appearance of a total of nineteen titles, rather than seventeen. As a result, separate lines are listed for the individual state files and groups of states files on Tables 1 and 2; however, because these particular titles were issued under one Su-doc number each, for statistical purposes the total title count is seventeen.

DISCUSSION:
THE SURPRISES OF MYTHS AND REALITIES

A close examination of the RLIN and OCLC cataloging records for the seventeen depository CD-ROM document titles and the completed tables revealed that the nine initial assumptions con-tained both myth and reality. The findings also revealed three other important findings that had not been accounted for in the initial nine assumptions.

The myths and realities regarding the initial nine assumptions are:

(1) *REALITY.* As assumed, no cataloging records for the seven-teen depository CD-ROM documents were found in books format. This finding is due to the introduction and, by now, general use and acceptance of the MARC computer files format. Prior to the

introduction and acceptance of the format in the early 1980's, some computer files had initially been cataloged in books format.

(2) *MYTH*. Contrary to the second assumption that approximately half (or less) of the depository CD-ROM documents would have cataloging records in the RLIN and OCLC databases, records for all seventeen (100%) documents were found in both databases.

(3) *MYTH*. The third assumption was based on the presumption that most depository CD-ROM documents were serial in nature and that the Library of Congress had previously ruled that serial-type items, irrespective of their format, should be cataloged as a serial in the MARC serials format.[12] The third initial assumption that there would be a low percentage of cataloging records (approximately 25%-30%) for the seventeen depository CD-ROM documents in the MARC computer files format proved to be false. In both the RLIN and OCLC databases, 100% of the document titles had been cataloged in the computer files format. Some titles even occurred more than once. This happened in the case of the *Census of Population and Housing* and the *Tiger/Line Files*. Both titles were issued in multi-disk sets with one or more states represented on each CD-ROM. Cataloging records with attached holdings exist in the RLIN and OCLC databases for each individual CD-ROM and for the series as a whole.

(4) *REALITY AND MYTH*. It was assumed that the cataloging records for depository CD-ROM documents in the MARC computer file format would cover all of the variations permitted in the format. The assumption proved true, but with some twists. CD-ROM items can be cataloged in the MARC computer file format as a monograph, utilizing the monograph-specific elements of the format for date type and dates (USMARC field 008, character positions 06 and 07-14; RLIN MARC fixed fields "PC" and "PD" and OCLC MARC fixed fields "Dat tp" and "Dates"). Monographic sets (open entries) can also be accommodated in the computer file format, by entering the appropriate dates in the same USMARC fields and the same RLIN and OCLC fixed fields, as well as in the MARC 260 field (Imprint), delimiter "c" (date of publication, distribution, etc.).

CD-ROM items can further be cataloged in the MARC computer file format as serials, utilizing the serial-specific elements of the format, including USMARC field 008, character positions: 18 (frequency), 19 (regularity), 06 (publication status) and 07-14 (publication dates. These serial-specific elements correspond to RLIN fixed fields "FRQ," "REG," "PSC" and "D" and OCLC fixed fields "Frequn," "Regulr," and "Dat tp" and "Dates." RLIN makes more of a distinction between a computer file/monograph and a computer file/serial than does OCLC.

As anticipated, the choice of MARC cataloging format varied widely for cataloging records found in RLIN and in OCLC. The wide variations are a direct result of three factors, including: (1) the continuing conflict between choice of MARC cataloging format (computer file versus serials format) for materials issued in CD-ROM format, as well as for other computer files; (2) the range of choice within the computer files format alone; and (3) the continuing difficulty in the determination if a CD-ROM or other computer file item is a serial or monograph, based on the conflicting or lack of information listed on the title screen(s), the disk itself, the disk containers or other accompanying print materials. The situation is even further complicated by the mixed signals about format choice given by one of the lead cataloging agencies, the Government Printing Office. The Government Printing Office cataloging records showed that no titles (0%) were cataloged in the computer files format and five titles (29%) were cataloged in the serials format in the RLIN database, while six titles (35%) were cataloged in the computer files format (as computer file/serials) and five titles (29%) were cataloged in the serials format in the OCLC database. The assumption regarding the percentages cataloged in each computer file variation proved not to be on target.

Of the cataloging records found in the MARC computer files format for the seventeen depository CD-ROM document titles: nine titles (53%) in the RLIN database and four titles (24%) in the OCLC database were cataloged as computer file monographs (see Tables 1 and 2, under CF/M); nine titles (53%) in the RLIN database and no titles (0%) in the OCLC database were cataloged as computer file monographic sets/open entries (see Tables 1 and 2, under CF/MOE) and nine titles (53%) in the RLIN database and thirteen titles (76%) in the OCLC database were cataloged as computer file serials (see Tables 1 and 2, under CF/S).

(5) *REALITY AND MYTH.* The assumption that the majority (approximately 60-74%) of the cataloging records for the seventeen depository CD-ROM documents would be in the MARC serials format, proved to be partly true and partly false. Of the seventeen depository CD-ROM document titles, eleven titles (65%) in the RLIN database and eight titles (47%) in the OCLC database were cataloged in the MARC serials format (see Tables 1 and 2, under Serials). The issue of MARC format choice for CD-ROM titles is complicated by the fact that there is so much choice in format—choice that is not available for other types of materials, such as books. In addition to the three variations in the MARC computer files format, serial-type CD-ROMs can be cataloged in the MARC serials format.

The issue of format choice is further complicated by the fact that it is not always easy to determine the nature of the CD-ROM in hand. This seems particularly true of the depository CD-ROM documents. The determination of "serialness" under the *AACR2R* definition ("*Serial.* A publication in any medium issued in successive parts bearing numeric or chronological designations and intended to be continued indefinitely . . . *Series.* 1. A group of separate items related to one another by the fact that each item bears, in addition to its own title proper, a collective title applying to the group as a whole. The individual items may or may not be numbered . . .")[13] is frequently not an easy one. *Library of Congress Rule Interpretations* Rule 12.0A are somewhat more helpful regarding the definition of "serialness," but are still not as easily applied to materials issued in CD-ROM format, as to items issued in print.[14] Serial indications are not always supplied or readily evident on the item, its internal sources of information or on the printed documentation. Serials indication, even when supplied, often conflicts on the various internal and external sources of information. Some of the depository CD-ROM documents (such as *1987 Economic Census*) did clearly indicate a date (serial-type designations) that could be a clue to the document's "serialness." None of the documents, however, clearly stated (on any source of information, internal or external) that the document in CD-ROM format was definitely intended to be issued indefinitely (or ever again), making it difficult to establish "serialness" under the *AACR2R* or *Library of Congress Rule Interpretations* definitions.

The continuing confusion of choice between cataloging a CD-ROM serial in the MARC computer file/serials format and serials format should be alleviated when the USMARC format integration project is completed, adopted, and utilized during the next several years. Format integration will not, however, make it any easier to determine an item's "serialness."

(6) *MYTH*. The assumption that all of the depository CD-ROM documents with cataloging records in the RLIN and OCLC databases would have been entered by either the Library of Congress or the Government Printing Office proved false. The disparity created as a result of the different methods of and assorted times of entry of cataloging records for the documents is a handicap. RLIN tapeloads the cataloging records from the Government Printing Office (for items cataloged in the MARC book, serials and map formats) every four weeks. Library of Congress tapes are loaded weekly (for books), every four weeks (for maps, recordings, scores, serials and visual material) and quarterly (for computer files).[15] The Government Printing Office catalogs directly on OCLC.

It was somewhat surprising to find that so few of the cataloging records were entered by the Library of Congress. Only two (12%) of the seventeen titles had been cataloged in the RLIN database and two (17%) in the OCLC database by the Library of Congress. Even more surprising, despite the fact that both RLIN and OCLC load Library of Congress MARC tapes, is that the two records found in the RLIN database (the *Congressional Record* and *County Business Patterns*) were not the same two records found in the OCLC database (*U.S. Imports of Merchandise* and *U.S. Exports of Merchandise*). In order to account for the possibility that RLIN and OCLC loaded the Library of Congress MARC tapes at different times, the two databases were searched for cataloging records for all seventeen depository CD-ROM document titles monthly during the course of the study. The findings remained the same.

It was not only surprising, but also disappointing to find that the Government Printing Office had not cataloged all of the titles. Five cataloging records (29% of the seventeen titles) had been entered in the RLIN database and eleven cataloging records (11% of the seventeen titles) had been entered in the OCLC database by the Government Printing Office. Although there was some overlap (e.g., *County Business Patterns, DOD Hazardous Materials* and *National Trade Databank*) once again, the titles with cataloging records entered by the Government Printing Office in the RLIN database were different from the titles in the OCLC database. Both the RLIN and OCLC databases were searched monthly during the course of the study; the findings, remained the same.

Ernest states that, "OCLC and RLIN include the Government Printing Office [cataloging] records from 1976 to the present and neither differentiates government publications from other materials."[16] It would certainly be more advantageous if the Government Printing Office cataloged the depository CD-ROM documents in a more timely manner, and if the Office's cataloging records (along with those provided by the Library of Congress) appeared at similar times in the RLIN and OCLC databases.

(7) *REALITY.* The assumption that the titles cataloged by the Library of Congress would be cataloged in the MARC serials format was, indeed, true. The initial assumption was based on the fact that the Library of Congress treats items as serials, irrespective of their format, or as Sandberg-Fox (Computer Cataloging Specialist, Special Materials Cataloging Division, Library of Congress) notes, ". . . it is the policy of the Library to catalog all serials in the serials format regardless of medium."[17]

(8) *MYTH.* It was originally assumed that the cataloging records (irrespective of MARC format choice) that had been entered by either the Government Printing Office or the Library of Congress would have the largest number of holdings attached to them. The assumption proved false, on several counts. The presence or absence of cataloging records entered by either the Library of Congress or the Government Printing Office had no discernible impact on other RLIN or OCLC libraries choosing to catalog a document title or not. If a Library of Congress or the Government Printing Office cataloging record were not already present, RLIN and OCLC member libraries entered cataloging records and master records anyway, soon after the receipt of the CD-ROM disk.

Also, RLIN and OCLC member libraries were not shy in using the cataloging records entered by member libraries to copy catalog a document. The member libraries were just as likely to use member library cataloging copy as they were to use Library of Congress or Government Printing Office cataloging copy. For example, the cataloging records in the MARC computer files format (see under CF/S, Table 2) for the *Congressional Record* in the OCLC database, contained twelve master records (all entered by member libraries) with the most number of holdings (189).

(9) *REALITY.* It was disappointing, but not unexpected to find that title entries in the cataloging records for depository CD-ROM documents varied widely. It was even more disappointing to discover what a significant impact title variation and selection made in the ability to successfully locate the item in the RLIN and OCLC databases. Identification and selection of a title for a depository CD-ROM document can be a confusing and frustrating struggle. Depository CD-ROM documents are shipped in jewel cases or in cardboard mailers imprinted with title information. The CD-ROM disk itself is generally also imprinted with sometimes identical, sometimes differing title information. To complicate this further, printed materials, accompanying the CD-ROM disks also have similar, yet differing title information.

Additionally, the titles listed on the title screens of the documents often also vary from the title printed on the other three locations. The title information is determined by the issuing agency of the document (rather than by the Government Printing Office), and there is, subsequently, little chance of developing a standard procedure for listing such information. Despite the fact *AACR2R* Rule 9.0B1 requires that title information be taken from the chief source of information (internal source or title screen) when possible,[18] this frequently is more easily said than done. For example, the depository CD-ROM document, titled *County & City Databook* runs on a software package titled *Extract.* Loading the CD-ROM disk presents the user with a title screen for *Extract,* rather than the title screen for *County & City Databook.* Also, the *Tiger/Line Files* arrived at depository libraries with no software at all. It was, therefore, impossible for many depository libraries to load the *Tiger/Line Files* and to access the title screen.

Even in cases where the title screens were relatively easy to access, it was evident that libraries cataloging the titles frequently derived the title entries from the information printed on the jewel case, the CD-ROM disk itself or from the accompanying print material, rather than from the internal title screen. Bypassing *AACR2R* Rule 9.0B1 creates inconsistencies in title access, rendering titles difficult, if not impossible to find in the RLIN and OCLC databases. For example, *1:2,000,000–Scale Digital Line Graph (DLG) Data* is the title entered on the internal title screens, while *U.S. Geodata* is the title listed on the CD-ROM disk itself. This title is only entered in the RLIN and OCLC databases under the title *U.S. Geodata*, with no entries (main or added) for the *AACR2R* prescribed longer title.

Presented with such varying title information in so many different locations, catalogers frequently choose differing titles as main entries and added entries. Such differences account, in part, for the large number of clusters (in the RLIN database) and master records (in the OCLC database) for the depository CD-ROM documents. Title inconsistencies and difficulty in title entry selection, can make the search for the documents in the RLIN and OCLC databases complex and confusing.

After consideration of our nine initial assumptions, a closer look at the cataloging data collected in this study, revealed three other findings about the current state of cataloging records for depository CD-ROM documents in the RLIN and OCLC databases, including: (1) the absence of SuDoc numbers in many cataloging records, (2) the absence of technical notes in many cataloging records, and (3) the short lag-time between the distribution of the disk and the entry of cataloging records in both the RLIN and OCLC databases.

The most dismaying finding was that SuDoc numbers were not present in many of the records entered by RLIN and OCLC member libraries. The inclusion of SuDoc numbers in cataloging records (particularly in RLIN and OCLC cataloging records) takes on increased importance for depository CD-ROM documents, particularly when title access is complex or unclear, as is the case with the seventeen titles included in this study. RLIN does not require the inclusion of the MARC field 086;[19] however, OCLC does require it in both the computer files and serials formats for full or "I" level cataloging records.[20, 21]

Determining a SuDoc number for depository CD-ROM documents is not easy, and may be impossible for non-depository libraries. Unfortunately, SuDoc numbers are either not included or not readily apparent in the data listed on the title screens of the documents or printed on the CD-ROM disks themselves, the jewel cases or accompanying print. Although a library could create a SuDoc number, there is no guarantee that the number created by the library would be exactly the same as or similar to the number already assigned by the Government Printing Office. Also, the creation of a SuDoc number is not an easy task, requiring the cataloger to utilize the instructions contained in the *GPO Classification Manual: A Practical Guide to the Superintendent of Documents Classification System*. Many non-depository libraries do not have easy access to this manual.

The second dismaying finding was the lack of complete or consistent technical notes in the cataloging records. The distribution of documents in CD-ROM format demands that cataloging records include technical notes, specifying technical information about the software and hardware required to load and use each CD-ROM document. Unfortunately, such information has not been consistently included in cataloging records for CD-ROM and other computer files in the computer files format, and such information is not required at all in the serials format (although it can be added in MARC field 500 for general notes). This is true for cataloging records contained in both the RLIN and the OCLC databases. It was, therefore, not surprising to find inconsistencies in the cataloging records themselves for the seventeen depository CD-ROM documents, particularly in regard to the inclusion or exclusion and content of the two technical notes fields, MARC field 538 (Technical Details Note) and MARC field 753 (Technical Details Access to Computer Files).

The third finding, rather than being dismaying, was encouraging. All seventeen of the depository CD-ROM document titles had full cataloging records in both the RLIN and the OCLC databases, and that the RLIN and OCLC member libraries (rather than the Library of Congress or the Government Printing Office) had entered the full cataloging records very quickly after the distribution of the CD-ROM disks (at the least a week after distribution and at the most a month after distribution). This finding clearly indicates the importance that the member libraries place on the depository CD-ROM documents. It also indicates the libraries' keen interest in providing access to the depository CD-ROM documents for their own patrons, as well as for the wider audience on the shared bibliographic utilities.

CONCLUSIONS:
DEALING WITH "POST-QUAKE" REALITIES

The "earthquake" (or, at least, the first tremor) created by the distribution of the first depository CD-ROM documents is past, and it is time to deal specifically and realistically with quality of the cataloging for depository CD-ROM documents entered in the two most prominent, shared databases, RLIN and OCLC.

The distribution of depository document publications in CD-ROM format poses a number of exciting prospects. The distribution of the depository CD-ROM documents also poses a number of problems, including issues related to service to patrons, storage of the CD-ROM disks themselves and access to the depository CD-ROM document titles in bibliographic utility databases (such as RLIN and OCLC) and in local online systems.

Depository CD-ROM documents are not different from other CD-ROM and computer file titles, and their cataloging treatment need not be any more mystifying than the cataloging treatment for any other item. The information contained in the depository CD-ROM documents is important and vital. Access is the most pressing problem associated with depository CD-ROM documents. Service to depository library patrons cannot be considered as an issue, if a depository CD-ROM document is inaccessible because the cataloging access provided is inadequate or nonexistent. If access to this information is to be made readily available, then excellent cataloging records need to be entered, not only in the RLIN and OCLC databases, but in other shared databases and in each library's own local system or print catalog. Storage of the CD-ROM disks is only practical and possible if the title first has proper access in online databases and catalogs.

In addition, accurate and consistent title information and SuDoc numbers should be included, not only on the title screens of the CD-ROM documents, but also on the disks themselves, the jewel cases and all accompanying print materials. The title of a document should not be clouded in mystery.

Prompt, precise full-level cataloging, particularly in automated environments, is the essential key to access for depository CD-ROM documents, as well as other items issued in CD-ROM format. Prompt, precise and full-level cataloging is, therefore, the tool that can tame the depository CD-ROM document "earthquake."

Finally, the lack of information in the library literature regarding cataloging depository CD-ROM documents and other CD-ROM titles, in general, must be remedied. More research and case studies, as well as up-dated "how-to" articles and books are needed. Knowledge and discussion regarding cataloging the documents issued in CD-ROM format will bring realities to the fore and dispel the myths.

NOTES

1. Superintendent of Documents, "CD-ROM Distributed to Selected Depository Libraries," *Administrative Notes* 9 (October 1988): 11-13.

2. Pamela R. Mason, "Planning the National Agricultural Library's Multimedia CD-ROM *Ornamental Horticulture*," *Government Publications Review* 18 (1991): 137-146.

3. Kathy Jackson, "CD-ROM Databases from the U.S. Government: Some with Minimal Software," *The Laserdisk Professional* 3 (March 1990): 94-97.

4. Lisa Sanchez, "Dissemination of United States Federal Government Information on CD-ROM: An Issues Primer," *Government Publications Review* 16 (1989): 133-144.

5. Raeann Dossett, "For Those Few of You Who Still Aren't Confused: An Introduction to Government Information and CD-ROM," *Illinois Libraries* 71 (November 1989): 492-494.

6. Anna M. Wang, "The Challenge of Cataloging Computer Files," *The Serials Librarian* 15 (1989): 99-116.

7. Patricia S. Vanderberg, "CD ROMs and Seriality," *RLG Computer Files Workshop* (Emory University, Atlanta, Georgia, 18 June 1991).

8. Sue A. Dodd and Ann M. Sandberg-Fox, *Cataloging Microcomputer Files: A Manual of Interpretation for AACR2* (Chicago, IL: American Library Association, 1985).

9. Nancy B. Olson, *Cataloging Microcomputer Software: A Manual to Accompany AACR2 Chapter 9, Computer Files* (Englewood, CO: Libraries Unlimited, 1988).

10. The primary cataloging sources include: *Anglo-American Cataloging Rules*, 2nd edition, 1988 revision [hereafter cited as *AACR2R*] (Chicago, IL:

American Library Association, 1988); *USMARC Format for Bibliographic Data* (Washington, DC: Library of Congress, Cataloging Distribution Service, 1988–); *Library of Congress Rule Interpretations* (Washington, DC: Library of Congress, 1990–); *RLIN Supplement to USMARC Bibliographic Format: Variable & ARC Fields* (Mountain View, CA: Research Libraries Group, Inc., 1991–); *RLIN Supplement to USMARC Bibliographic Format: Fixed Fields* (Mountain View, CA: Research Libraries Group, Inc., 1991–); *Serials Field Guide* (Stanford, CA: Research Libraries Group, Inc., 1982–); *Computer Files Format* (Dublin, OH: Online Computer Library Center, Inc., 1989–); *Serials Format*, 3rd ed. (Dublin, OH: Online Computer Library Center, Inc., 1986–); *Government Printing Office Cataloging Guidelines*, 3rd ed. (Washington, DC: U.S. Government Printing Office, 1990); and *GPO Classification Manual: A Practical Guide to the Superintendent of Documents Classification System* (Washington, DC: U.S. Government Printing Office, 1988).

11. *AACR2R*, p. 222.

12. Ann Sandberg-Fox, [Cataloging CD-ROM Serials in the Serials Format at LC]. Message to: AUTOCAT (Cataloging and Authorities Discussion Group) [electronic bulletin board], July 23, 1991. Available at: LISTSERV@UBVM.

13. *AACR2R*, p. 622.

14. *Library of Congress Rule Interpretations* (Rule 12.0A), 1.

15. Karen Smith-Yoshimura, [On-going RLIN Dataloads]. Message to: RLIN-L (A Forum for RLIN Issues) [electronic bulletin board], December 9, 1992. Available at: LISTSERV@RUTV1.

16. Douglas J. Ernest, "Accessing Federal Government Publications with RLIN," *Government Publication Review* 15 (1988): 237-243.

17. Sandberg-Fox, [Cataloging CD-ROM Serials].

18. *AACR2R*, p. 222.

19. *RLIN Supplement to USMARC Bibliographic Format: Variable and ARC Fields*, 086/3 (5/5/89).

20. *Computer Files Format*, MRF/INTRO/6.

21. *Serials Format*, SERIALS/INTRO/7.

CASE STUDIES

Processing of Government Publications in the State Library of New South Wales

Mark Hildebrand
Richard Fell-Marston
Edwina Rudd

SUMMARY. In 1989 the State Library of New South Wales restruc-
tured its Acquisitions and Cataloguing Department to combine all
processing functions in a merged Materials Processing Branch. Specialist teams of 10 to 12 staff were established to process material
using redesigned workflows. At the same time the automated cataloguing and acquisitions processes were linked using an integrated
system. Government publications are processed by specialist teams
within the Monographs Processing Branch and Serials Processing

Mark Hildebrand is Team Leader in the Serials Processing Branch, Richard
Fell-Marston is Team Leader in the Monographs Processing Branch, and Edwina
Rudd is Government Publications Librarian, all with the State Library of New
South Wales. Address all correspondence to Mark Hildebrand, Serials Processing
Branch, State Library of New South Wales, Macquarie Street, Sydney, Australia
2000.

[Haworth co-indexing entry note]: "Processing of Government Publications in the State Library of
New South Wales," Hildebrand, Mark, Richard Fell-Marston, and Edwina Rudd. Co-published simul-
taneously in *Cataloging & Classification Quarterly* (The Haworth Press, Inc.) Vol. 18, No. 3/4, 1994,
pp. 155-165; and: *Cataloging Government Publications Online* (ed: Carolyn C. Sherayko) The Haworth
Press, Inc., 1994, pp. 155-165. Multiple copies of this article/chapter may be purchased from The
Haworth Document Delivery Center [1-800-3-HAWORTH; 9:00 a.m. - 5:00 p.m. (EST)].

Branch. The work of these specialist teams is described along with the challenges and new issues currently being addressed to provide effective access to government information.

BACKGROUND

"We are creating for the community a thriving dynamic organization, leading the New South Wales library system so that it becomes one of the world's best in collecting, conserving and communicating information" is the Library's mission statement which was developed through extensive staff consultation and highlights the leadership role that the Library takes in providing access to all information, including government publications and government information.

The Library has its foundation in the establishment of the Australian Subscription Library in 1826 and is now a large and diverse organization of over 400 staff providing a wide variety of information products and services. The services include telephone inquiry services, loans of materials in over forty languages to public libraries throughout New South Wales, educational tours, exhibitions on topics as diverse as Bligh and the Bounty mutiny, and Sport in Australia, business information services, a legal information access centre, newspaper services, and a family history service. The Library's services extend throughout New South Wales, serving clients directly from the Macquarie Street site, and indirectly through public and other libraries. The Library's collections are also wide-ranging, with over 3,800,000 items valued in excess of $500,000,000, and including heritage materials such as First Fleet diaries and colonial oil paintings, CD-ROMs, newspapers, photographs, and videodiscs as well as books and journals. There are two main divisions in the Library's collections: the General Collections (including the General Reference Library, special needs materials, and multicultural materials), and the Australian Research Collections (including the world-renowned Mitchell and Dixson Libraries).

The State Library has demonstrated its leadership role in providing access to government information through the implementation of two of the Library's corporate strategies. These are: "Develop and implement strategies . . . for improved use of information within government and improved access to government information" and "Acquire items for the Collection and create related automated records which provide effective intellectual access and physical access."[1]

GOVERNMENTS IN AUSTRALIA

There are three levels of government in Australia. The Commonwealth Government, with authority derived from a written constitution for areas such as defence and trade; the state governments with residual powers for areas such as police and law enforcement; and the local government authorities with powers for local town planning and the delivery of local services based upon state acts of parliament. The Commonwealth of Australia was established on 1st January 1901 and is a federation of six states, New South Wales, Queensland, Victoria, Tasmania, South Australia and Western Australia and two territories, the Australian Capital Territory and the Northern Territory.

Australia is currently debating the advantages and disadvantages of becoming a republic and the possible effects a republic would have on the role of the state governments and the Governor-General who is the representative of Her Majesty Queen Elizabeth II in Australia.

ACQUIRING GOVERNMENT PUBLICATIONS

The direction and strength of the State Library's government publications collection is outlined in the Library's collection development policy.[2] Management of the collection development policy is the responsibility of the Library's Resource Networking and Collection Development Branch. The Government Publications Librarian is part of this Branch.

Government publications are actively sought by the Government Publications Librarian who identifies, selects, and obtains government publications, especially those published by the New South Wales state government. The difficulty in obtaining government publications is well known to all librarians. Problems include the identification of published material, difficulties in contacting the officer responsible for the publication through the maze of government departments and continuing placement on a mailing list for the department's commercial and non-commercial publications.

The Library has a large collection of government publications that have been acquired by deposit, exchange with other State Libraries in Australia, and through purchase and donation. Major collections are held of the publications of the Australian Government Publishing Service, the Australian Bureau of Statistics, the United Nations and some of its specialist agencies, the European Communities, and the Organization for Economic Co-operation and Development. The publications of the Australian Government Publishing Service are deposited with the State Library.

Under the terms of the New South Wales Premier's Memorandum no. 91-27 (issued 17th October, 1991) entitled "Requirements for all N.S.W. Government Publications," three copies of all New South Wales government publications in all formats are deposited by government departments and declared authorities with the State Library. Two of the three copies received are held by the State Library for on-site use, loan and preservation. The third copy is acquired on behalf of New South Wales universities and forms part of the Universities' Co-operative Collection and is lent to the universities via the interlibrary loan network. One copy of New South Wales local government publications is deposited with the Library under the library deposit provisions of the New South Wales Copyright Act, 1879-1952.

SYSTEMS USED WITHIN THE STATE LIBRARY

The State Library uses URICA as its local system and runs a PEGASUS PLUS Series 9 minicomputer supplied by McDonnell-Douglas. The local system has the usual library modules, Inquiry, Acquisitions, Cataloguing, Serials, and Circulation. The State Library is linked to the Australian Bibliographic Network (ABN), based in Canberra (the national capital), and bibliographic records are found or created on ABN and downline loaded to URICA. In practice about 80 percent of monographs and 45 percent of serials received by the State Library already have full ABN records. Manuscripts, pictures, and posters are catalogued on PICMAN which is a local database running on AWAIRS software on the same computer as URICA. The State Library has implemented local area networks to allow access to URICA, PICMAN, ABN, and other internal databases throughout the Library. A switched data network connects the computer catalogue (OPAC) and technical services workstations to the central minicomputer. The Library's personal computers and the CD-ROM workstations in the Reading Rooms are linked by ETHERNET networks using NOVELL software.

The State Library follows international standards for creating bibliographic records. These are AACR2, DDC 20 and LCSH. Pictures, posters and manuscripts are described using a locally developed subject thesaurus based on LCSH. Maps are given Boggs and Lewis classification numbers. The level of bibliographic description is mostly AACR2 level 2 enhanced.

WORKFLOWS

As a result of the reorganization of the Acquisitions and Cataloguing Departments in 1989, a single Materials Processing Department was created with merged cataloguing and acquisition workflows. There are now four serial processing teams and three monograph processing teams, one team consisting of four members and the other six teams of nine to twelve members. There are teams in both the Serials and Monographs Processing Branches specialising in government publications. In Monographs Processing one team processes all government publications. In Serials Processing one team processes all Australian, state, and local government publications as well as a part of the general serials collection and another team processes all overseas government publications and a part of the general serials collection. Each team carries out all functions, ordering non-deposit material and accessioning, cataloguing, and end processing all material received. Deposit titles obtained by the Government Publications Librarian are passed on to the appropriate serials or monographs team.

The merged workflows give staff an opportunity to acquire a wide variety of skills. This multiskilling of staff and the creation of small teams have had a positive impact on the level of job satisfaction of staff. One of the greatest advantages of the team structure was the elimination of double handling. All staff have been trained and given the responsibility to undertake many of the tasks associated with the processing of a monograph or serial. To ensure continuing improvement of these processes and a client focus, the Library has introduced total quality management principles in the Materials Processing Branch.

When a monograph or serial is ordered, ABN is searched and if a bibliographic record is found it is downline loaded to the local system (URICA). If no record is found, a brief record is added to ABN and then downline loaded to URICA. The order details are then added to the URICA record. Orders for monographs are compiled fortnightly and forwarded to our suppliers. Orders for serials are placed with the Library's suppliers within a week of the request being received.

If the brief ABN records are "bumped" by full national agency records (e.g., LC, BNB, ANB, NZBN, etc.) or a full record created by other ABN participants, the URICA record will be upgraded automatically. As stated earlier, 80 percent of monographs and 45 percent of serials received will already have full bibliographic records on ABN. However, New South Wales government publications have even lower "hit" rates. The librarians within the teams are responsible for original cataloguing when full records are unavailable on ABN. All cataloguing takes place on ABN and the records downline loaded to URICA.

When ordered material arrives, it is accessioned on URICA and the bibliographic record is assessed for completeness. Deposited material is processed in the same fashion, that is, ABN is searched for a bibliographic record. If a record is found, it is downline loaded. If no record is available, a brief record is put onto ABN and downline loaded to URICA. Items with brief records are given to the librarians within the team for original cataloguing. End processing consists of labelling, shelflisting, stamping, adding location details to ABN and carrying out some binding. Barcoding and security tagging are undertaken for monographs, and heavily used serials are security tagged.

Four years after the restructure, the productivity of the Monographs Processing Branch and the Serials Processing Branch has risen substantially, with the number of monographs processed rising by over 70 percent during this period.

CATALOGUING OF GOVERNMENT PUBLICATIONS

Formats

Government publications come in a variety of formats. Maps, pictures, and posters have been mentioned earlier. Microfiche and microfilm are often reproductions of a paper copy government publication. Where the Library receives both the paper copy and the microform of a serial, the Library's holdings are placed against the one bibliographic record with a note of the format if it is non-print. Holdings in different formats are attached to one record because the intellectual content of the publications is the same and the microform is a true reproduction of the paper copy. The Library's clients find this approach more effective when using the computer catalogue.

Ephemera presents its own unique problems. Government published ephemera is stored with other ephemera according to its subject in acid free boxes. Ephemera is defined as a publication of fewer than five pages where specific access to an individual item is not warranted. Bibliographic records for different ephemera subjects are placed on ABN and downline loaded to URICA. Subjects include banks and banking, AIDS, and alternative lifestyles.

Community language versions of government publications are all catalogued individually. This is consistent with the Library's philosophy of equity of access to information because it allows retrieval in the computer catalogue of all works in a particular community language covering a desired subject area. The New South Wales and Australian governments may produce as many as 16 community language translations of their publications. Community languages are the languages of the ethnic communities who have come to Australia through immigration.

All other formats of government publications such as CD-ROMs and discs are catalogued on ABN, downline loaded to URICA, and accessed through the Library's computer catalogue. There is no separate government publications collection; all material is integrated into the one collection and similar formats are stored together.

Name Authorities

To enhance access to government publications the State Library's cataloguers carry out authority work on ABN. The Materials Processing Branch holds the latest editions of the New South Wales and Australian government directories and is aware of all announcements detailing the reorganization of government departments and agencies. Authority records for New South Wales government names contain a full reference structure and detailed history notes. The endless reorganization of government departments and agencies makes this an important but never ending task.

As records on ABN are input from many sources, there are many authority conflicts and the State Library has successfully tendered for authority work contracts with the National Library. These contracts include the maintenance of headings for New South Wales state and local government departments and agencies, as well as some Australian government departments. A new contract with the National Library covers the maintenance of New South Wales geographic names.

Another challenge faced by the Library is that a number of government enterprises are taking trading names such as Pacific Power which is the trading name of the Electricity Commission of New South Wales. Following is a quote from the 1992 annual report: "Meeting the challenge of change, Pacific Power, the new trading name for the Electricity Commission of New South Wales is a major participant in Australia's energy industry and the nation's largest provider of electric power."[3] Several government enterprises have taken trading names. The guidelines for describing an organization which has a long established name but has also adopted a trading name has been referred to the Australian Bibliographic Network's Standards Committee.

ACCESS TO GOVERNMENT PUBLICATIONS

In keeping with the Library's policy of improving access to government publications, several initiatives have been undertaken for some categories of publications.

Parliamentary papers are those annual reports and reports of government departments, declared authorities, committees and commissions presented to parliament. Over 500 parliamentary papers can be published each year by either the Australian government or the New South Wales government. Each government deposits two sets of their parliamentary papers with the Library. One set is kept together in paper number order and the parliamentary papers in the other set are catalogued individually as monographs or serials under their originating body and classified with relevant subject headings to their appropriate Dewey classification.

The Australian Bureau of Statistics is the major statistical publisher in Australia producing over 500 individual statistical titles each year, a majority of which are serial titles. Heavily used titles are kept in the Library's reference collection at the one call number, NQ319.406/4, and filed by the Australian Bureau of Statistics' own catalogue number. It is essential that all these publications be kept together because they form a unique and accessible collection of Australian statistics. Access to the publications is through the Bureau's annual publication, *Catalogue of Publications and Products*.[4] To enhance access to these reference publications the Library is downline loading the appropriate bibliographic records from ABN into URICA and inputting our holdings along with the Bureau's catalogue number. Therefore the Library is creating detailed index entries to some important statistical publications.

To improve access to government publications the Library has commenced using genre headings for "common" government publications such as statutes, parliamentary debates, parliamentary papers, etc. This enables clients of the Library to locate through the computer catalogue the parliamentary publications of all jurisdictions held by the Library.

NEW SOUTH WALES GOVERNMENT PUBLICATIONS

As part of the State Library's contribution to the Distributed National Collection, the Australian Bibliographic Network and to the Australian National Bibliography (ANB), the Library gives priority cataloguing to all New South Wales government publications. Over 95 percent of these publications are catalogued within

two weeks of receipt. Records created by the State Library on ABN
are incorporated into the publication ANB.

New South Wales government publications received by the Library are listed in the Library's publication, *New South Wales Government Publications Received in the State Library of New South
Wales.*[5] This publication is sent to 280 information agencies both in
Australia and overseas and is used primarily as a selection tool. It
includes all newly received monographs, new serial titles, annual
reports of government departments and declared authorities, and
each act and bill issued by the Parliament of New South Wales.
Annual reports, bills and acts are included because they do not have
individual entries on the Australian Bibliographic Network. The
publication is produced using DBASE IV and WORD. To increase
access to this bibliography and to the publications themselves, the
possibility of having the database available to information agencies
via the State Library's ILANET and therefore through AARNET
and the INTERNET is being considered. ILANET (Information and
Libraries Access Network) has over 600 clients and is an electronic
messaging and database access service. ILANET facilitates information exchange and interlibrary loans within Australia and
overseas, enables material to be ordered from library suppliers and
facsimiles to be sent to any Fax mail facility.

Libraries throughout Australia have access to the majority of the
Library's holdings through the Australian Bibliographic Network.
Further access to the Library's collection is provided by a dial-in
facility and a CD-ROM version of the Library's computer catalogue
is also available.

THE FUTURE

What does the future hold for the processing of government
publications in the State Library? A number of developments have
taken place or will take place in the near future which will challenge
the way the Library provides access to government publications.

Developments over the next few years include:

(1) The debates of the New South Wales parliament will become
available online. Recently the recommendations of the State Library's working party on how to provide access to electronic jour-

nals were accepted and many of the features of these recommendations will be incorporated to provide access to the debates.

(2) New South Wales statutes and important Australian Bureau of Statistics titles will be available in full text on CD-ROM. The Library has already implemented procedures for providing access to the titles on Business Periodicals on Disc, General Periodicals on Disc and Social Sciences Index Full Text. These procedures which give access to the specific titles available will be adapted to give access to these government titles on CD-ROM.

(3) Although indexes and abstracts have been available online through hosts such as Dialog for some time, the Library would like to increase client awareness and access to some of these databases such as the Federal Register. Clients who rely solely on the computer catalogue do not realize some information is available online. The Library plans to alert clients to the existence of all the services and information available to them through the computer catalogue.

(4) Another development is the provision of access to information held by government agencies in New South Wales and Australia. The number of databases held by government agencies is vast and includes such areas as land information databases containing both text and graphic information. Once physical access is provided, the next challenge is to make potential clients aware that it is available.

The issues raised in this paper show the essential role the Library has taken and will continue to take in the development and implementation of strategies for the effective use and access of government information.

NOTES

1. State Library of New South Wales. *Realising the Vision: Corporate Plan, 1991-1994.* (Sydney: The Library, 1991.)

2. State Library of New South Wales. *State Library of New South Wales Collection Development Policy.* 2nd edition. (Sydney: The Library, 1993.)

3. Pacific Power (Electricity Commission of New South Wales). *Annual Report 1992.* (Sydney: The Commission, 1992.)

4. Australian Bureau of Statistics. *Catalogue of Publications and Products 1993.* (Canberra: The Bureau, 1993.)

5. State Library of New South Wales. *New South Wales Government Publications Received in the State Library of New South Wales.* (Sydney: The Library, 1993.)

The Online Cataloguing
of Government Publications
# of Southern Africa
at the State Library, Pretoria

Ria Stoker
Barbara Kellermann

SUMMARY. The State Library in Pretoria, South Africa, receives all South African government publications as legal deposit as well as those from the independent and self-governing states within its borders. To improve access to these publications, a retrospective online cataloguing project was implemented in 1985. Some aspects having specific influences on the cataloguing are discussed.

INTRODUCTION

The State Library, Pretoria, was established in 1887, and with the promulgation of the Copyright Act of 1916, which included a section on legal deposit that was later repealed by the Legal Deposit Publications Act, of 1982, the State Library became one of the five legal deposit libraries of the then Union of South Africa.

Ria Stoker, B.A.Bibl. (UP), is Cataloguer, responsible for the retrospective cataloguing of government publications and Barbara Kellermann, B.Bibl., is editor of the South African National Bibliography, both at the State Library, P. O. Box 397, Pretoria, 0001, Republic of South Africa.

[Haworth co-indexing entry note]: "The Online Cataloguing of Government Publications of Southern Africa at the State Library, Pretoria," Stoker, Ria, and Barbara Kellermann. Co-published simultaneously in *Cataloging & Classification Quarterly* (The Haworth Press, Inc.) Vol. 18, No. 3/4, 1994, pp. 167-180; and: *Cataloging Government Publications Online* (ed: Carolyn C. Sherayko) The Haworth Press, Inc., 1994, pp. 167-180. Multiple copies of this article/chapter may be purchased from The Haworth Document Delivery Center [1-800-3-HAWORTH; 9:00 a.m. - 5:00 p.m. (EST)].

167

In the capacity of legal deposit library, the State Library developed a comprehensive collection of South African publications which includes a large collection of government publications dating back to the 19th century. This includes government publications of the former British colonies that were later to become the four provinces of the Union of South Africa in 1910, and then the Republic of South Africa in 1961. For the government publications in its collections and those received as legal deposit, the State Library through the years built up a card catalogue that was separate from the main catalogue, mainly in order to facilitate retrieval. Various cataloguing styles and rules were applied through the years (i.e., ALA rules and AACR.)

Cataloguing of the government publications was done by the general cataloguing department of the State Library, although some was also done by the staff of the *South African National Bibliography* (SANB), which was first published in 1959 and which also included records for South African government publications. Due to staff shortages in the late 1970s and early 1980s, the general cataloguing department was closed down and a gap developed in the cataloguing of government publications. The card catalogue was no longer comprehensive and therefore no longer a reliable tool for information retrieval. It was also difficult to use due to inconsistencies in filing, the application of various cataloguing rules, and the variety of entries and headings for the government departments and institutions.

In 1978 the State Library acquired the DOBIS/LIBIS computer system (Dortmunder Bibliothekssytem/Leuvens Integraal Bibliotheek Systeem), and started in late 1981 with online cataloguing. Government publications, together with all other legal deposit material, were catalogued by the division responsible for the compilation of the SANB, which meant that only the new and currently published government publications were added to the database.

The State Library's collection of South African government publications is one of the most complete in the country. To have it all accessible in one catalogue or database would have tremendous advantages and in 1985 it was decided to commence a project of retrospective cataloguing in order to place the whole collection on the computer database. At present, the collection of government publications of the State Library consists of approximately 108,000 bound volumes, monographs, serials, and monographic series.

The retrospective work is being done at a rate of about 3,300 records per year by one full-time staff member, and about forty percent of the work was completed by the end of 1992. At a rough estimate, the collection of publications of the central government of South Africa should be completed by the year 1999, while the cataloguing of the publications of the four provincial administrations, the four independent states (Transkei, Bophuthatswana, Venda and Ciskei) and the six self-governing states (Gazankulu, KaNgwane, KwaNdebele, KwaZulu, Lebowa and QwaQwa) should take another five years. Some of the current titles of the latter have already been catalogued. With the retrospective cataloguing of all these publications, some interesting facts became evident.

The history of South Africa and the constitutional development had a marked effect on the kind of government publications that were published since 1652 (when the Dutch landed at the Cape and established an outpost for the sea route to the East). The oldest publications are only available as transcripts from the State Archives, but from 1806, with the second British invasion, more publications were published and distributed. The Colony of the Cape of Good Hope then started with the publishing of the first *Government Gazette*. From the 1850s each of the four colonies had its own parliament ("Volksraad") with its own government publications.

In 1910 these colonies were merged to form the Union of South Africa with the Parliament consisting of the House of Assembly and the Senate, as well as the Provincial Councils for each of the four provinces of the Cape of Good Hope, Natal, Orange Free State and Transvaal. The South Africa Act of 1909, the constitution of the country, included an entrenched clause decreeing English and Dutch as the two official languages. Dutch, however, was developing into the new language Afrikaans, and in 1925 Afrikaans replaced Dutch as one of the official languages. Having two official languages meant that all government publications had to be published in both languages, but this clause was not always adhered to. Today it is very difficult to ascertain whether a publication was indeed published in both languages.

Initially the government publications were published separately in English and Afrikaans (or Dutch), but since approximately 1942, only one bilingual publication was published (perhaps due to paper shortages during the Second World War). At present, government publications are published in all forms: bilingually (usually tête-bêche), or separately, or in one language only. From 1938 onwards, there was a significant interest in Afrikaans and it was obvious that more publications were published in Afrikaans than before, and more were specifically bilingual.

Since the 1970s after the establishment of the self-governing and independent states, a new kind of government publication emerged. Each state has its own parliament (or legislative assembly), and the vernacular of each area is one of the official languages of that state (e.g., Zulu is spoken in the KwaZulu Legislative Assembly). English is the second official language in eight of the states, with Afrikaans as a third official language in seven of the states. The publications of these states are therefore in many cases multilingual. The State Library receives all these government publications as legal deposit; in the case of the four independent states in terms of an agreement between the governments. This collection constitutes about ten percent of the government publications in the State Library's possession.

The cataloguing of the government publications on the DOBIS/LIBIS system now makes the collection more accessible to a greater group of users. There exists as yet no comprehensive subject index to the government publications of South Africa, although subject headings have been assigned to these records since the beginning of 1992 by the staff of the SANB. These latter records are usually only the latest government publications included in the current issues of the national bibliography, and retrospective indexing or subject analysis has not yet been planned. The Department of National Education compiled and published a number of bibliographies of the publications of a few selected government departments in the 1970s and early 1980s.

The government publications are distributed by a number of state departments on their own behalf, while others are distributed by the Government Printer's offices in Pretoria and Cape Town on behalf of the departments. The departments, however, are responsible for the legal deposit of the publications.

The government publications are catalogued as follows:

* serials as an open entry with the library's holdings given in a copy record (this includes annual publications such as annual reports, estimates of expenditure, reports of the Auditor-General, etc.);
* individual records for issues in monographic series and monographs.

Government publications for which the records have to appear in the current issue of the SANB have to be included in the somewhat lengthy processing of all the publications catalogued and classified for the SANB, which takes five weeks. The publications not included in this process are returned to the shelves immediately after cataloguing on the computer.

THE DOBIS/LIBIS COMPUTER SYSTEM

DOBIS/LIBIS is an integrated online system that is used by the State Library for the compilation and production of the SANB, and as an in-house system, used among others by the reference and interlending sections to provide them with access to the State Library's collections. The version of DOBIS/LIBIS is 1.4, and it has been adapted to the South African MARC format, known as SAMARC. Producing the printed SANB from DOBIS/LIBIS has an influence on some aspects of cataloguing and classification such as adding labels to the classification number entries on the classification file to provide the captions in the printed bibliography.

Although DOBIS/LIBIS provides the State Library with many of the advantages of computerisation, such as a wider range of access points, immediacy of access, and duplication of records for speedier cataloguing, there are some disadvantages as well such as limited length of records. The SAMARC format has also been extended in some areas of the bibliographic description to make provision for records in more than one language.

The ISBN was one of the added access points that the computer provided. In creating a record on DOBIS/LIBIS the cataloguer is forced to refer to the various authority files for the access points.

Names, if already present in the authority file, can be pulled into the record, which eliminates time-consuming retyping and the possibility of typing errors. The same applies to titles, publishers and the ISBN. For the latter this has the added advantage that it enables the cataloguer to check for duplicate ISBNs.

The State Library is the national ISBN agency for South Africa. The ISBN facilities on DOBIS/LIBIS are also used for the administration of the ISBN system, which includes picking up incorrectly printed ISBNs in publications, and passing this information on to the publisher. Especially with government publications which have a number of recurring or similar titles it is important that the ISBN be correct, as it is an aid in identifying publications uniquely. With this aim in mind, there is close co-operation between the cataloguers and the staff of the ISBN agency.

Since the State Library is both a legal deposit library and the ISBN agency, entries on the publishers' authority file on DOBIS/LIBIS have been extended to include information such as addresses, country of location and ISBN identifiers, and in the authority file notes the telephone or fax numbers and names of contact persons at the various organisations. South Africa has a Government Printer that assigns ISBNs with his own identifier to government publications, but there are also some government departments that prefer to have their own ISBN identifiers, and therefore their own range of ISBNs. Continuity at departments in the assigning of ISBNs can become a problem with changes in staff, and having the ISBN identifier added to the department's entry in the publisher's file enables the State library to keep track of inconsistencies or errors.

RETROSPECTIVE CATALOGUING

Retrospective online cataloguing can be done by copying the existing card catalogue records onto the computer system. At the State Library it was found unpractical as the card catalogue of government publications was no longer a reliable retrieval tool. The decision was taken to recatalogue the whole collection by physically retrieving the complete set of every series from the shelves, checking the series for missing numbers, requesting missing issues from the South African Book Exchange Centre (SABEC), and after recataloguing, having the complete series bound. Monographs are also retrieved from the shelves for recataloguing.

For the retrospective cataloguing, the duplication facility on DO-BIS/LIBIS was found to be a very useful tool. For monographic series where the individual publications are much alike, the previous record is duplicated for a new record, requiring only certain elements to be changed, such as title, ISBN number, series number, the number of pages and the date. The author or issuing body (the government department) and the publisher remain the same. This means that a large number of similar publications can be catalogued per day, up to sixty items by one cataloguer. The retrospective cataloguing project also brought with it the opportunity of verifying name changes and mergers of departments through the years, as reflected in annual reports. Older records on DOBIS/LIBIS which were incompletely entered in the early years after acquiring the system, could be upgraded.

A primary function of the State Library is the bibliographic control of South African publications. In spite of this, there is no single complete bibliography of South African government publications, although bibliographies for certain sections of the publishing output exist, and the national bibliography (SANB) lists government publications published after 1959, when the SANB was first issued. The retrospective cataloguing project is therefore an opportunity to compile a complete record of all South African government publications on one database.

LANGUAGES

The diversity of languages in South Africa as used in the central, provincial and other governments is perhaps the most significant aspect which influences the cataloguing of these publications. With two official languages (English and Afrikaans) most of the publications issued by the central government are available in both languages. Cataloguers at the State Library are expected to be bilingual as far as English and Afrikaans are concerned, as the SANB maintains a bilingual catalogue, with entries in both languages for the name access points of most government departments and institutes. Bilingual publications usually also have a longer bibliographic description and more added access points, which can become a problem as a computer record is limited as to its length.

Bilingual publications in South Africa are of course not restricted to government publications. Publishers issue them in various ways with either one bilingual title page or more than one title page. Most of the libraries in South Africa use AACR2 (now AACR2R) as their cataloguing standard, and in 1987 the Subcommittee for Cataloguing and Classification of the South African Institute for Librarianship and Information Science looked at the AACR2 rules (specifically rule 1.0H),[1] and issued the following additional guidelines for dealing with bilingual or multilingual publications with more than one title page:

- if the text is in only one language, or one language is predominant, choose the title page in that language as the chief source of information, (AACR2 rule 1.0H 4(a);
- if no one language is predominant, choose the first occurring title page as the chief source of information, regardless of whether the different title pages are facing or following each other, or are distributed throughout the publication;
- for tête-bêche publications, choose the title page that is in the language of the catalogue as the chief source of information, and provide information on the other title in a note, as well as all the necessary access points.[2]

Although having a bilingual catalogue, the SANB division decided to create only one record for tête-bêche publications, using the English title page as the chief source of information, with the Afrikaans title given in a note and as an access point.

When cataloguing, for example, an annual report of a department of the central government, the cataloguer sometimes encounters the following:

- two language versions published separately: as Annual report in English, and the Afrikaans or Dutch version with varying titles such as Rapport, Jaarrapport, Verslag or Jaarverslag; and/or
- at a certain point (approximately 1942) some annual reports began to be published jointly, with the languages of the parallel titles alternating each year.

In order to cope with these and similar problems, a separate serial record is created for each changed title proper. Where the wording of the titles of the bilingual publications remains the same but the order of the titles on the title page alternates each year, one record is created based on the earliest issue and the alternation explained in a note (according to a Library of Congress Rule Interpretation).[3]

On DOBIS/LIBIS the different records for one serial publication are linked chronologically, with the State Library's holdings for each title provided in the copy records. Unfortunately retrieval is sometimes cumbersome.

The cataloguing of the trilingual or sometimes multilingual publications of the independent and self-governing states is more intricate. The philological structures of the nine indigenous languages differ vastly from each other, so that knowledge of one language does not necessarily enable one to understand the other languages.

Where all the languages are published together in one document, the meaning can be derived from the English or Afrikaans titles given on the title page. Where the different language versions are published separately, however, the cataloguer would not be able to identify the indigenous version unless the publications were received simultaneously. Title changes in the indigenous languages can present a real problem. As the number of cataloguers at the State Library conversant in one or more of the indigenous languages is limited, staff members in other departments of the library are consulted as to title or content of a publication.

The publications of the independent and self-governing states are similar to those of the central government in that they are either printed separately in each language, or with languages together: two languages bound together with two following title pages, or bound tête-bêche, or all three languages bound together in one consecutive sequence with only one title page in one language, with no indication that the text consists of more than one language. All these variations could occur in the same series.

Inconsistencies in title, language, format and name of the department often compel the cataloguer to create numerous records for one serial, even to the extent of one record per annual issue of a report. These records are linked chronologically.

The DOBIS/LIBIS system permutes on the significant words in

titles and names to facilitate searching on these words. Insignificant words such as articles and prepositions are entered on a stop list to prevent permutation. In the indigenous languages in South Africa, a classifying prefix is often grammatically linked to the noun, with the result that these prefixes cannot be entered on a stop list for non-permutation purposes, and searching on the pure form of the noun is not possible. At present English is mostly used for retrieval purposes.

The indigenous languages Northern Sotho and Venda make use of diacritical symbols that are not provided in the DOBIS/LIBIS system. These include the circumflex below the letter (e.g., ḓ) and the dot above the letter (e.g.,ṅ), which indicate the pronunciation. Titles and names including these diacritics are entered on the database without them with no adverse effect on retrieval, as their omission does not change the meaning of the word.

ACCESS POINTS

Computerising the government publications catalogue enabled the State Library to build up an authority name list for the names of government departments. Like many other countries, South Africa suffers from the malaise of name changes as far as government departments are concerned. One example is the present Department of Agriculture, which in the period from 1910 when it was established until 1982, went through seven name changes, split into three departments and consolidated again into the Department of Agriculture in 1982.

In the name authority file on DOBIS/LIBIS, the name changes are linked by cross-references, indicating the chronology as well as translated forms in other official languages. The authority files notes on DOBIS/LIBIS include information on dates of establishment or cessation, dates of name changes, descriptions of mergers or splitting, and references to the official notices on new names of government departments that are published in the South African *Government Gazette*. The State Library as the national bibliographic agency for South Africa, has the duty of keeping track of government department names through the receipt of all government publications by legal deposit, and by regularly perusing the *Government Gazette* to pick up any relevant notices of name changes.

Since January 1984 South Africa has had a tricameral parliament, consisting of the House of Assembly, the House of Delegates and the House of Representatives. The departments residing under these three houses mostly have the same names. Although rule 24.18 in AACR2R provides for the shortening of a name entered subordinately through the omission of intervening subdivisions,[4] we found that it could not always be applied to these particular cases. Most of the hierarchy had to be included in the name so as to distinguish between the different Houses of Parliament and the result was sometimes a long and cumbersome entry (e.g., South Africa. Administration: House of Assembly. Directorate Cultural Affairs. Homemaking Division.) (Full hierarchy: South Africa. Administration: House of Assembly. Department of Education and Culture. Directorate Cultural Affairs. Homemaking Division).

There is a tendency in South Africa to name important Commissions of Enquiry or their published reports after the chairman of the commission, and it was found that library users ask for them under these names. With the online cataloguing of the various commissions' reports it was decided to add the chairman's name in a note, as well as giving it as an access point.

Government publications which are published in a serial format are given a serial entry on DOBIS/LIBIS. The State Library's reference section, however, found that the individual fiscal numbers given to the individual issues of some serials such as estimates or annual reports, were important access points for the users. In the period of the Union of South Africa (1910-1961), publications of the government departments had UG (Union Government) numbers with the date attached (e.g., UG 5-1917) or given as UG 5-'17. When the Union became the Republic of South Africa, the series was changed to RP (Republic Publications) numbers (e.g., RP 10-1971 or RP 10-'71). To aid the user, it was decided to add these individual numbers to the serial records as access points.

Unfortunately, the particular field on DOBIS/LIBIS provided for these numbers is limited to fourteen access points per record. Where a series consists of more than fourteen issues, we considered the contraction of numbers into a single or a few access points (UG

1 1916-1918), but the same number was not always used for the consecutive annual issues of the same report. Some reports are issued with a different number every year (the numbers are assigned chronologically as reports are published), and we have been exploring the method of duplicating records to enable us to add the numbers of the next fourteen consecutive issues as access points. The disadvantage is a proliferation of the same record, but with the user's needs in mind we are continuing with this practice at present.

Publications in the South African treaty series sometimes have extremely long titles, or have lengthy titles and are bilingual. Since title access points on DOBIS/LIBIS are allowed only 250 characters, the handling of lengthy title information is a problem. An example of such a title:

Agreement between the Government of the Republic of South Africa and the Government of the Republic of Bophuthatswana for the recovery of amounts payable by the Government of the Republic of South Africa with respect to insurance business of the South African Special Risks Insurance Association in the Republic of Bophuthatswana.

Rule 1.1B4 in AACR2R permits the cataloguer to abridge the title, provided this can be done without omission of the first five words and without loss of essential information.[5] The limited number of characters allowed on DOBIS/LIBIS sometimes compels the cataloguer to do this where loss of information is inevitable. With abridgement a title like the example given above will lose some of its retrievability, as the significant part of the title is in the last fifteen words. To aid the user, the State Library provides the full title in a note in the record, although this title cannot be used as an access point.

For lengthy titles of publications such as "Estimates of expenditure" it was decided to drop that part of the title indicating the period covered by the publication, from the title access point, even though it is supposed to be read as part of the title. For example, in the title *Estimates of the additional expenditure to be defrayed from revenue and loan funds and the Defence Endowment Account dur-*

ing the year ending 31st March . . . , the words "during the year ending 31st March . . . " are left out in the title access point.

MULTILEVEL DESCRIPTION

For the records that are included in the SANB for monographs that are part of a set, rule 13.6 of AACR2R is applied,[6] and multilevel descriptions consisting of two levels are entered on DOBIS/ LIBIS. This applies to both government publications and ordinary monographs. Records of more than two levels were found to be cumbersome and not feasible.

For the internal processing of the output programming for the SANB it was necessary to set a limit to the length of records (2,000 characters), which meant that we had to limit the number of second-level records linked to any one first-level record. This limit was set at fifteen links. To accommodate further second-level records a duplicate of the first-level record is created.

In terms of the existing output programming for the SANB, titles added as access points to second level records do not appear in the index of the printed SANB volumes, and significant titles of parts therefore are lost as access points to users of the printed SANB. The SANB has only been produced from DOBIS/LIBIS from 1988 onwards, and the previous batch programme that was used did not have this problem. To find a solution to this we have been investigating the alternative of creating individual records applying the AACR2R rule 1.1B9[7] where feasible, instead of using the multilevel method. This enables us to add the title of the part as a significant access point in order to have it included as an entry in the index of the printed SANB.

CONCLUSION

Despite some obstacles encountered along the way, the retrospective cataloguing project for government publications at the State Library is steadily showing progress. An added advantage is the thorough knowledge of the collection built up by the cataloguer responsible for the project, which proves to be of great help to users' enquiries at the State Library's reference section.

NOTES

1. *Anglo-American Cataloging Rules,* 2nd ed. (Chicago: American Library Association, 1978), p. 16.

2. South African Institute for Librarianship and Information Science. Subcommittee for Cataloguing and Classification. Minutes of seventh meeting held on 5 August 1987, Appendix 1.

3. *Cataloging Service Bulletin* no. 50 (Fall 1990), p. 33. Library of Congress Rule Interpretation 21.2C.

4. *Anglo-American Cataloging Rules,* 2nd ed., 1988 rev. (Chicago: American Library Association, 1988), p. 465.

5. Ibid. 1.1B4, p. 19.

6. Ibid. 13.6, p. 302.

7. Ibid. 1.1B9, p. 20.

Ball State University Libraries and OCLC GOVDOC Service

Diane Calvin

SUMMARY. Ball State University Libraries began adding records for depository government publications to its online catalog in mid-1990. Marcive was chosen for retrospective records, and OCLC GOVDOC Service for ongoing records. GOVDOC records were compatible with NOTIS, the Libraries' online system. The GOVDOC profiling ensured that only records for documents selected from the Government Printing Office (GPO) would be received. The few problems encountered since beginning the Service are the result of GPO cataloging practices. After three years, the GOVDOC Service continues to provide an efficient, cost-effective way to add records to an online catalog.

BACKGROUND

Bracken Library of Ball State University has been a selective federal depository since 1960. Although the percentage of items selected was once as high as 65 percent, the library currently selects 47 percent. For fiscal year 1993, this meant an addition of 2,511 paper titles, 4,092 microfiche titles, and 91 electronic (diskette and CD-ROM) titles.

Diane Calvin is Government Publications Librarian at Ball State University, Muncie, IN.

The author wishes to thank Sharon Roberts for her help in the preparation of this article.

[Haworth co-indexing entry note]: "Ball State University Libraries and OCLC GOVDOC Service," Calvin, Diane. Co-published simultaneously in *Cataloging & Classification Quarterly* (The Haworth Press, Inc.) Vol. 18, No. 3/4, 1994, pp. 181-188; and: *Cataloging Government Publications Online* (ed: Carolyn C. Sherayko) The Haworth Press, Inc., 1994, pp. 181-188. Multiple copies of this article/chapter may be purchased from The Haworth Document Delivery Center [1-800-3-HAWORTH; 9:00 a.m. - 5:00 p.m. (EST)].

181

From 1960 to 1970, most depository monographs and many depository serials were cataloged and placed in the library's general collection. After 1970, virtually all documents received were housed uncataloged in the government publications collection. Since the Government Printing Office (GPO) began distributing depository microfiche in the late 1970's, these fiche have been housed uncataloged in the library's microforms collection.

In mid-1988, the library began exploring the idea of adding document records to its Carlyle online public access catalog (OPAC). A committee was formed to investigate catalog record sources and to calculate the monetary and personnel costs of various options. The committee consisted of the Head of Cataloging, the Government Publications Librarian, a serials cataloger, and the Director of Automated Library Systems.

VENDOR SELECTION

The committee read extensively in the current literature, then contacted two vendors of document catalog records (Brodart and Marcive) for price and service information. The committee also wrote and distributed a survey asking other libraries about their experiences in loading document records into an online catalog. After several months' work, the committee recommended purchasing retrospective and ongoing records from Marcive. At that point, however, the committee's work was put on hold while the library switched its online catalog from the Carlyle system to the NOTIS system.

By the time the committee resumed its work in the spring of 1990, OCLC had announced its GOVDOC Service to supply current records of depository publications. The committee investigated the new service and modified its earlier recommendation, selecting the GOVDOC Service for current acquisitions while retaining the earlier recommendation of using Marcive-supplied records for the retrospective collection.

RATIONALE

The Ball State University Libraries had subscribed to OCLC since early 1976, and with good results. We knew their records would be compatible with NOTIS. The committee's earlier research indicated that cataloging documents individually by searching OCLC would be too expensive and labor-intensive. An ongoing service based on a profile method seemed more cost-effective, and pricing structures at that time favored OCLC GOVDOC over the Marcive service.

PROFILING

The profiling experience for the GOVDOC Service was fairly painless because we had just completed the Marcive profile for retrospective records. That procedure had required a thorough review of our depository item number cards and shelflist records.

For the Marcive profile, we determined when an item number had been added to and/or dropped from our depository selection and indicated by location code which item numbers had documents that were housed outside Government Publications Service, namely in the Maps or Microforms collections. Once the Marcive profile was finished, the same information was used to complete the OCLC GOVDOC profile.

OCLC provided us with a printed list of item numbers that we currently selected extracted from the GPO item selection records (see Figure 1). As with the Marcive profile, we typed our local location codes next to item numbers for documents housed outside Government Publications Service. Item numbers for serials were excluded from the profile by indicating them with an "X" on the profile sheets.[1] This profiling paperwork was completed in a few days.

Both Marcive and OCLC GOVDOC allowed only one location code per item number. This was a dilemma for an item number that corresponded to multiple titles housed in more than one area. We chose to use the location that housed most of the titles. Since then, we have created local procedures for changing location codes for new documents housed elsewhere. Another dilemma resulted from GPO's practice of issuing titles in either paper or microfiche format under the same item number. Again, we chose the location that we expected would house most of the documents. As new records arrive, government publications staff change any erroneous locations.

FIGURE 1

GOVDOC Order Form   Page: 2

These are the items you are currently receiving from GPO. If you have new item numbers which do not appear on this list, please add them to the last page of this form. After the initial file is set up the library is responsible for notifying OCLC about any changes. This can be done on a Product Status Change Report Form from your network.
- If the GOVDOC Default Holding Library Code (HLC) is to be assigned, leave the HLC space blank.
- If the GOVDOC Default Holding Library Code (HLC) and others are to be assigned to an item, all must be listed.
- If an item is not to be included in the profile place an 'X' in the blank.

Sample: (assume XYZA is the GOVDOC default HLC)

Item Code	HLC(s)	Item Code	HLC(s)
1234		1234-B-01	*X*
	(blank will use default)		(will not be inlcuded in GOVDOC)
1234-A	*XYZB*	1234-C-56	*XYZA, XYZB*
	(use this non-default HLC)		(use default HLC and another)

∙ ∙

Item Code	HLC(s)	Item Code	HLC(s)
0001	X	0014-A	
0003		0015	IBSF
0004		0017	
0006	X	0018	X
0006-K	X	0018-A	X
0006-R	X	0018-C	X
0009		0019	X
0010		0021-B	X
0011		0021-D	X
0012		0021-E	X
0013-A		0021-H	X
0013-A-01	X	0021-I	X
0013-H-01	IBSF	0021-K	X
0013-H-02		0021-L	X

Used with the permission of OCLC

In mid-August 1990, the first GOVDOC tape arrived and was loaded into NOTIS with no problems.

ISSUES

Maps

Map records posed the biggest problem, once the profiling was completed and GOVDOC records began to arrive. Large numbers of map records containing the same OCLC control number were being added to the database because of GPO's practice of modifying and reusing the set record for each state to create availability records for the individual quadrangles within the state. This situation made it difficult for Cataloging Services to identify duplicate records in the local database. It also resulted in many identical or nearly identical online catalog displays, which confused library patrons. We dropped map item records from the OCLC GOVDOC profile in late 1991; we will catalog current depository maps on an individual basis in a future project.[2]

Time Gaps

There is a time gap between receipt of a depository document and the arrival of its bibliographic record on the OCLC GOVDOC tape. The gap is usually from two to six months, although occasionally a record for a one- to three-year old document appears on the tape. The OCLC GOVDOC Service has no control over the time lag since GPO is responsible for creation of the catalog record and its addition to the OCLC online union catalog.

As yet, we have not automated our check-in procedure, and have no link between new depository acquisitions and the online public catalog. This means new documents can go undetected by most users until catalog records are loaded. This is a definite disadvantage, as many government agency and commission reports are highly publicized and therefore in demand by patrons. Often, the only access to a document during this time lag is a government publications employee's memory of the document's receipt and its Superintendent of Documents (SuDoc) classification number.

This time lag has been shortened in part by subscribing to a CD-ROM, the Government Documents Catalog Service (GDCS) from Auto-Graphics Incorporated. The GDCS is a clone of GPO's *Monthly Catalog of United States Publications*, and includes bibliographic records of documents cataloged by GPO since July 1976. In early 1993, Auto-Graphics enhanced the GDCS by adding document entries from the daily depository shipping lists. The GDCS now includes complete bibliographic records for cataloged documents plus brief records for the documents distributed but not yet cataloged on OCLC.

The brief records include the Sudoc number, title, item number, and shipping list number for each document. *All* items on a shipping list are included, individual issues of serials as well as monographs. This brief entry information is indexed and thus can be easily searched. The title or keyword search is the only one likely to be of use to the general public, but a SuDoc search would yield new titles from a specific agency. Granted, this is not the full author/title/subject/keyword approach available for fully cataloged documents, but it does provide more timely access. The time lag between distribution of the shipping lists and the lists' appearance on GDCS seems to be about six weeks. Auto-Graphics deletes these shipping list entries after six months on the GDCS in the belief that GPO will have produced a catalog record by then.[3]

Access

Bracken Library's Government Publications Service does what it can to alert patrons to new documents not yet included in the online catalog. Selected documents on popular or topical issues are kept on a new publications display near the documents collection. The documents are moved to their regular shelving location when the catalog records arrive. Government Publications Service also maintains in-house bibliographies on topics such as AIDS, smoking, and the homeless. New documents on these topics are added immediately, making them available to any patron who uses the bibliographies.

Circulation

The time lag between a document's receipt and the receipt of its catalog record has also affected automated circulation. All new documents have a random barcode code inserted. When a new monograph has a catalog record, the government publications librarian attaches an item record containing the document's barcode number to the catalog record for circulation purposes. Except for those new monographs placed on display, item records are not routinely created for documents that lack cataloging records. But if a new monograph is presented for circulation prior to its receiving a catalog record, a temporary unlinked item record is created for it by a circulation employee. Later, when the catalog record for the document is received, the government publications librarian deletes the unlinked item record and creates a permanent item record.

Many government publications serials do not yet have their holdings on OPAC, and do not have linked item records; therefore, government publications staff often create temporary unlinked item records for popular serial issues as they are received. As with monographs, an unlinked serial presented for circulation has a temporary item record created for it at that time by a circulation employee.

Holdings Gap

Because Ball State used different vendors to acquire retrospective and current records, a space of time between the cut-off date of Marcive records and the beginning of OCLC GOVDOC records occurred. This meant about four months of documents issued in early to mid-1990 received no catalog records in either tapeload. Government publications staff identified many of these by spot-checking entries from the mid- and late-1990's *Monthly Catalog of United States Government Publications*. We photocopied the document entries and forwarded them to Cataloging Services, which provided machine-readable catalog records for us through our regular OCLC service. This proved to be a satisfactory way of closing the gap.

CONCLUSION

Our past experience with OCLC was good, and was one factor for choosing the GOVDOC service. The customer support at OCLC is excellent.

It is true that cataloging a documents collection in-house would provide the best match between holdings and online catalog records, and would ensure correct location codes. But this is a very time-consuming and expensive method of adding records. The GOVDOC service provides automatic addition of records at a reasonable cost.

The GOVDOC profiling ensures we receive catalog records for only those documents selected from GPO. In the past three years of service, we have observed no problems in the match between the profile item numbers and the records received. The only mismatches are minor ones, and are not errors on OCLC's part: the mismatches generally occur when we receive a record for a missing document that we selected but did not receive from GPO. Changing the profile is an easy matter: we change it once yearly, when item numbers are added and dropped from our GPO selection.

Overall, we are pleased with the OCLC GOVDOC service. We believe the advantages for GOVDOC that have been outlined in this article outweigh any disadvantages for the service.

NOTES

1. We excluded item numbers for serials because at the time of our profiling, choosing them meant we would receive dozens of monthly availability records. However, OCLC GOVDOC can now offer collective records for serials.

2. Since December 1991, GPO has changed its map cataloging practices and now creates separate map cataloging records, each with its own OCLC control number. (See *Administrative Notes*, v. 12, no. 20, p. 4-5.)

3. Vendors such as Bernan and Marcive offer similar records for items distributed but not cataloged, and also sell temporary shelflist cards.

University of California, San Diego's Experience Creating and Updating Machine-Readable GPO Records

Joanne Donovan
Roberta A. Corbin

SUMMARY. One of the major collections for which libraries are beginning to automate processes is U.S. government documents. The conversion is generally in two parts: conversion of the retrospective collection to machine-readable records and the creation of online records for the ongoing new titles received. Various options for automating document collections are currently available. UC San Diego selected a commercial vendor (Marcive, Inc.) and is working with that vendor and our automated system vendor (Innovative Interfaces, Inc.) to: (1) improve bibliographic access to the collections; (2) increase the efficiency of interfaces between the automated processes and the library staff; and (3) to reduce the staff time and effort required to process these materials.

Once a library's initial database has been loaded using tapes from its bibliographic utility (e.g., OCLC, RLIN), libraries begin to look at other collections which are not reflected in the online public catalog (OPAC). For the University of California, San Diego (UCSD), a major collection falling into this category was U.S. government doc-

Joanne Donovan is Assistant Head, Acquisitions, Documents and Serials and Roberta Corbin is Acting Head, Library Systems, both at the University of California, San Diego.

[Haworth co-indexing entry note]: "University of California, San Diego's Experience Creating and Updating Machine-Readable GPO Records," Donovan, Joanne, and Roberta A. Corbin. Co-published simultaneously in *Cataloging & Classification Quarterly* (The Haworth Press, Inc.) Vol. 18, No. 3/4, 1994, pp. 189-195; and: *Cataloging Government Publications Online* (ed: Carolyn C. Sherayko) The Haworth Press, Inc., 1994, pp. 189-195. Multiple copies of this article/chapter may be purchased from The Haworth Document Delivery Center [1-800-3-HAWORTH; 9:00 a.m. - 5:00 p.m. (EST)].

189

uments. Automation of documents was done in two phases—one to get machine-readable records for the retrospective collection and one to provide records for current receipts on an ongoing basis.

BACKGROUND

UCSD became a selective Federal Depository in late 1963, selecting approximately 92 percent of documents available from the Government Printing Office (GPO). At the time of our proposal to provide online access to the collection, we were an 82 percent selective, and the collection contained approximately 150,000 titles. In 1991/92, 8,200 new titles were received on deposit. The collection, as with many document collections, was separate and uncataloged, arranged by the Superintendent of Documents (SuDoc) classification numbers. Bibliographic access to the depository collection was dependent on the department's manual shelflist and printed indexes. Many library users were thus unaware of the vast resources available in this collection.

The implementation of the local OPAC (Innovative Interfaces, Inc. [I.I.I.] Innopac system) combined with the availability of machine-readable records for federal documents led to the decision to incorporate the federal documents into the OPAC. A proposal to mainstream the collection, providing equal access with other library materials was developed in 1989.

VENDOR SELECTION

Although machine-readable records had been available since mid-1976, few libraries had local systems on which to load them at that time. In addition, GPO cataloging policies and a variety of technical difficulties with the tapes provided major obstacles to loading the records. By the mid-1980s more options were beginning to appear. Options available to us were:

- Catalog or convert federal documents on a utility;
- Purchase GPO tapes from the Library of Congress;
- Purchase tapes from a commercial source.

Cost was a major factor in the decision to select a commercial vendor. In-house cataloging of a collection of this size was prohibitively expensive, and staffing was simply not available for a manual conversion project. Purchase and loading of GPO tapes from the Library of Congress would require extensive programming, and the tapes had many errors and contained availability records (a new record for each serial issue, parts of sets, etc.) rather than a single catalog record appropriate for the type of material.

Two major commercial sources of the tapes were Marcive and Brodart. OCLC GovDoc Service was not available in 1990, and the GPO, itself, did not begin providing cataloging tapes until 1991. In 1989 Marcive had sponsored a project for cleaning up the GPO tapes: deleting unwanted duplicate and availability records; correcting tags, item, and SuDoc numbers; and running name, subject, and series headings against the Library of Congress authority file. Marcive offered this version of the GPO file for sale for a reasonable price, and this is what UCSD purchased.

Once the vendor selection was complete, a contract was sent to the library by Marcive. The contract was a challenge, from understanding tape specifications, obtaining vendor permission to have our records on the University-wide system (Melvyl) to tracking the contract through the campus bureaucracy. Fortunately, cataloging and systems staff were available for consultation, and Business Services followed the process through the campus contract procedures.

PROFILING

With the contract negotiation complete, we began the next step—profiling the collection (i.e., matching our holdings with the Marcive GPO tapes). The GPO tapes contain all titles issued by the Government Printing Office 1976 to date, but as a selective depository we received only a portion of these items. Profiling options included receiving all GPO records from 1976 to date or acquiring only those records for materials we owned based upon our collection profile. Resources were not available to inventory the collection. Our profiling match was based on GPO item numbers rather than SuDoc numbers (which would have been much more expensive). While this method does not allow for perfect matching of holdings and records, it is a feasible method for large collections. Additional considerations in developing a profiling strategy concerned the treatment of voluminous series such as bills, House/Senate reports, slip treaties and reprints; maps and posters; serials; and multiple locations and formats.

In addition to collection profiling done to insure we would get only the bibliographic records for those materials we select for deposit, the profiling included setting up separate OCLC location codes (MARC field 049) for printed materials, microforms, and maps so these materials could be assigned appropriate location codes and item types for our local Innopac system's circulation module. In order to facilitate OPAC indexing and later processing, Marcive agreed to place the last 086 field (i.e., the latest SuDoc classification) in the bibliographic record in an 099 call number field with a special indicator so these call numbers could be indexed separately in Innopac and be moved into the call number field in later processing.

RECORD PROCESSING FOR TAPELOADING

Once the profiling was complete, the next step was to have our data conversion vendor (Amigos Bibliographic Council) program to prepare the Marcive tapes for loading. This step was necessary because it was our intention to create both bibliographic and item records upon load into our Innopac system. This process allowed both easier immediate ability to charge items out through the circulation module and, with the exception of serials, to send the records to the University of California Division of Library Automation (DLA) for loading into the University's union catalog, Melvyl. Records must have item or summary holdings information to load into Melvyl from our local system.

Amigos processed the records to create a standard 940 field for each of the three 049 codes described above. This allowed the load program to create the appropriate Innopac fixed fields including the branch location, material type (e.g., monograph, serial), and government publication code. In addition, a 945 field was devised to provide the needed information for Innopac to create item records containing the appropriate item type, shelving location, and call number during the load of the tapes. Even though the holdings information was not always complete because only one item record was created for each title, it did provide, for non-serials, a record which could be sent to DLA for the Melvyl catalog and easily charged out through the circulation module in our local system.

Serials are slightly different since they require check-in records with a summary holdings statement in order for DLA to load them into the periodicals database of the Melvyl catalog. Due to the large number of serials and lack of staff, we have not yet been able to enter all of our serial holdings. We currently have a project with I.I.I. to create a generic check-in record for the retrospective inactive serials, so they can also be loaded into the Melvyl catalog.

POST-LOAD CLEANUP

It is axiomatic that what one does not clean up before the load, one will have to clean up afterwards. We are still cleaning up, in part due to the nature of the match and in part to the nature of the cataloging records. GPO cataloging practices and the idiosyncratic nature of some documents are major challenges in a project of this type. Cataloging decisions need to be made concerning the treatment of multiple classification numbers, serials within series, mother-daughter records, authorities, and the time lag between receipt of a document and the corresponding record (e.g., how long to hold a document without a record.)

CURRENT CATALOGING

Initially, procedures for receiving the current Marcive GPO records for U.S. government documents included UCSD's staff keying a brief bibliographic record which contained the 086 field (the SuDoc number). The Marcive tape was sent to Amigos for creation of the item record information. The records were loaded into our local system using a profile to overlay on the existing brief record matching on the SuDoc number. At the beginning, our Innopac system ran Innovacq (the acquisitions module) and Innopac on separate machines, so keying a brief bibliographic record on Innovacq would have to be followed by keying an item record on Innopac. The easier solution was to key only the brief bibliographic record on Innovacq and then to create the item record as part of the load of the full cataloging records. It was thought that this would reduce workload for the staff in Documents, but as a result of not having a barcoded item record, the Circulation staff had a difficult time identifying the correct bibliographic record for charge outs during the three- to four-month period while we waited for the cataloged records. There were so many mis-matches that it turned out to be more advantageous for the item records to be keyed at the time the brief records were created and the barcode number entered into the record. This became more reasonable once the Innovacq and Innopac systems were merged into one.

The merged system enabled the procedures to change, eliminating the Amigos processing since default settings could be used for the bibliographic record Innopac fixed fields. Furthermore, the records which did not overlay could be identified by a special code which both highlighted them for the staff doing the processing and prevented them from going to the Melvyl catalog.

While these new procedures have allowed us to provide vastly increased access to our federal document collections, and it would have been impossible to get machine-readable records for so many records in such a short time without the automated shortcuts described here, the process is still far from perfect. Matching to overlay the brief records is dependent on staff keying the SuDoc number perfectly. Non-matches (i.e., brief records not overlaid) also occur for those items which contain SuDoc numbers corrected after depository distribution, those which contain specific volume and part information (e.g., TD 1.2:C 3 v.1), those items claimed, rainchecked or transferred, and those records representing voluminous series for which we have not entered minimal brief records, such as "Nuregs."

Additionally, we chose not to attempt to overlay serials records because of the problems this caused. The problems include title changes which retain the same SuDoc number and would overlay the original title, decision records created in the system to give a specific treatment to the title which would be removed from the record if overlaid, and the possibility of overlaying a serial on a series record.

FUTURE PLANS

While we have provided immensely increased access to this collection, we're still developing improved workflows. For the future we plan to continue to refine our Marcive profile in order to eliminate monographic records for which we provide serial records only. We are currently developing criteria for searching the database to create lists for claiming, retention review, de-selection review, and identification of missing items for possible replacement. In addition, we are developing procedures to do online statistical reports of the collection. At some point we hope to get our pre-1976 records into the system and finally be able to inventory the collection using our automated system. Once our plans are finalized, we anticipate major time saving for our staff in addition to the vastly expanded access to the collection for the library patrons.

Online Processing
of Government Publications
at the University Library System,
University of Pittsburgh

Debora A. Rougeux
Rebecca L. Mugridge

SUMMARY. In 1992 the University Library System of the University of Pittsburgh loaded the entire file (approximately 276,000 records) of the U.S. Government Printing Office (GPO) machine-readable cataloging records as supplied by Marcive, Inc. into its NOTIS online system. A monthly Marcive tapeload updates this file which is used to catalog retrospective and current receipts of U.S. government publications. This article describes in detail the workflow used in this process as well as the workflows used to catalog the library's holdings of Pennsylvania and Canadian depository documents, and United Nations and European Communities publications.

BACKGROUND AND HISTORY OF COLLECTION

The history of the selection practice for U.S. Government publications at the University of Pittsburgh figured largely in the decisions concerning how to perform retrospective conversion and

---

Debora A. Rougeux is Head, Government Documents Technical Services Unit and Rebecca L. Mugridge is Government Documents Retrospective Conversion Librarian, University Library System, University of Pittsburgh, Pittsburgh, PA.

[Haworth co-indexing entry note]: "Online Processing of Government Publications at the University Library System, University of Pittsburgh," Rougeux, Debora A., and Rebecca L. Mugridge. Co-published simultaneously in *Cataloging & Classification Quarterly* (The Haworth Press, Inc.) Vol. 18, No. 3/4, 1994, pp. 197-208; and: *Cataloging Government Publications Online* (ed: Carolyn C. Sherayko) The Haworth Press, Inc., 1994, pp. 197-208. Multiple copies of this article/chapter may be purchased from The Haworth Document Delivery Center [1-800-3-HAWORTH; 9:00 a.m. - 5:00 p.m. (EST)].

197

current processing on the collection. Until 1987, the University Library System (ULS) was a 75 percent depository, after which date the percentage dropped to approximately 50.1 percent. Also, in 1987, a large weeding project took place to accommodate other library materials. The University Library System is made up of Hillman Library and many departmental libraries. Some of these departmental libraries receive depository materials, and others have made a practice of ordering specific materials that they wanted for their own collections through firm orders. For these libraries the Catalog Department catalogs the materials and assigns LC call numbers. The bibliographic records appear in the NOTIS-based online catalog. Because of this practice of firm ordering and the history of item selection, the Government Documents Retrospective Conversion Subcommittee of the ULS NOTIS Implementation Task Force determined that profiling (i.e., selecting categories of records to acquire) with a vendor service such as Marcive would not be the most efficient method of retrospective conversion.

A visit to another depository library by several members of the Task Force convinced them that the cleanup required after loading profiled Marcive tapes would be very time-consuming and an inefficient use of limited staff resources. For Pittsburgh, the primary cleanup issue was the fact that some items come in microfiche, some in paper format. The experience of other libraries indicated that after profiling and loading the records into the online catalog, a staff member still had to go through the shelflist and determine which items were actually owned by the library and in which format.

The Task Force recommended that the University of Pittsburgh hire one librarian and one paraprofessional (Library Specialist III/ LS III) on a temporary basis for the retrospective conversion project and that a Government Documents Technical Services Unit be formed to perform current processing. These units are located administratively within the Serials and Acquisitions Department. The entire tape of bibliographic records marketed by Marcive, Inc., representing everything cataloged by the U.S. Government Printing Office since 1976, was loaded into the online catalog. At the time of the load, the file consisted of 276,000 bibliographic records, and was loaded into its own processing unit (processing unit code: D1), with the records set to display and index in staff mode only. Several recommendations from the Task Force influenced these choices for the following reasons:

1. It would be difficult to profile accurately for a collection that was weeded heavily in the past, has drastically changed its item selection profile, and that distributes depository items to departmental libraries.
2. We wanted to display to users accurate holdings, location and format information, especially microform holdings.
3. There is a lack of staff to perform major database cleanup expected for GPO records that would be loaded directly into the OPAC based on the profiling process.
4. We would avoid duplication of records for documents that are already cataloged in various other collections in the ULS.

RETROSPECTIVE CONVERSION
OF THE U.S. COLLECTION

Getting Started

Retrospective conversion of the U.S. Government publications collection began at the University of Pittsburgh's University Library System in June of 1992, after the bibliographic records were loaded into NOTIS. The first task for the newly hired librarian was to assess the reliability of the shelflist. The Task Force had determined that a 90 percent accuracy rate of the shelflist would be acceptable to allow us to work from the shelflist most of the time. After checking approximately 600 items, the librarian found that 93.5 percent of the items were accounted for; therefore, the decision was made to work straight from the shelflist when possible.

A second priority agenda item for the new librarian was to poll all librarians for recommendations about which agencies' publications were most heavily used by library patrons. The following agencies were requested by librarians for priority treatment: State Department (S), Congressional hearings (Y4), Labor Department (L), Census Bureau (C3), Department of Education (ED), Smithsonian

Institution (SI), Geological Survey (I19), Bureau of Indian Affairs (I20), Environmental Protection Agency (EPA), and NASA (NAS). Since the Y4s were such a large collection, the librarian determined that the LS III, after initial training, would work almost exclusively with these materials, so that we would not spend months on only one area of the shelflist. Other priority areas of the shelflist were handled by the librarian.

Hiring the staff was another priority. One LS III was hired as well as 2 (now 3) student assistants working a total of 13 (now 23) hours per week. Initial training of the LS III took about one month. This involved teaching the LS III procedures such as identification of the correct records for books and serials based on the shelflist card or book-in-hand, identification of problems, and entering the copy and volume holdings data in NOTIS. The training was done by the librarian in charge of the project. Students pull books and microfiche, reshelve books and microfiche, check holdings on serials, file shelflist cards, and do some simple authority work in support of the work performed by the librarian.

Basic Procedures

Monographs

The LS III takes a drawer from the shelflist to the NOTIS terminal and searches for bibliographic records in NOTIS by title. It is necessary to do title searches because of the large number of U.S. Government publications purchased for other collections within the ULS. Since these items often have LC call numbers already assigned, a SuDoc call number search will not find these records. If a C1 (Central Processing Unit, indicating that we already own a copy) record is found for an item, the LS III enters the government publications holdings information on the copy holdings record, using the appropriate NOTIS location code and the SuDoc call number. If the item is a multi-volume monograph, the volume holdings information is entered at this time also. If only a D1 (processing unit code assigned to the retrospective tapeload) record exists for an item, the LS III copies it into the C1 processing unit, where the record is immediately searchable by the public. At this point, changes can be made to the bibliographic record if necessary. This editing generally consists of correcting indicator values in certain fields in which mistakes are common, such as the 245, and removing extraneous 590 fields that have been mistakenly left on the records.

Serials

Procedures for serials differ only in that the University Library System has had a long-standing policy of not entering volume holdings data without actually doing a shelf check first. This practice continued with the government publications materials. Students help with this part of the project by pulling all of the issues of a serial so that the LS III or librarian can enter the information into the volume holdings record.

Authority Control

Part of the duties of the librarian in charge of the government publications recon project involves helping the authorities librarian with some of the authority work generated by the project. In addition to the 276,000 bibliographic records we purchased from Marcive, we bought 94,000 authority records. We loaded them into NOTIS at the same time as the bibliographic records. After loading, approximately 20,000 were found to be duplicates of records already in the authority file. The LS III and the librarian helped to delete these by examining each and retaining only the most current record.

All of the authority records were loaded into NOTIS with the heading use codes set so that none of the headings appeared in PITTCAT, our OPAC. These are changed manually by staff and librarians in the Catalog Maintenance Department, or in the case of series, also by the government publications recon librarian. When a record which has a series statement on it is copied into the C1 processing unit, a printout of the bibliographic record is made. Later, a student searches for an authority record in NOTIS, changes the heading use codes as appropriate, and adds 690 fields with initials, date, and NOTIS record number. The librarian checks these later for the presence of the 644 and 646 fields. Many of the series authority records that were in this tapeload seem to be lacking these fields, so they are added at this point, bringing them into conformity with all of the other series authority records in the database. Searches are also made of the cross-references to ensure that all occurrences of the series were traced correctly.

CURRENT PROCESSING

The Government Documents Technical Services Unit currently consists of 1 full-time librarian, 3 full-time library specialists, (LS II, III, and IV) and 2 student assistants who work approximately 10 hours per week each. The unit is responsible for all United States Federal publications (depository, firm order and gift items), United Nations publications received through a standing order program and firm orders, and European Community, Canadian, and Pennsylvania publications received through depository agreements or firm ordered. This responsibility includes handling these items from time of order and/or receipt until they are ready to be shelved in the public stack areas. Workflows for processing items from the various organizations follows.

GPO Depository Receipts

When depository shipments arrive from GPO, the student assistants unpack them and verify that they are complete. This verification includes checking the shipping lists against our *List of Items to Be Received* and indicating on the shipping list which items were and were not received. Materials in each shipment are property and date stamped with the date of the shipping list. Student assistants then write the Superintendent of Documents (SuDoc) classification number (listed on the shipping list), along with any special location code, on the piece. They then place the item on a shelf for further processing by the library specialists. Shipping lists are forwarded to the librarian for review and claiming of missing items as appropriate and then filed.

The Library Specialist II takes items from the processing shelf and searches the local NOTIS database for a matching bibliographic record. If such a record is found in the central processing unit (C1), the LS II adds or updates the appropriate copy line on the copy holdings record and adds or verifies the Superintendent of Documents call number. He/she then creates or updates Order/Pay/Receipt and volume holdings records as needed, barcodes the item, creates a linked item record for it, and prints call number labels for all items except microfiche.

If the LS II does not find a matching C1 record on the NOTIS database, he/she copies a D1 or other processing unit record into the C1 processing unit, checks all authority controlled fields for accuracy and proceeds as above. If no matching bibliographic record is found, he/she barcodes the item and creates an unlinked item record (i.e., a circulation record) for it. The ACTIONDATE on this unlinked item record is set for six months in advance of the date of creation. The creation of the unlinked item record allows for online shelflist access to these items until a complete bibliographic record is available, either from the monthly Marcive tapeloads or from OCLC. We are currently investigating the feasibility of creating brief provisional records for items not found in our database at the time of receipt. This would provide more complete access than the unlinked item record does. We would then overlay these provisional records with full bibliographic records as they become available from Marcive using NOTIS' Derive Overlay (AOVL/BOVL) program.

When all NOTIS processing is completed, the student assistants put a call number label on all items except microfiche and place these items on a book truck. Once a week they take this truck to the U.S. Government Documents bibliographer, who reviews the items before shelving.

A NOTIS "Operations report" is generated daily which lists unlinked item records with expired action dates. The LS III searches these lists for matching bibliographic records in the Marcive file in our NOTIS database. If an appropriate record is found in NOTIS, the record is copied into C1, the copy holdings record is updated, Order/Pay/Receipt and volume holdings records are created as necessary, and the item record is linked to the new bibliographic record. If no matching record is found on NOTIS, the LS III then searches OCLC. If he/she finds a matching record, he/she edits it as necessary, updates it, and then transfers it to our NOTIS database using GTO (Generic Transfer/Overlay) and proceeds with the processing. If no matching record is found, the LS III resets the AC-TIONDATE in the unlinked item record to expire in three months, at which time he/she re-searches the item. If no appropriate bibliographic record is found at that time, the item is forwarded to the librarian for original cataloging.

Orders for U.S. Government Publications

Any bibliographer in the University Library System may request that a particular U.S. government publication be ordered from GPO or the National Technical Information Service (NTIS) and sends such requests to the librarian in charge of the Government Documents Technical Services Unit for processing. The librarian, after getting approval from the Collection Development bibliographer responsible for the GPO and NTIS depository accounts, generates purchase orders for these items on NOTIS and sends them to the appropriate distributor. When the items are received, the librarian updates the order records and processes the items for the appropriate collection.

Processing United Nations Publications

When shipments of U.N. publications requested through our standing order program arrive, the student assistants unpack and check the contents of the shipment against the shipping list for completeness. Missing items that are identified from the shipping list are claimed by the librarian. The student assistants then give the shipping list to the LS IV to be matched against the bill when it arrives and place the items received on a processing shelf. Next, LS IV searches them on our NOTIS database. If he/she finds a matching record, he/she updates the copy holdings, the Order/Pay/Receipt, and the volume holdings records as needed. For serials and multi-part monographs, this includes checking the paper shelflist and public stacks for retrospective holdings and adding them to the NOTIS record. In addition, volume holdings information for serials is passed on to the person in the Serials Cataloging unit who is responsible for updating our local data records on OCLC for union listing purposes. The LS IV then barcodes the item, creates a linked item record and call number label for it, and passes it back to the student assistants for end processing. The final step before shelving is the review by the Government Documents Bibliographer.

If no matching record is found on NOTIS, the LS IV searches OCLC. If he/she finds a record, he/she edits it as necessary, updates it, and then transfers it to our NOTIS database using GTO and proceeds with the processing. If no record is found on OCLC, the LS IV puts a dated flare in the item and places it on a processing shelf. The item will be re-searched in three to six months and if no record is found at that point, it will be forwarded to the librarian for original cataloging.

Collection development bibliographers may also submit order requests for U.N. publications not received through our standing order. The librarian searches these titles on OCLC, transfers the appropriate record to our NOTIS database (or creates a provisional record if no OCLC record is found), and places the order. When the ordered items are received, the librarian searches NOTIS and updates the matching records as needed to indicate receipt. He/she then searches OCLC, edits matching records as needed, produces a shelflist card, exports the record to NOTIS if necessary, and proceeds with the processing. If the librarian does not find an OCLC record, he/she does original cataloging for the piece.

Processing Pennsylvania and Canadian Publications

Government Documents Technical Services staff search NOTIS for records matching government publications received through Pennsylvania and Canadian government depository programs. If a matching record is found, the LS IV updates holdings information on NOTIS and communicates appropriate data to the person in the Serials unit responsible for updating our union list records on OCLC. The LS IV then barcodes the item, creates an item record and spine label for it, and passes it on to the student assistant for final processing. When processing is completed, items are sent to the appropriate areas for shelving.

If no NOTIS record is found, staff place the publications on a shelf for review by the appropriate bibliographers, who then make the decision on whether or not to add the item to the collection. The LS IV searches those items to be added to the collection on OCLC. If no matching record is found, the LS IV passes the item on to the librarian for original cataloging. If the LS IV does find a matching record, he/she edits it as necessary, produces a shelflist card, and exports the record to our NOTIS file. He/she then adds holdings information and an Order/Pay/Receipt record as necessary, barcodes the item, creates an item record and spine label for it, and passes it on to the student assistant for final processing. When processing is completed, items are sent to the appropriate areas for shelving.

Some Canadian government publications are ordered through the Canadian weekly and special checklists. When received, these lists are checked in on NOTIS and are then reviewed by bibliographers and departmental librarians with collection development responsibilities. After the lists have been reviewed, the LS III or IV searches OCLC for matching records for those items selected to be added to the collections and exports them into NOTIS. If no OCLC record is found, he/she creates a provisional record in NOTIS. He/she then inputs the proper location code and a note that the title is a Canadian government publication into the copy holdings record. He/she writes the appropriate NOTIS record number next to the title in the Checklist, completes the order form on the back of the Checklist, and mails the form to the given address. He/she then files the Checklist for future reference.

When the above ordered publications arrive, the LS III or IV searches NOTIS and updates the matching records as needed to indicate receipt. He/she then searches OCLC, edits matching records as needed, produces a shelflist card, exports the record to NOTIS if necessary, and proceeds as with the items received on depository. If the staff person does not find an OCLC record, he/she passes the item to the librarian for original cataloging.

Processing European Community Publications

When shipments of European Community (EC) publications requested through our depository program arrive, the student assistants unpack them and put them on the processing shelf. The LS IV then takes these items and searches them on our NOTIS database. If he/she finds a matching record, he/she updates the copy holdings, the Order/Pay/Receipt, and the volume holdings records as needed. For serials and multi-part monographs, this includes checking for retrospective holdings and adding them to the NOTIS record. The volume holdings information for serials is passed on to the person in the Serials Cataloging unit who is responsible for updating our local data records on OCLC for union listing purposes. The LS IV then barcodes the item, creates a linked item record and call number label for it, and passes it back to the student assistants for end processing. These items are then sent to the appropriate area for shelving.

If no matching record is found, the LS IV places the item on a shelf for review by the appropriate subject bibliographer. After the bibliographer has made retention and location decisions, the LS IV searches the approved items on OCLC. If he/she finds a record, he/she edits it as necessary, updates it, and then transfers it to our NOTIS database using GTO and proceeds with the processing. If no record is found on OCLC, the LS IV puts a dated flare in the item and places it on a processing shelf. The item will be re-searched in three to six months and if no record is found at that point, it will be forwarded to the librarian for original cataloging.

CONCLUSION

We are optimistic about the future of online bibliographic access to government publications at the University of Pittsburgh's University Library System. We are working on plans to provide online access to our Map Collection (most of which are government publications) and are talking about the steps needed to initiate the online processing of currently received maps. We are also developing proposals for the retrospective conversion of United Nations and League of Nations publications, and are eagerly monitoring the progress of a group of libraries working to create a machine-readable file containing full MARC records for pre-1976 GPO-cataloged materials.

We hope to take advantage of new technologies and access methods being developed by OCLC and of improvements to the NOTIS system to streamline some of our current procedures. Additionally, one of the responsibilities of the Government Documents Technical Services librarian is to periodically review and evaluate sources of machine-readable bibliographic records for government publications to ensure that we receive the best and most cost-effective products available.

Overall, we think that both the current processing and retrospective conversion units are performing very well and we are pleased with the positive response from our patrons about the progress we have made in providing access to a very important part of our collection.

Index

Page numbers in italics indicate figures; page numbers followed by t indicate tables

AACR2
    bilingual or multilingual
        publications, 174
    chief source of information rule,
        134-135,148
    description of CD-ROM, 113
    multilevel description, 179
    New South Wales library system,
        159
    serial cataloging records, 16
    title source identification, 114
ABN (Australian Bibliographic
        Network), 158,160,
        162,164
Abridged cataloging
    document categories, 129
    purpose, 129
Afrikaans, 169-170
AGRICOLA database, 102-103
Agricultural information
    FAIRS CD-ROM
        cataloging, 102-118
        development, 99-100
        software description, 100-102
        system requirements, 100
    Florida publications, 98-99
ALA (American Library
        Association), 22
Alan, Robert, 92
Alm, Mary, 39
American Library Association, 22
Amigos Bibliographic Council,
        192-194
Australia
    government system, 157

State Library of New South
    Wales, 155-165. *See also*
    State Library of New South
    Wales
Australian Bibliographic Network
    (ABN), 158,160,162,164
Australian Bureau of Statistics,
    163,165
Authority work
    cooperative efforts, 72
    Florida Agricultural Information
        Retrieval System, 104
    GPO tapes, 50
    New South Wales library system,
        162
    State Library, Pretoria
        DOBIS/LIBIS system,
            171-172
        name, 176-177
        publishers, 172
    University of Pittsburgh
        University Library System,
            201-202
Auto-Graphics, Inc., 186
Availability records (GPO tapes)
    elimination, 64
    Marcive, Inc., 63
    for serials, 46

Bahr, Alice, 60
Ball State University Libraries,
        181-188
    collection, 181-182
    OCLC GOVDOC service
        access, 186

advantages, 187-188
circulation, 186-187
holdings gap, 187
maps, 185
profiling, 183, *184*
selection, 182-183
time lags, 185-186
vendor selection, 182-183
Barcodes
Ball State University Libraries,
187
Claremont Colleges, 53
Northern Michigan University,
78,81,82
San Jose State University, 23
Bibliographic records. *See*
Cataloging; GPO catalog
tapes
Bindery modules, 51
Binding operations, 90
Boggs and Lewis classification
numbers, 159
Brief records
Government Documents Catalog
Service, 186
New South Wales library system,
160
University of California, San
Diego, 193-195
Brodart, Inc., 41,123
Bushing, Mary C., 85

Caldocs (California State
Documents classification
scheme order), 38
CALDOCS (software), 38
California State Documents
classification scheme order
(Caldocs), 38
California State University at
Fullerton, 45
Call numbers. *See* Classification;
SuDoc numbers
Calvin, Diane, 181
Canadian documents

Montana State University
Libraries, 88,90
University of Pittsburgh
University Library System,
205-206
Card catalog, State Library, Pretoria,
168
Carmack, Norma, 57
Carrington, Bradley, 93
Case, Mary M., 93
Catalogers
GPO Library Program Service,
129
Montana State University
Libraries, 87-88
Northern Michigan University,
77-84
Trinity University, 67-71
Cataloging. *See also* Classification;
GPO catalog tapes; OCLC
GOVDOC; SuDoc
numbers
Canadian publications, 205-206
CD-ROM and printed out
version, 106, 114-115
contributions of government
agencies, 125-128
Florida Agricultural Information
Retrieval System, 102-119
institutions involved, 102-103
process, 103-106,*105*
record, 106-119,*107,108-109,*
110,117
GPO CD-ROMs
computer file format, 143-144
by GPO, 146-147
as key to access, 151-152
Library of Congress, 146-147
literature review, 133-134,152
in MARC format, 143-147
vs. non-document CD-ROMs,
135-136
OCLC, 136-151,140t-141t,
142
RLIN, 136-151,138t-139t

serials format, 145-146
source of records, 146-148
SuDoc numbers, 149-150
technical notes, 150
time lag, 150-151
titles, 134-145,148-149
use of books format, 142-143
GPO publications
history, 59-64
problems, 40-41
in-house vs. vendor, 188
New South Wales library system,
159-163
Pennsylvania publications,
205-206
State Library, Pretoria
authority work, 176-177
bilingual or multilingual
publications, 173-176
history of, 168
monographs, 171
multilevel description, 179
retrospective, 168-169
serials, 171,177-178
subject headings, 170
titles, 178-179
traditional vs. tapeloading, 39-41
United Nations publications,
204-205
*Cataloging Microcomputer Files: A
Manual of Interpretation
for AACR2* (Dodd and
Sandberg-Fox), 133
*Cataloging Microcomputer
Software: A Manual to
Accompany AACR2
Chapter 9, Computer Files*
(Olson), 133
"CD-ROM Databases from the U.S.
Government: Some with
Minimal Software" (Jackson), 133
CD-ROMs
descriptions, 113
Florida Agricultural Information
Retrieval System, 99-119

cataloging, 102-119,*107*,
108-109,110,117
characteristics, 100-102,*101*
development, 99-100
GPO
accessibility, durability, and
standards, 133
cataloging, 131-152. *See also*
GPO distribution of
CD-ROMs
New South Wales library system,
161-162,165
"CD-ROMs and Seriality"
(Vanderberg), 133
"The Challenge of Cataloging
Computer Files" (Wang),
133
Check-in. *See* Serials check-in
Circulation
Ball State University Libraries,
186-187
impact of GPO tapeloading,
53-54
Northern Michigan University,
81,82
Trinity University, 65
University of California, San
Diego, 194
University of Pittsburgh
University Library System,
199-200
University of
Wisconsin-Madison, 15
Claiming modules, 51
Claremont Colleges, 37-54
collection and classification, 38
GPO tapeloading
authority control, 50
call numbers, 44-45
duplicate records, 45-46
holding locations, 44
microfiche, 43
phases, 42
planning task force, 39
quality control, 52-53

retrospective, 43-44
serials check-in, 50-51
time lag, 47-49
vs. traditional cataloging,
    39-41
Clark, Mae M., 97
Classification. *See also* Cataloging;
    SuDoc numbers
California State Documents
    (Caldocs), 38
Claremont Colleges, 38,44-46
Florida Agricultural Information
    Retrieval System (FAIRS),
    111
GPO catalog tapes, 49-50
call numbers, 44-45
changes and errors,
    49-50,52-53
Innovative Interfaces, Inc., 44-45
Library of Congress call
    numbers, 111
National Agricultural Library
    (NAL), 111
New South Wales library system,
    159,163
San Jose State University, 25
State Library of New South
    Wales, 159
University of California, San
    Diego, 192
University of Pittsburgh
    University Library System,
    200
University of
    Wisconsin-Madison, 3
Cole, Jim, 94
COM catalog, Trinity University,
    64-65
Commerce Department, 127
Community languages, Australia,
    161
Computer file format in CD-ROM
    cataloging, 133,137-141,
    143-146
Congressional publications

as cataloging priority, 122
format, 69-70
lack of bibliographic records,
    125,127t
CONSER numbers for serials, 46
Cooperation
among libraries, 54
cataloging and maintenance, 72
in GPO tapeloading
    San Jose State University, 29
    Trinity University, 59,69-71,73
    University of
        Wisconsin-Madison, 15
librarians and FAIR developers,
    99-100
processing and bibliographic
    control, 77-84
Copeland, Nora S., 115
Copy cataloging
RLIN and OCLC member
    libraries, 147-148
Trinity University, 65,67-68
Corbin, Roberta A., 189
Cornwell, Gary, 72
Crawford, Josephine, 1

dBase IV, 38
Decision table, University of
    Wisconsin-Madison,
    4-5,6,7,8-9
Defense Department, 125
Department of Energy, 47
Diacritical marks, 176
"Dissemination of United States
    Federal Government
    Information of CD-ROM:
    An Issues Primer"
    (Sanchez), 133
DOBIS/LIBIS computer system, 168
advantages and disadvantages,
    171-172
authority work, 171-172
bilingual or multilingual
    publications, 175-176
multilevel description, 179

retrospective cataloging, 173
serials, 177-178
titles, 179-180
Documents librarians. *See also*
Personnel
Northern Michigan University,
77-84
Trinity University, 66-67,
70-71
Dodd, Sue A., 133
Donovan, Joanne, 189
Dossett, Raeann, 133
Downing, Thomas A., 129
Duplicate records in GPO tapes
Claremont Colleges, 45-46
Marcive, Inc., 63
University of Wisconsin-
Madison, 10-11,15
Dutch language, 169

Edge, Sharon, 59
English language, 169-170
Ephemera, 161
Esman, Michael D., 97
European Community publications,
206-207
Extension agents in Florida, 98-99

FAIRS. *See also* Florida Agricultural
Information Retrieval
System
Fell-Marston, Richard, 155
Financial issues in GPO tapeloading
in-house vs. vendors, 191
Northern Michigan University,
81-82
San Jose State University, 26
vs. traditional cataloging, 60
University of California, San
Diego, 191
University of
Wisconsin-Madison, 15,16
Florida, agricultural publications,
98-99
Florida Agricultural Information

Retrieval System (FAIRS),
98-119
cataloging
call numbers, 111
description of CD-ROM, 113
document retrieval
information, 115
edition, 112-113
environment, 102-103
file name, 116
fixed fields, 111
imprint information, 113
main entry, 111-112
personal name tracing,
116,118
printed out version,
106,114-115
process, 103-106,*105*
publication information, 118
record, 106-118,*107,108-109,*
110,117
series/stock number, 115-116
statement of responsibility,
112,114
summary notes, 115
system requirements, 113-114
title, 114
computer equipment, 100
decision making aids, 101,102
development, 99-100
information provided, 100-101
menu system, *101*
printed out version, 106,114-115
Foggin, Carol M., 92
"For Those Few of You Who Still
Aren't Confused: An
Introduction to Government
Information and
CD-ROM" (Dossett), 133
Fry, Bernard, 60,64

Gammon, Julia, 92
General Accounting Office, 125
GOVDOC. *See* OCLC GOVDOC
GOVDOC-L, 22,26

Government Documents Catalog
    Service (GDCS), 186
Government enterprises in Australia,
    162
GPO catalog tapes. *See also* OCLC
    GOVDOC; Serials;
    Vendors
abridged cataloging, 129
academic library survey, 28,34-36
access, 186
advantages and disadvantages,
    15-16,20,64,83-84
authority control, 50
availability records, 46
Ball State University Libraries,
    181-188
bibliographic records vs.
    collection, 124-129,
    126t,127t,128t
call numbers, 44-45
circulation, 53-54,78,81,186-187
Claremont Colleges, 37-54
classification changes, 49-50
cooperative cleanup project,
    22,46-47,63
corrections, 80-81
documents included, 24
documents not distributed, 9
duplicate records, 10-11,
    15,45-46,63
error rate, 77
government agency contributions,
    125-128,130
history, 62-64
holding locations, *8*,44,124
increasing access to documents,
    21
integration, 9-11,*11*,17,124
item numbers, 4-5,*6,7*,16
legal responsibility of depository,
    81
literature review, 20-23
maps, 185
matrix processing, 5,8-9
methods, 21

microfiche handling
    Claremont Colleges, 43
    Trinity University, 64-65
    University of
        Wisconsin-Madison,
        11-13,*12*
missing records, 46-47
Northern Michigan University,
    75-84
number of libraries using, 63-64
objectives and initiatives,
    129-130
personnel
    communication, 79
    cooperation, 69-71,73
    impact on, 53-54,58-59
priorities, 122
problems, 21-22
processing
    Northern Michigan University,
        78,81-83
    University of California, San
        Diego, 192-195
    University of Pittsburgh
        University Library System,
        202-204
profiling
    Ball State University
        Libraries, 183-185,*184*,188
    Claremont Colleges, 42-47
    University of California, San
        Diego, 191-192
programming objectives, 3-4
purpose, 61-62
quality control, 52-53
record selection, 76
retrospective projects, 22
    Claremont Colleges, 43-44
    Trinity University, 65-68
    University of Pittsburgh
        University Library System,
        198-202
survey of academic institutions,
    28-31,34-36
testing

Northern Michigan University,
79-80
University of
Wisconsin-Madison, 5,13-15
time lag, 47-49,122,185-186
title changes, 92-94
vs. traditional cataloging, 39-41
Trinity University, 57-72
University of California, San
Diego, 189-195
University of New Mexico,
121-130
University of Pittsburgh
University Library System,
197-204
University of
Wisconsin-Madison, 1-17
GPO distribution of CD-ROMs,
131-152
cataloging, 133-152
book format, 142-143
computer file format, 143-144
by GPO, 146-147
as key to access, 151-152
Library of Congress, 146-147
literature, 133-134
MARC format, 143-147
vs. nondocuments, 135-136
OCLC, 136-152,140t-141t
RLIN, 136-152,138t-139t
serials format, 145-146
source of records, 146-148
SuDoc numbers, 149-150
technical notes, 150
time lag, 150-151
titles, 134-135,148-149
history, 131-132
literature review, 132-134
GPO publications
cataloging history, 59-64
cataloging problems,
40-41,115-116
integrating into routing
operations, 86-87
special nature, 86

Hildebrand, Mark, 155
Holding location
Ball State University Libraries,
183
Claremont Colleges, 44
Northern Michigan University,
80-81
University of New Mexico, 124
University of Wisconsin-Madison
item number matrix, 6,7
microfiche, 13
Honnold Library, 37-54. *See also*
Claremont Colleges
Huffard, Jon R., 93

ILANET (Information and Libraries
Access Network), 164
Innopac. *See* Innovative Interfaces,
Inc.
Innovative Interfaces, Inc.
brief records, 48
California state documents, 38
call numbers, 44-45
claiming modules, 51
location code, 44
San Jose State University, 25
University of California, San
Diego, 192-194
University of New Mexico,
123-124
ISBN, 171
Item numbers, GPO tapes, 16
Ball State University Libraries,
183
missing records, 47
profiling for record selection, 44
University of California, San
Diego, 192-194
University of
Wisconsin-Madison,
4-9,6,7,13

Jackson, Kathy, 133
Johnson, Bonnie, 85
Johnson, Linda, 19

Keating, Kathleen, 121
Kellermann, Barbara, 167
Kinney, Thomas, 72
Labor Department, 125
Languages
    AACR2 rules, 174
    Australia, 161
    South Africa, 169-170,173
Latest entry cataloging, 93-94
Legal responsibility in depository
    management, 81
Library of Congress
    cataloging of GPO publications,
        60-61
    CD-ROM cataloging records,
        146-147
    GPO tapes, 190,191
Library of Congress Call Numbers
    Claremont Colleges, 45-46
    Florida Agricultural Information
        Retrieval System, 111
    San Jose State University, 25
    University of Pittsburgh
        University Library System,
        200
Library of Congress Classification,
    Claremont Colleges, 38
Library of Congress Subject
    Headings
    Florida Agricultural Information
        Retrieval System, 104
    Florida state agricultural
        publications, 102
    New South Wales library system,
        159
LIBROS, 123-125,126t
Location. *See* Holding location
Louisiana State University, 22,47

McKay, Beatrice, 57
Mackay, Jane, 64
Maddux Library, 57-72. *See also*
    Trinity University Library
Manuscripts, New South Wales
    library system, 159

Maps
    Ball State University Libraries,
        185
    New South Wales library system,
        159
MARC format
    CD-ROM cataloging records
        computer file vs. serial format,
        143-146
    nondocument material, 136
    OCLC, 136-137,140t-141t
    RLIN, 136-137,138t-139t
    file identification, 116
    GPO/Marcive records, 16
    item numbers, 17
    State Library, Pretoria, 171
Marcive, Inc., 3,5
    Ball State University Libraries,
        182,183
    Claremont Colleges, 41
    cooperative cleanup project,
        22,47,191
    Montana State University
        Libraries, 92
    number of libraries using, 63-64
    records provided, 16
    services offered, 63
    survey of academic institutions,
        29-32,34-36
    Trinity University microfiche
        catalog, 65
    University of California, San
        Diego, 191-192
    University of New Mexico, 123
    University of Pittsburgh
        University Library System,
        198
MARC records. *See also* GPO
    catalog tapes
Martin, Mary, 37
Mason, Pamela R., 152
Melvyl, 38,192-193
Meyer, Christine, 50
Microfiche
    GPO tapes

Ball State University
　　Libraries, 183
Claremont Colleges, 43
　　problems, 69
　　time lag, 42
Trinity University, 64-65
University of
　　Wisconsin-Madison,
　　11-13,*12*
New South Wales library system,
　　161
Microform. *See* Microfiche
MicroLinx, 90,94
Missing records, GPO tapeload,
　　46-47,66
Monographs
　　Ball State University Libraries, 187
　　CD-ROM cataloging, 137-141,
　　　143-146
　　Florida state agricultural
　　　documents, 102
　　Montana State University
　　　Libraries, 88-89
　　New South Wales library system
　　　cataloging, 158-159
　　　processing, 159-161
　　State Library, Pretoria, 171,173,179
　　University of New Mexico, 124-129,
　　　126t,127t,128t
　　University of Pittsburgh
　　　University Library System,
　　　200-201
　　University of
　　　Wisconsin-Madison, 11-13
Montana State University Libraries,
　　85-94
　　GPO tapeloading
　　　changes, 92-94
　　check-in, 89-91
　　monograph and serial
　　　processing, 88-89
　　OPAC, 91-92
　　processing, 89
　　technical service reorganization,
　　　87-88

*Monthly Catalog of United States
　　Government Publications.
　　See also* GPO catalog
　　tapes
　　availability records, 63
　　corrections in GPO/Marcive
　　　records, 16
　　Government Documents Catalog
　　　Service (GDCS), 186
　　purpose, 61-62
　　time lag, 122
Mooney, Margaret, 38,122,125
Mother-daughter records, 46
Myers, Judy, 22,47,58

NAL (National Agricultural
　　Library), 102-103,111,118
Name authorities
　　New South Wales library system,
　　　162
　　State Library, Pretoria, 171-172,
　　　176-177
NASA records, 47
National Agricultural Cooperative
　　Cataloging Program,
　　102-103
National Agricultural Library (NAL)
　　call numbers, 111
　　Land-Grant State Publication
　　　Program, 103
　　National Agricultural
　　　Cooperative Cataloging
　　　Program, 102-103
　　personal name tracings, 118
*New South Wales Government
　　Publications Received in
　　the State Library of New
　　South Wales,* 164
New South Wales library system,
　　155-165
　　access to government pub-
　　　lications, 156-157, 162-163
　　acquisition of government
　　　publications, 157-158
　　Australian Bureau of Statistics, 163

bibliographic standards, 159
cataloging
    authority work, 162
    formats, 161
    CD-ROMs, 165
    collection, 156
    computer technology, 158-159
    online information, 164-165
    parliamentary papers, 162-163
    processing, 159-161
    services, 156
    state publications, 158,163-164
Northern Michigan University GPO
    tapeloading, 75-84
    circulation, 78,81
    communication among staff,
        79
    corrections, 80-81
    error rate, 77
    legal responsibility, 81
    outcomes, 83-84
    personnel, 75-76
    physical processing, 78,81-83
    record selection, 76
    testing, 79-80
Northern Sotho, 176
Northwestern University, 93
NOTIS
    Ball State University Libraries,
        182,183
    Northern Michigan University, 78
    Trinity University, 67
    University of Pittsburgh
        University Library System,
        200-207
    University of
        Wisconsin-Madison, 3,6,16

OCLC
    CD-ROM cataloging records
        access, 151-152
        format, 136-137,140t-141t,
            143-146
        lag time, 142,150-151
        source of, 146-148

SuDoc numbers, 149-150
        technical notes, 150
        title entries, 148-149
    GPO tapes, 20,41
        copy cataloging, 65,67-68,
            125-128,127t
        history of, 61,62
        microform cataloging, 12
    University of
        Wisconsin-Madison, 1-17
    National Agricultural
        Cooperative Cataloging
        Program, 102-103
    numbers
        Claremont Colleges, 45-46
        GPO/Marcive records, 16
    survey of academic institutions,
        29-32,34-36
OCLC GOVDOC, 191
    access, 186
    advantages, 187-188
    Ball State University Libraries,
        181-188
    circulation, 186-187
    maps, 185
    number of libraries using, 63-64
    profiling, 183,184
    selection process, 182-183
    time lag, 185-196
Olson, Nancy, 113,133
Olson Library, 75-84. See also
        Northern Michigan
        University
Online Computer Library Center.
        See OCLC
Online public access catalogs. See
        OPACs
OPACs
    Claremont Colleges, 44-45
    Montana State University
        Libraries, 91-94
    New South Wales library system,
        158-159
    Northern Michigan University,
        76-77,81,82

San Jose State University, 23,25
Trinity University Library
  inclusion of government
  documents, 58
  microfiche, 64-65
University of California, San
  Diego, 192-193
University of New Mexico,
  123-124
University of
  Wisconsin-Madison, 3,16

Parliamentary papers, 162-163
Partnerships. *See* Cooperation
Patrons
  staff cooperation, 59
GPO tapeloading
  access before automation, 20
  circulation, 13,23,65
  impact on, 53-54
  latest entry vs. successive entry
    cataloging, 93
Pennsylvania publications, 205-206
Personnel
  GPO Library Program Service, 129
  GPO tapeloading, impact, 27,54
  Montana State University
    Libraries
      department reorganization, 87
      processing GPO materials,
        88-90
  New South Wales library system,
    159-161
  Northern Michigan University,
    75-84
  processing teams, 159-160
  San Jose State University, 28-29
  traditional cataloging, 39-40,60
  Trinity University
    cooperation, 69-71
    impact of GPO tapeloading,
      58-59
    workflow, 66-68
  University of Pittsburgh
    University Library System

current processing, 202-208
  retrospective project, 198-202
  University of Wisconsin-
    Madison, 5
  training, 13-15
  working relationships, 15
  workload, 15
Phantom documents, 15,17
PICMAN, 159
Picture cataloging, 159
Pierce, Darlene M., 75
"Planning the National Agriculture
  Library's Multimedia
  CD-ROM *Ornamental
  Horticulture*" (Mason), 133
Poster cataloging, 159
Pretoria, 167-179. *See also* State
  Library, Pretoria
Printed materials, 54
  Florida Agricultural Information
    Retrieval System,
    106,114-115
  Florida agricultural publications,
    98-99
  New South Wales library system,
    161
Publishers' authority files, 172

Quality control, GPO tapes, 52-53

Reference service, Claremont
  Colleges, 41
Retrospective cataloging projects
  Ball State University Libraries, 182
  Claremont Colleges, 42-44
  literature review, 22
  San Jose State University, 26
  State Library, Pretoria, 168-169,
    172-173
  Trinity University, 65-68
Rice University, 22,47
RLIN, CD-ROM cataloging records
  access, 151-152
  format, 136-137,138t-139t,
    143-146

lag time, 142,150-151
source of, 146-148
SuDoc numbers, 149-150
technical notes, 150
title entries, 148-149
Rudd, Edwina, 155

SAMARC (South African MARC)
    format, 171
SANB (*South African National
    Bibliography*). *See* State
    Library, Pretoria
Sanchez, Lisa, 133
Sandberg-Fox, Ann M., 133
San Jose State University
    classification system, 25
    collection, 24-25
    OPAC, 25-26
    personnel, 24
    planning model for GPO
        tapeloading, 23-36
    barcoding and security
        tagging, 23-24
    future directions, 24
    integration, 25-26
    personnel, 28-29
    site visit and final proposal,
        31-32
    survey of academic
        institutions, 28,29-31,
        34-36
    system or vendor
        requirements, 26-27
    vendor comparison, 36
    serials, 25
Scott, Sharon, 93
Sea Grant publications, 98
Security tagging, 23
Selness, Sushila, 19
Serials
    Ball State University
        Libraries, 187
    CD-ROM cataloging,
        137-141,143-146
    Claremont Colleges

availability records, 46
    cataloging, 40
    CONSER numbers, 46
    customizing GPO tapes, 42
    microfiche, 43
    European Community
        publications, 207
    Montana State University
        Libraries
        check-in, 90-91
        GPO tapeloading, 92-94
        latest entry vs. successive
            entry cataloging, 93-94
        processing, 88-90
    New South Wales library system
        cataloging, 158-159
        processing, 159-161
    State Library, Pretoria,
        171,177-178
    United Nations publications,
        204-205
    University of New Mexico,
        124-129,126t,127t,128t
    University of Pittsburgh University
        Library System, 201
    University of
        Wisconsin-Madison, 13
Serials check-in
    Ball State University Libraries,
        185
    Claremont Colleges, 50-51
    Montana State University
        Libraries
        procedures, 89-91
        serials vs. monographs, 88-89
    Northern Michigan University,
        80-81
    problems with automated, 50-51
    University of California, San
        Diego, 193
Series notes, Claremont Colleges, 51
Series/stock number, 115-116,
    177-179
Series tracings, Trinity University, 70
Shelflist

Montana State University
Libraries, 90
Northern Michigan University, 78
University of Pittsburgh University
Library System, 199
Shipping lists, GPO publications
Government Documents Catalog
Service (GDCS), 186
Montana State University
Libraries, 89
Northern Michigan University,
80-81
University of Pittsburgh University
Library System, 202
South Africa, 167-179. *See also*
State Library, Pretoria
South African National Bibliography
(SANB). *See* State Library,
Pretoria
Staff. *See* Personnel
State documents
Claremont Colleges, 38
Montana State University
Libraries, 88,90
University of Pittsburgh
University Library System,
205-206
State Historical Society of
Wisconsin, 2-5. *See also*
University of
Wisconsin-Madison GPO
tapeloading
State Library, Pretoria, 167-179
cataloging
card catalog, 168
DOBIS/LIBIS computer
system, 168,171-172
languages, 172-176
multilevel description, 179
name authority files, 176-177
retrospective, 168-169,172-173
serials, 177-178
*South African National
Bibliography*, 170-171
titles, 178-179

collection, 168
establishment, 167
impact of South African history,
169
languages of documents, 169-170
State Library of New South Wales,
155-165. *See also* New
South Wales library system
Statement of responsibility, FAIRS,
112,114
Stoker, Ria, 167
Student assistants
Northern Michigan University,
78,81-82
University of Pittsburgh
University Library System,
200-208
Subject headings, 170. *See also*
Library of Congress
Subject Headings
Successive entry cataloging, 93-94
SuDoc numbers
CD-ROM cataloging records,
149-150
Claremont Colleges, 43,44-45
classification scheme, 16
errors and changes, 49-50,
52-53
Government Documents Catalog
Service (GDCS), 186
GPO/Marcive records, 16
missing records, 46-47
Montana State University
Libraries, 90
Northern Michigan University,
80-81
San Jose State University, 25
Trinity University, 67
University of California, San
Diego, 193-194
University of Pittsburgh
University Library System,
200-201
University of
Wisconsin-Madison, 3,6,*9*

Summary notes in cataloging, 115
Superintendent of Documents
    numbers. *See* SuDoc
    numbers
System requirements in CD-ROM
    cataloging records,
    113-114,149-150

Technical notes
    CD-ROM cataloging records,
    149-150
    Florida Agricultural Information
    Retrieval System, 113
Technical services
    Montana State University
    Libraries, 87-88
    Northern Michigan University
    GPO tapeloading, 77-84
Temporary records, GPO tapes
    Claremont Colleges, 48-49
    vendors, 49
Testing GPO tapes
    Northern Michigan University,
    79-81
    Trinity University, 67
    University of Wisconsin-Madison,
    5,9, 13-15
Texas A&M University, 22,47
Theodore-Shusta, Eileen, 75
Time lag in GPO cataloging, 80,122
    Ball State University Libraries,
    185-186
    CD-ROMs, 142,150-151
    priorities in cataloging, 47
    temporary records, 48-49
Titles
    bilingual or multilingual
    publications, 174-176
    CD-ROMs, 134-145,148-149
    multilevel description, 179
    serials, 178
Trading names, Australia, 162
Training in GPO tapeloading, 27
University of Pittsburgh
    University Library System,
    200

University of
    Wisconsin-Madison, 13-15
Translations, 161
Transportation Department, 125
Treasury Department, 125
Treaty series, 178
Trinity University Library, 57-72
    collection, 57-58
    GPO tapeloading
    cooperation of personnel,
    69-71,73
    impact on personnel, 58-59
    microfiche catalog, 64-65
    retrospective project, 65-68
    personnel, 58
Tull, Laura, 69

United Nations publications, 204-205
University of California, San Diego,
    189-195
    collection and access, 190
    OPAC, 190
    overlaying the brief record,
    193-195
    post-load cleanup, 193
    profiling, 191-192
    record processing, 192-193
    vendor selection, 190-191
University of Florida. *See also*
    Florida Agricultural
    Information Retrieval
    System (FAIRS)
    cataloging process, 102
    GPO tapeloading, 53-54
    National Agricultural Library,
    102-103
    personal name tracings, 118
    publications, 98,99
University of Illinois Library, 60
University of New Mexico, 121-130
    collection
    description, 123
    vs. GPO tapes, 124-129,
    126t,127t,128t
    database description, 123-124

GPO tapes
  circulation, 53
  holding locations, 124
  selection, 121-122
University of Pittsburgh University
  Library System, 197-208
  collection, 197-198
  current processing, 202-208
  retrospective cataloging, 198-202
University of Wisconsin-Madison
  GPO tapeloading, 1-17
  benefits vs. limitations, 15-16
  bibliographic database system, 3
  holding locations, 2-3,*8*
  integration, 9-11,*11*,17
  item number matrix, 4-9,*6,7,8,9*
  microform handling, 11-13,*12*,17
  normalization and automatic
    truncation, *9*
  programming objectives, 3-4
  systems analysis and
    communication, 5
  testing, training, and reports,
    13-15
Upper Peninsula Region of Library
    Cooperation (UPRLC), 76
URICA, 158-159,160
U.S. Geological Survey publications,
    70
Users. *See* Patrons

Vanderberg, Patricia S., 133
Van De Voorde, Philip E., 39
Venda languages, 176
Vendors, 3,5
  advantages, 26
  authority control, 50
  Ball State University Libraries,
    182-183
  Claremont Colleges, 41
  cooperative cleanup projects,
    22,47,191
  history, 63
  Montana State University
    Libraries, 92

  number of libraries using, 63-64
  products and local online
    systems, 42
  records provided, 16
  San Jose State University, 26-27
  services provided, 41,63
  survey of academic institutions,
    28,34-36
  temporary records, 49
Trinity University, 65
University of California, San
    Diego, 190-191
University of New Mexico, 123
University of Pittsburgh
    University Library System,
    198

Wang, Anna M., 133
Weston, Claudia V., 97
WLN bibliographic network, 91
WordPerfect, 102,106,114,116

Zulu language, 170

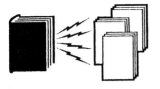

Haworth
DOCUMENT DELIVERY
SERVICE
and Local Photocopying Royalty Payment Form

This new service provides (a) a single-article order form for any article from a Haworth journal and (b) a convenient royalty payment form for local photocopying (not applicable to photocopies intended for resale).

- *Time Saving:* No running around from library to library to find a specific article.
- *Cost Effective:* All costs are kept down to a minimum.
- *Fast Delivery:* Choose from several options, including same-day FAX.
- *No Copyright Hassles:* You will be supplied by the original publisher.
- *Easy Payment:* Choose from several easy payment methods.

Open Accounts Welcome for . . .
- Library Interlibrary Loan Departments
- Library Network/Consortia Wishing to Provide Single-Article Services
- Indexing/Abstracting Services with Single Article Provision Services
- Document Provision Brokers and Freelance Information Service Providers

MAIL or *FAX* THIS ENTIRE ORDER FORM TO:

Attn: **Marianne Arnold**
Haworth Document Delivery Service
The Haworth Press, Inc.
10 Alice Street
Binghamton, NY 13904-1580

or **FAX:** (607) 722-1424
or **CALL:** 1-800-3-HAWORTH
(1-800-342-9678; 9am-5pm EST)

PLEASE SEND ME PHOTOCOPIES OF THE FOLLOWING SINGLE ARTICLES:

1) Journal Title: _____
   Vol/Issue/Year:_____Starting & Ending Pages:_____
   Article Title:_____
   _____

2) Journal Title: _____
   Vol/Issue/Year:_____Starting & Ending Pages:_____
   Article Title:_____
   _____

3) Journal Title: _____
   Vol/Issue/Year:_____Starting & Ending Pages:_____
   Article Title:_____
   _____

4) Journal Title: _____
   Vol/Issue/Year:_____Starting & Ending Pages:_____
   Article Title:_____
   _____

(See other side for Costs and Payment Information)

COSTS: Please figure your cost to order quality copies of an article.

1. Set-up charge per article: $8.00
  ($8.00 × number of separate articles) _____

2. Photocopying charge for each article:
  1-10 pages: $1.00 _____
  11-19 pages: $3.00 _____
  20-29 pages: $5.00 _____
  30+ pages: $2.00/10 pages _____

3. Flexicover (optional): $2.00/article _____

4. Postage & Handling: US: $1.00 for the first article/
  $.50 each additional article _____
  Federal Express: $25.00 _____
  Outside US: $2.00 for first article/
  $.50 each additional article _____

5. Same-day FAX service: $.35 per page _____

6. Local Photocopying Royalty Payment: should you wish to copy the article yourself. Not intended for photocopies made for resale. $1.50 per article per copy
  (i.e. 10 articles x $1.50 each = $15.00) _____

GRAND TOTAL: _____

METHOD OF PAYMENT: (please check one)

❑ Check enclosed   ❑ Please ship and bill. PO # _____
  (sorry we can ship and bill to bookstores only! All others must pre-pay)

❑ Charge to my credit card: ❑ Visa; ❑ MasterCard; ❑ American Express;

Account Number: _____ Expiration date: _____

Signature: *X*_____ Name: _____

Institution: _____ Address: _____

City: _____ State: _____ Zip: _____

Phone Number: _____ FAX Number: _____

MAIL or *FAX* THIS ENTIRE ORDER FORM TO:

Attn: **Marianne Arnold**
Haworth Document Delivery Service
The Haworth Press, Inc.
10 Alice Street
Binghamton, NY 13904-1580

or **FAX:** (607) 722-1424
or **CALL:** 1-800-3-HAWORTH
(1-800-342-9678; 9am-5pm EST)